IRREVERENT guide to Walt Disney World® & Orlando

6th Edition

By
Chris Mohney

1807 WILEY 2007 BICENTENNIAL
Wiley Publishing, Inc.

other titles in the

IRREVERENT GUIDE

series

Irreverent Amsterdam

Irreverent Boston

Irreverent Chicago

Irreverent Las Vegas

Irreverent London

Irreverent Los Angeles

Irreverent Manhattan

Irreverent New Orleans

Irreverent Paris

Irreverent Rome

Irreverent San Francisco

Irreverent Seattle & Portland

Irreverent Vancouver

Irreverent Washington, D.C.

About the Author

Chris Mohney has edited, contributed to, and written numerous guidebooks about Walt Disney World, Las Vegas, and other destinations, including the *Irreverent Guide to Las Vegas,* 3rd edition (Wiley Publishing, Inc.). He is the editor of Gridskipper.com.

Published by:
Wiley Publishing, Inc.

111 River St.
Hoboken, NJ 07030-5774

ISBN-13: 978-0-470-04308-0
ISBN-10: 0-470-04308-3

Interior design contributed to by Marie Kristine Parial-Leonardo

Editor: Jennifer Moore
Production Editor: Katie Robinson
Cartographer: Guy Ruggerio
Photo Editor: Richard Fox
Anniversary Logo Design: Richard Pacifico
Production by Wiley Indianapolis Composition Services

For information on our other products and services or to obtain technical support, please contact our Customer Care Department within the U.S. at 800/762-2974, outside the U.S. at 317/572-3993 or fax 317/572-4002.

Wiley also publishes its books in a variety of electronic formats. Some content that appears in print may not be available in electronic formats.

Manufactured in the United States of America

5 4 3 2 1

A Disclaimer

Prices fluctuate in the course of time, and travel information changes under the impact of the varied and volatile factors that influence the travel industry. We therefore suggest that you write or call ahead for confirmation when making your travel plans. Every effort has been made to ensure the accuracy of information throughout this book and the contents of this publication are believed correct at the time of printing. Nevertheless, the publishers cannot accept responsibility for errors or omissions or for changes in details given in this guide or for the consequences of any reliance on the information provided by the same. Assessments of attractions and so forth are based upon the author's own experience and therefore, descriptions given in this guide necessarily contain an element of opinion, which may not reflect the publisher's opinion or dictate a reader's own experience on another occasion. Readers are invited to write to the publisher with ideas, comments, and suggestions for future editions.

Your safety is important to us, however, so we encourage you to stay alert and be aware of your surroundings. Keep a close eye on cameras, purses, and wallets, all favorite targets of thieves and pickpockets.

CONTENTS

INTRODUCTION

If you're reading this book, you've probably already made up your mind to visit Walt Disney World, the attraction that started the whole ball rolling here in Orlando. Before WDW, Orlando was a pass-through from Miami to Atlanta with a few settlers and a lot of swamps. On the West Coast, Walt Disney was looking to expand, and with Anaheim closed in around Disneyland, the Great Mouseketeer set his eyes on Central Florida. With its temperate climate and cheap land, Walt Disney knew he had a winner on his hands.

Love it or loathe it, the Walt Disney Company has become a giant, mouse-eared symbol of American culture. Last year, Disney attractions logged more than 38 million visitors from around the globe. Of course, there are still a few holdouts: Like people who brag that they don't own a television set, some snobbier-than-thou types enjoy snorting that they've never, ever done Disney. "It's so fake, so...happy," shuddered one colleague when asked why he'd never set foot in the theme parks. Another decidedly anti-Mickey chum summed up the Walt Disney World experience with three words: "Grotesque and appalling." You betcha. And those are just two of the many things we love about the place.

Indeed, what's not to love? Orlando is faux, it's fun, it's blissfully over the top. Think Vegas, without the sleaze: Instead of battling with one-armed bandits, you're kept busy dodging dinosaurs and evading spookhouse ghosts; here, the unreal becomes completely real, if only for a few seconds. The big trend in theme parks nowadays is "total immersion" adventures, where the line between the real world and virtual reality becomes disconcertingly blurred. (Like doing drugs without all the nasty side effects—except the dent to your wallet.) The newest, most cutting-edge rides recently launched at Orlando's theme parks take this concept to dizzying heights. Disney's Mission: Space has convinced so many would-be astronauts that they are actually flying, they now have "lunch bags" installed in each capsule. The Journey into Narnia: Creating the Lion, the Witch, and the Wardrobe attraction at Disney–MGM Studios walks you through a giant wardrobe and into a re-created mythical land, just as in C. S. Lewis's Narnia books. Universal's Amazing Adventures of Spider-Man, considered one of the most technically complex of the park's attractions, aims to give riders the illusion that they're flying through the air, as they leap from the tops of skyscrapers, narrowly escaping destruction at every turn. And its newest attraction, Revenge of the Mummy, uses technology devised to make you feel like you're out of control, pitching forward and backward at rapid speeds.

Talk for a few minutes to the ride-engineering types who build these attractions and you'll hear high-flying phrases like "simulation technology," "roving base simulator," "hydraulic physics," and "space-age robotics." Child's play, it ain't. All this and giant, pants-wearing rodents, too.

Of course, kids go along with this concept from the get-go. Adults, on the other hand, can't help but feel a tad cynical about a place that, after all, is designed chiefly to separate them from large sums of hard-earned cash. It's all intensely, crassly commercial—where else can you buy pasta shaped like Mickey Mouse ears?—and the presentation is all so slick and seamless that it's a little scary. Just check out Disney's wholly owned, operated, and micromanaged community of Celebration for a glimpse into what a real "total immersion" lifestyle could be like. It's hard to get past the fact that these theme parks are shrewdly calibrated utopias where every thrill is manufactured, every lawsuit anticipated, every cost subjected to yield-management analysis. Long lines may be the only problem they haven't solved yet. Then again, perhaps to a park pro with a movie mentality, a long line may just be proof that you've got a hit on your hands.

But hey, you're going to Disney World—so lighten up, already. It's time to suspend your politically correct outrage at the homogenization of American culture, and your ecologically based horror at the fact that, since your last visit, a few more of Florida's last remaining undeveloped acres have disappeared. Look at the bright side: The park is wholesome, it's clean, and it's highly unlikely that you'll be massacred by machete-wielding locals on *this* vacation. How petty to complain about a place where Mickey Mouse and Cinderella get to live happily ever after! Take a cue from the kids, and let the magic do its number on you. No matter what their parents' attitude, for youngsters, the Disney Magic is just that: *magic.* Disney's Imagineers know imagination is the primary engine that drives the parks, and they fuel that engine—on kids and adults alike—with expert abandon. Many people remember their first Magic Kingdom vacation with the same reverence reserved for their first two-wheel bike and visit from the tooth fairy. Whatever you think of the Disney mystique, it's hard not to feel good watching kids' eyes widen as they crane their necks up at Big Thunder Mountain Railroad, or whirl, thrilled, on the Magic Carpets of Aladdin. Disney counts on this appeal to keep pulling in visitors year after year, but who cares when you're having this much fun?

The fact that Walt Disney World built a wild-animal park carries a certain irony, considering that the company is responsible for drastically altering Orlando's natural landscape. Surrounded now by high-maintenance foliage shaped like Mickey, it's difficult to imagine this area when it was all mangrove swamp, orange groves, and grasslands. Those vistas are long gone by now, gobbled up not only by manicured resorts but by strip malls, restaurants, motels, gator shows, water parks, and go-cart tracks. Kissimmee, the town closest to Disney World, was once populated with cattlemen and their herds. Today, the closest you'll get to a cow in these parts will be at the Ponderosa Steakhouse All-U-Can-Eat buffet.

So bring your sense of humor with you, and accept the fact that you may feel ambivalent about this theme-park version of virtual reality. Just three pieces of practical advice: 1) Once you do make your peace and dive in, don't, as sometimes happens, get sucked into the we-gotta-do-everything compulsion that can prevail around here. Concentrate on your must-sees, and take in the rest only if you have the time and energy. Skip the lines if they look too long and you can't get a FASTPASS (damn it). It'll still be there on your next visit (probably). Unless you've allotted a good 5 days just for theme parks, you won't see everything anyway. 2) Don't confuse fun with free-spirited spontaneity. (After all, Disney certainly doesn't.) Take a fairly

Map 1: Orlando Neighborhoods

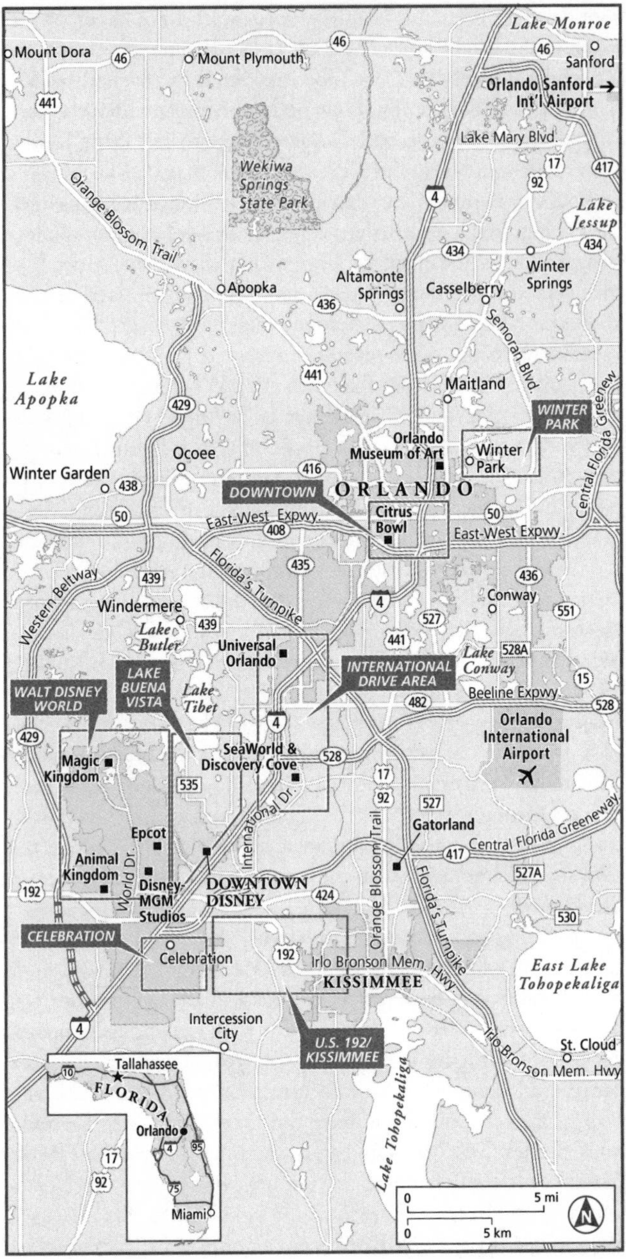

organized approach, or else you'll end up wandering around, eyes glazed over, by midmorning. 3) Don't let a thwarted itinerary ruin your mood. If it rains, grab a poncho and enjoy the rides without lines. If you get sunburned, ride all the indoor rides or go after dark.

But most of all, remember that it's okay to act silly. Not only are you paying for that right, but whom out of the thousands of people you'll encounter at the park will you ever see again? Besides, nowhere else is it more forgivable—perhaps even mandatory—to get back in touch with your inner child.

YOU PROBABLY DIDN'T KNOW

What do Viagra and Walt Disney World have in common?... Answer: Both require you to wait an hour for a 2-minute ride. Unless you take a VIP tour (p. 141) or you just won the Super Bowl, you can't avoid waiting in lines around here. During the busiest weeks of the year (spring break/Easter; Christmas till New Year's), the Disney parks can suffer gridlock so severe it would shock even Manhattanites. There are times when the searing Florida heat and the endless tank-topped crowds can seem like a preview of hell on Earth, rather than "The Happiest Place on Earth," as Disney calls itself. The lines are especially hideous at Disney's most popular park, the Magic Kingdom, or maybe it just seems that way because you're dodging double strollers at every turn. And it's not just Disney, either: When Universal's Islands of Adventure is busy—which it nearly always is—waits of 90 minutes to get into rides are not uncommon. Long lines are also a fact of life at

Disney–MGM Studios, though the process seems to run a tad more efficiently there. On the other hand, you'll spend very little time waiting in lines at SeaWorld compared to the other theme parks, a big plus for those who'd rather avoid this particular stress-inducer while on vacation. The action at SeaWorld centers on scheduled shows; you plan your itinerary around them, and spend the rest of your time touring walk-through exhibits such as Manatees: The Last Generation? and Penguin Encounter. Most likely, you'll only have to queue up at two places: the Kraken roller coaster and the Atlantis thrill rides. The big SeaWorld shows are held in outdoor stadiums, too, so you can see how big the crowds are as you walk up to enter. Elsewhere, seemingly short lines can be deceiving. You'll soon discover that for most shows, getting in the door is only the first step—once inside, you're herded into three more rooms before hitting the main theater. In each "preshow area," as they call them, there are attractions (or, more accurately, distractions) to keep you amused while you wait for the main event. If all this hurry-up-and-wait causes you to burn out by midday, here's our advice: Take an afternoon break (for a late lunch, a swim, or a nap) and then return to the park around 5 or 6pm. You'll feel refreshed, perky, and ready for action—just when most everyone else is heading home.

How far in advance should I plan my trip?... Planning a Disney/Orlando vacation entails about as much spontaneity as throwing a Martha Stewart Christmas party. Rental cars are often booked well in advance, while reservations at the best-deal resorts must be made a year ahead of time (and sometimes more); Disney takes reservations up to 2 years in advance for some of its dinner shows; and if you simply want to receive information from **Orlando's Official Visitor Center** (Tel 407/363-5872 or 800/551-0181), you'll have to give them 3 weeks to mail it to you. Of course, if you're Web-savvy, you can accomplish all of this with a few clicks of the mouse. Visit **www.disneyworld.com** and make reservations online; for Orlando info and links, go to **www.orlandoinfo.com**. If you're the adventurous type, wait until the last minute and take your chances. With 114,000 hotel rooms (and counting), you'll find someplace to stay, provided you're not too picky.

Is it possible to do Disney on the cheap?... Aside from shady maneuvers, there are several ways to see Cinderella Castle for less than a princely sum. For example: 1) Be flexible and a bit adventurous. If you absolutely must stay in a specific hotel or resort, you'll most likely pay through the nose. Instead, look around and negotiate. Better yet, when you pull into town, head straight for the Orlando Visitor Center on International Drive and ask for their "little black book." This book is a list of hotels that have dumped vacant rooms for the night, often at discounts of up to 50% or more off regular rates. 2) Time your vacation for off-peak value seasons (for the best times to go, see below). 3) Look for hotels that offer extras, such as free breakfast (at some hotels, such as Holiday Inn, kids eat free with paying adults), free shuttles to the major parks and attractions (this will save on parking fees), and free shuttles to and from the airport. 4) Finally, whatever you do, avoid buying souvenirs at the park. I know, every ride dumps you smack into the gift shop, but you can pick up your Mickey hats and Goofy ears at any one of the gazillion discount shops in Orlando.

When is the best time to visit Disney World?... Picking the best time to visit Disney World is becoming more and more of a crapshoot. It's always crowded, and you can invariably count on lines. If you can travel in the off season (anytime school is in session), you can save big bucks and enjoy the parks when they're not choked with little guests. The downside to off-season visits? The parks close earlier, and some of the evening pageants are suspended. If you're really crowd-phobic, go the week after Labor Day (or right after any major holiday) or during the period between Thanksgiving weekend and the week before Christmas—that's the slowest time at Disney World. At all costs, no matter what you have to do, *do not* plan your trip for the Christmas holiday week. This is Disney's busiest week of the year—a time when you don't want to be anywhere near this place. Summer (yes, when Central Florida turns into a sweltering sweatbox) is also busy, as kids are out of school and family vacations are underway. In January and February, the international crowd rolls into town, and the prices are lower ("super-value season," in Disney parlance), but once you start getting into those February, March, and April school breaks, look out. Not to mention that March has become the unofficial "cheerleader competition" month at Disney...they bring them in by the busloads. "So what," you say? Nothing will have you feeling more homicidal than standing in line for 20 minutes listening to endless variations of "Ready? Okay!" as the cheerleaders practice in line. Easter? Forget about it. May is better than most months, although Florida school kids arrive in droves on their end-of-year field trips. September through early December is value season again. If there's a big convention in town, though, all bets are off. The convention high season runs from January through June.

Am I hallucinating, or does that corn flake have mouse ears?... Call it cute, or call it subliminal seduction, but Disney's Imagineers subtly hide Mickey Mouse silhouettes in plain sight all over Disney World. Way Hitchcockian, no? These "Hidden Mickeys" are an inside joke among pranksterish Disney cast members (that is, employees). You'll catch them lurking about where you'd least expect them: There's a plush Mickey tucked away in the Tower of Terror, a broccoli Mickey in the Body Wars mural in Epcot, a Viking sporting mouse ears in Epcot's Maelstrom, and so on (if you happen to be flying a jet over Disney–MGM Studios, you'll notice the entire park is one giant Mickey!). So, if you're sharp-eyed, Mickey-obsessed, or just bored silly, see if you can ferret out a Hidden Mickey or two along the way. You can even post your sighting on the official **Hidden Mickey** website (www.hiddenmickeys.org); they'll tell you if it's the real thing or just wishful thinking on your part.

I can skip the lines?... Credit Disney for trying to do something about the horrendous lines at their theme parks. They've instituted their miraculous line-jumping FASTPASS system at all major attractions. Here's how it works: You go to the FASTPASS kiosk (located at the ride's or show's entrance), insert your park ticket into a slot, and out comes a free FASTPASS ticket, telling you what time to return. At the appointed time, simply return to the attraction and head for the FASTPASS entrance, leaving the poor chumps in the regular line choking on your dust. Instead of waiting, say, an hour to board Test Track, you only have to wait about 15 minutes. Not bad...until everybody catches on to the scheme (although they may not; the system's been around for years and the lemmings are still standing in lines). Even now, your FASTPASS may well instruct you to come back in 5 hours if all the earlier FASTPASS times are filled, and during busy times, it's entirely likely that all FASTPASSES for the day will be allocated before lunch. On the plus side, using the FAST-PASS gives some structure to your agenda—it's perfect for type-A personalities and those prone to line rage. On the negative side, your fun day at the theme park will take on all the spontaneity of Marine boot camp. Note that you can only get up to two FASTPASS slips at a time. Until you use one, you won't be able to get another. Universal Orlando introduced its own version of a fast-track ticket to its theme parks, called UNIVERSAL EXPRESS, that's a simpler version of line-breaking. In addition, guests at the on-site Universal hotels get to flash their room keys and walk the EXPRESS line for free (no 10 items needed!). Call it whatever you want; anything that reduces that cattle-drive feeling is okay by me.

Where can I get a room with an ocean view?... Don't laugh—this is reportedly the most frequently asked question at the Orlando Visitor Center. Apparently lots of folks don't realize that Orlando is landlocked. Sorry, folks, the closest oceanfront room is about 90 miles away, in Cocoa Beach. Still, if waterfront digs are what you crave, those you can have. (I just can't guarantee that the water is a natural feature of the landscape.) There are more than 125 lakes inside the Orlando city limits, while the surrounding region boasts a couple thousand more. And that doesn't even count the innumerable water parks, fountains, and pools. Many of Disney's resorts offer water views (ask about your options when you book), and two of Universal's three resorts offer water or pool views (and boat access to the theme parks). Take a peek behind some of the budget-priced lodgings on U.S. 192 in Kissimmee and you'll see bustling Lake Cecile.

I'm huggable. How do I get to be Mickey?... Yeah, and it's always been our dream to be Cinderella. Sad to say, even if you can tolerate being hugged by 10,000 children per day and can sign autographs wearing oversize rubber gloves—never mind wearing a huge head and a prickly costume in sweltering heat—you can't be Mickey. Or

Minnie, or Goofy, or any of the other big cheeses at WDW, for that matter. As a Disney PR person explained it, "You can't be Mickey. Mickey just...is." She stuck to this story, and I'm convinced she believes it. However, if your ambitions are a bit more realistic—say, you want to pick up trash at Epcot or work at one of the resort's restaurants—give a call to **Disney's Casting Center** (Tel 407/828-1000). You can listen to a tape recording of WDW's job opportunities, which are updated weekly, and arrange for an interview. Or—here's a real tip—you can walk right into the Casting Center (across the street from Downtown Disney Marketplace). You'll find postings with job offerings (some not available over the phone), and you might even be able to arrange an on-the-spot interview. But if you really have your heart set on being a character, it helps to be petite...most of the costumes, with the exception of Goofy, are made for those 5 feet tall or under.

Where can I get discounted tickets to the attractions?... The first rule of Orlando is never, ever pay full price. The next is to head online for discounts to the majors. **Disney** (www.disneyworld.com), **Universal Orlando** (www.universalorlando.com), and **SeaWorld** (www.seaworld.com) offer discounts for online ticket purchases. Note that you must purchase tickets from your home (not from a laptop or hotel business center once you have arrived), and that most tickets and passes have to be ordered at least 7 days in advance. You can also order discounted tickets at the **Orlando CVB** website (www.orlandoinfo.com). If you prefer to do your buying in person, you can forget Disney, although there are scads of deals to be had on admission tickets to SeaWorld, Universal Orlando, Gatorland, dinner theaters, clubs, golf courses, water parks, and more. Check with your hotel first; often the concierge or front desk will have discount coupons for guests. The Orlando Visitor Center always offers 10% to 25% off on SeaWorld and Universal admission, and on a handful of other local attractions as well. Pick up one of the many travel guidebooks and flyers you'll see lying around everywhere—they're full of offers. An even better idea is to call the visitor center ahead of time (Tel 800/972-3304; www.orlandoinfo.com), and they'll mail you a slew of their latest coupon books. Inquire about the free **Orlando Magicard,** which entitles you to a variety of savings at more than 100 attractions, stores, restaurants, and accommodations.

We're thinking about getting married at Disney.... You and the rest of the starry-eyed world, it seems. *Modern Bride* magazine has ranked Orlando as the number-one honeymoon destination in the world. (I won't even speculate why newlyweds would choose to stand in line for Pirates of the Caribbean rather than, well, do other things.) So why not have the whole ceremony here? For those who love prefab romance, Disney offers "fairy-tale" wedding packages: The ceremony takes place in a multimillion-dollar wedding pavilion built on an island in the Seven Seas Lagoon, with Cinderella Castle as the backdrop (loose wallets can rent Cindy's digs in the Magic Kingdom for the reception—the price starts at a princely $42,000). If you can imagine it—and can afford it—Disney will do everything it can to realize the day of your dreams. A variety of fantasy receptions are available, too, including ones with *Beauty and the Beast* or *Aladdin* themes. The ultimate (perhaps in insanity) is Cinderella's Ball: The bride arrives in a glass carriage drawn by six white ponies, a costumed fairy godmother and stepsisters mingle with the guests at the reception, and dessert is served in a white chocolate slipper. Kind of makes your teeth hurt, huh? I suppose it makes your special day a little more memorable, but it had better since you'll be paying it off for a while. To arrange your **Disney wedding,** call Tel 321/939-4610 or go to www.disneyweddings.com.

Is it worth getting up at the crack of dawn?... You betcha. Here's why: If you're staying at a Disney resort, you get a special incentive to rise and shine, in the form of the "Extra Magic Hours," when they open a Disney theme park an hour early and/or keep one open an hour later (on a rotating schedule) as a perk for *Disney resort guests only.* In spite of this, *everybody* rolls into the parks midmorning. So if you're hell-bent on doing the hottest rides without spending all day waiting in line, pass up your morning shower (thanks to the special effects, you'll wind up smelling like propane anyway), skip the 'do (you'll get soaking wet several times during the day on the river raft and "splash" attractions), and plan to arrive at the park a half-hour before its scheduled opening time. Hit the road at the crack of dawn, scarf down that bagel in the car, and sprint to those turnstiles. Immediately go to the hottest rides (the Rock 'n' Roller Coaster, Mission: Space, Space Mountain, Amazing Adventures of Spider-Man, Shrek, Men in Black, Incredible Hulk Coaster, Dueling Dragons, and so on) and have at it, while everybody else is still navigating the parking lots. If you time it right, you can get all the marquee attractions under your belt before the lines get too insane, freeing you up to explore the second-stringers at your leisure. Doing Disney can be great, but beating the system is sublime.

Which is better, Universal Studios Florida or Disney–MGM?... This is the question on everyone's lips. I like 'em both, being thrilled that there's something fun and escapist for adults to experience in Theme Park Land. The magic of the movies is an easy sell, of course, but the two parks are surprisingly different—you could do both in the same trip and not be bored. Universal is more of a working movie-and-TV studio than is Disney–MGM; you'll see more real production work going on in the back-lot sets, should you wish to pay attention. (With Islands of Adventure right next door, there's more going on in one location here, too.) Universal also has more of an edge than Disney–MGM. (Example: Islands of Adventure calls one dinosaur attraction "You Bet Jurassic." Walt would be turning over in his grave.) Both parks put on funny, engrossing shows. But—and this is big—Universal has wilder rides, packing an amazing amount of excitement into a few short minutes. Back to the Future...The Ride, Jaws, Revenge of the Mummy, Earthquake, and Terminator 2 3-D all feature special effects that are simply unparalleled. However, because there's so much to see at Universal Studios (it's bigger and more spread out than Disney–MGM), it's difficult to do it all in 1 day unless you power-tour. Given the time spent waiting in line for the hottest rides, and the amount of acreage you have to cover to get around the park, it can take a good 10 hours to see everything. In contrast, Disney–MGM is smaller and more compact, so you can see it all in a mere 8 hours or so. But with the exception of the Twilight Zone Tower of Terror and Rock 'n' Roller Coaster, Disney–MGM's rides aren't as intense or over-the-top thrilling as Universal's.

What happens when the sign says FULL at the theme park?... Of course, the best advice is to plan in advance such that this never happens with you on the wrong side of the fence. Simply put, the bigger crowds one can reasonably expect, the earlier you should get to the gate. The parks will fill to capacity at times during high season and during certain holidays, but everyone—including Disney employees—can tell you when these packed days are likely to happen. Disney water parks, too, often close to new arrivals just minutes after the doors open because of full-capacity crowds. If you get stopped at the parking-lot entrance because the lot is full, don't bother trying to get to the theme park via other means. Sure, the parking lot might have filled up before the theme park itself, but do you really want to be in that last group admitted before they slam shut the doors behind you? Of course, if you're staying at a Disney resort, it's no problem to simply take internal transportation into the theme park—you're guaranteed entrance. But if you do get shut out, the smartest move is simply to adjust your plans: Go back to the hotel and spend a lovely day at the pool. While everyone else is being driven mad as a hatter waiting 2 hours for a 5-minute ride on swirling teacups, you'll be sipping daiquiris and working on your tan. Then go back to the park later in the afternoon; the parking lot often opens as the early crowds thin. Or you could just pick another theme park to go to; hell, with nearly 100 attractions and amusements in the area, you certainly won't be left (God forbid!) with nothing to do.

Can I get Mickey to show me around?... Sort of. **Pal Mickey** is a talking 10½-inch-tall digital toy who serves as an often corny guide, telling guests about parades, showtimes, and so on. Designed for the kid set, he nevertheless gets toted around by adults, too (who usually get confused and go for their pagers when he vibrates to let them know he's got a message for them). His computer chips pick up wireless signals throughout the park and dispense fun facts; after you leave, you're stuck with the corny jokes. He's available for purchase only ($65). For that much money, I'd want the big guy instead of his little brother. Pal Mickey operates on three AA batteries—they're included!—and has hundreds of lines of "dialogue."

ACCOMM

ODATIONS

1

Basic Stuff

Deciding where you're going to stay during your Disney World vacation is probably the single toughest decision you'll make. I've seen perfectly calm, sane friends go absolutely mad after hours—no, days—spent looking over literature, talking to the Disney folks, listening to friends, and searching the Web, all to one purpose: where to stay? The range of options is truly dizzying. Orlando boasts more than 114,000 hotel/motel rooms, and by the time you finish reading this paragraph, there'll be more. Disney alone offers 24 full-scale themed hotel properties, with a total of more than 30,000 guest rooms. Universal Orlando has its own on-site destination resorts: **Portofino Bay Hotel, Hard Rock Hotel,** and **Royal Pacific Resort.** No doubt about it, folks, deciding where to bed down can suck the F-word (F stands for fun, okay?) right out of your vacation planning.

In Orlando you don't merely look for a room. No, no, no.... (Of course, if you're so inclined, that would make life easier. You'll find plenty of reasonable, ordinary options around town; think Red Roof Inn, Comfort Inn, Holiday Inn, Howard Johnson, Hilton, Doubletree, Days Inn, Marriott, Embassy Suites, Ramada, Radisson, Best Western.... Pick any of them—you know what to expect; they're all the same.) To do the Orlando experience right, you must first decide what theme you can live with, if only for a few days, and how much it's worth to you. Never mind that there are no mountains in Florida; you can still have a Rocky Mountain–high room at the Wilderness Lodge, a retreat overlooking bubbling hot springs and an erupting geyser. Choose between the Southern-style hospitality at Port Orleans Resort–Riverside, a spread of elegant manor homes complete with a Mississippi-style river, banjos strumming, and magnolias blossoming, or the New Orleans–themed Port Orleans–French Quarter complete with a waterslide that drops you out of the mouth of a sea serpent. At Marriott's Orlando World Center or the 1,500-acre Hyatt Regency Grand Cypress resort, you can swim in grottoes and under waterfalls. Sleep in a purple jester's bed studded with jewels at The Doubletree Castle, or with a three-story-tall Big Wheel parked outside your room at the Pop Century resort.

If you want to spend a fortune, the penthouse suite of Disney's Grand Floridian delivers two very nice bedrooms, a baby grand piano, surround-sound stereo, a full bar, a Jacuzzi tub, turndown service, high tea, hors d'oeuvres, and dessert—and there's a view of Cinderella Castle, too. (Oooh...restless heart, be still.) How about sleeping underneath the watchful eyes of five-story-tall stone fish and swans? You'll find it all at the side-by-side Walt Disney World Dolphin and Swan resorts, designed by world-famous architect Michael Graves. If you're looking for quiet elegance instead of hit-you-over-the-head decor, check in to the Peabody Hotel, where the atrium lobby soothes the soul with exotic plants, gentle waterfalls, and an eye-catching art collection. Alas, even the Peabody has a gimmick: the ducks (they're real). Each morning and evening, a 75-foot red carpet is rolled out, and the fabled Peabody Ducks—descendants of ducks that once graced the fountain of Memphis's original Peabody in the 1930s—waddle to the Orlando lobby's marble fountain, where they spend the day before heading back to the Royal Duck Palace for bed. (Turndown service at the Peabody also includes filling your bathtub and floating a yellow rubber ducky in it.) Here's where to start: Request the free **Planning Kit** (visitors guide, accommodations guide, coupon pack, and Orlando Magicard) from the Orlando/Orange County Convention and Visitors Bureau by calling Tel 800/551-0181 or heading online to www.orlandoinfo.com.

Let's Make a Deal

Orlando is a capital example of the laws of supply and demand. The $60 you paid for a room during "value season" will surely double—or more—in price when the kids are out of school. Location may be everything in the rest of the universe, but here, it's timing, timing, timing. Go off-season and you can almost name your price; come when everyone else does and you'd better make reservations at least 6 months ahead of time. Some of the more popular resorts book rooms up to a year in advance, especially during holidays. That said, you can nearly always negotiate a price, whatever the time of year, if you're flexible and persistent. Ask for a better deal, and chances are you'll get it. Disney properties, alas, are usually sticklers when it comes to room rates, but there are usually enough Disney discount codes floating out there to slash room rates by up to 33% or even more depending on the season. If you're really feeling adventurous, roll into town without a room reservation and head to Orlando's **Official Visitor Center** at 8723 International Dr. (at the corner of Austrian Row). Then ask if there are any rooms currently available. Orlando hotels phone the center each day, looking for folks to fill their properties. The visitor center's **"little black**

book" lists available hotel rooms, with prices often slashed 50% or more. On a recent visit during peak spring-break time, it was possible to snatch a two-bedroom, full-kitchen condo (nice digs), just minutes from Disney World, for $79 a night. The regular rate would have been double that.

Web-savvy surfers can get the latest prices and book airfare, lodging, even theme-park tickets online. Start with a visit to **Disney's official website,** www.waltdisneyworld.com. From there, **Mousesavers** (www.mousesavers.com) should be your next stop. If there are Disney resort discount codes available, they'll have them listed. Walt Disney World annual passholders and Florida residents usually get deeper discounted code rates, so if you don't live in Florida, it might be worth your time and money to get at least one annual pass for your group.

You might check out hotel brokers, too, who snatch unsold rooms and offer them at deeply discounted rates. A couple to try: **Hotels.com** (Tel 800/246-8357; www.hotels.com) and **Places To Stay.com** (Tel 800/390-4687; www.placestostay.com). If you don't mind doing a bit of calculation, check into the various Disney World/Universal Studios/Orlando package deals. Several airlines offer Orlando/Disney World packages complete with airfare and lodging, including **Southwest Airlines Vacations** (Tel 800/243-8372; www.swavacations.com), **Continental Airlines Vacations** (Tel 800/301-3800; www.covacations.com), and **Delta Vacations** (Tel 800/221-6666; www.deltaairlines.com).

For people who just can't get enough of the Mouse, the Disney experience extends beyond the Orlando area with the **Disney Cruise Line.** Two ships, ***Disney Magic*** and ***Disney Wonder,*** both docked at Port Canaveral, Florida, offer 3-, 4-, 7-, and 10-day cruises to the Bahamas, Mexico, and the Caribbean, as well as 7-day land-and-sea vacations. All cruises include a stop at Castaway Cay, Disney's private Bahamian island. This cruise is a magnet for families, so you might want to look elsewhere if you don't want to be trapped at sea with a swarm of kids. For information, call Tel 800/951-3532 or visit www.disneycruise.com.

Is There a Right Address?

There are four major lodging areas in Orlando to choose from: the **U.S. 192 strip,** situated southeast of Disney World along the road to **Kissimmee;** the **International Drive area,** which lies east of the World and includes the resorts of **Universal**

Orlando; the **Lake Buena Vista area,** which is just off WDW property and is also home to on-site hotels not actually owned by Disney; and **Walt Disney World** itself, which encompasses 21 on-site hotels.

The **U.S. 192 strip** offers the most economical choices—including not only all the major chain hotels, but also a selection of local mom-and-pop motels. You can find many rooms on the strip for $50 or less per night, and "high-end" here usually means under $150. Accommodations in this area, often referred to as "Main Gate" residences, are touted as being the closest to Disney attractions, with I-4 being the dividing line between East and West Main Gate. Technically speaking, the hotels at the Disney end of U.S. 192 are generally a lot closer than the lodgings on International Drive, and staying here may even get you closer to the Disney parks than the guests at some of the more remote Disney resorts. But don't read this as necessarily convenient—you still have to fight the inevitable traffic in this neighborhood. And even though you might save 10 minutes or so in the car getting to the Magic Kingdom, you'll make up for it trying to find a decent restaurant at the end of the day. If there is a fast-food chain in existence, you'll find it somewhere along this road. Living smack dab in the midst of tourist-gouging shops and cheap amusements (how 'bout a spin around the go-cart track after that All-U-Can-Eat buffet at Ponderosa?), you have to have a high tolerance for tacky to spend much time on U.S. 192. Still, if you're traveling *en famille,* who can argue with the convenience of an IHOP next door to your hotel and a Pizza Hut down the street? Besides, after a long day of fighting crowds and blowing your budget on admission tickets and a high-priced lunch at Disney, maybe all you need is a clean, cheap room and a clean, cool pool.

The on-site but non-Disney hotels command higher prices for their convenient location (right off Downtown Disney, but actually in Lake Buena Vista—see below). There are six independently owned hotels: the **Buena Vista Palace, Doubletree Guest Suites, Grosvenor Resort, Hilton WDW, Hotel Royal Plaza,** and **Best Western Lake Buena Vista.** (A seventh hotel in this group, the Holiday Inn at Walt Disney World, suffered extensive hurricane damage and had no planned reopening date at press time.) WDW parks and the restaurants and attractions on International Drive are relatively close and accessible. Free shuttle service is provided to WDW areas, and other Disney privileges like Extra Magic Hours are also available. Beware of what you book in this area, however; it's a mixed bag when it comes to value. You can pay up to $200 a night at cookie-cutter high-rise hotels, just for the Disney proximity. But make a reservation at the **Nickelodeon Family Suites by Holiday Inn** just down the road, and you'll get a two-bedroom suite, free breakfast, free meals for kids all day long, a fab pool, free shuttles to the Disney parks, and more—all for about the same price or less than what you'll get at the on-site non-Disneys, depending on the season.

The area just east of Downtown Disney is known as **Lake Buena Vista** and features a mixture of themed hotels and mid-priced all-suite properties. This is a good area for families on a budget who want to be as close as possible to Disney World but can't afford the Disney price tag (though note that some hotels on the far side from Disney aren't really that close to the park entrances).

International Drive (I-Drive to locals) offers some of the best lodging values in town, with rooms ranging from $50 to $200 a night. In case you're wondering, by the way, there's nothing international about International Drive: It's pure commercial Americana, with hundreds of restaurants, shops, amusements, and hotels. But you'll find some great places to stay—and generally they'll have a much smaller price tag than their Disney resort counterparts. Two additional advantages of staying on International Drive (or close to it): You'll have access to a few high-quality, reasonably priced restaurants, and you'll be closer to other top non-Disney attractions, such as SeaWorld and Universal Orlando. Most hotels on International Drive provide free shuttle service to these attractions, though you may have to pay to get to Mickey. If you stay on I-Drive, expect to spend some grueling time in the car trying to get anywhere besides the World. During afternoon rush hour and when the parks let out, it's not uncommon to spend about 45 minutes going less than 10 miles (are we having fun yet?).

When it comes to staying at **Disney World resorts,** you have to decide not only how much you're willing to pay, but also what theme you can tolerate best. Get ready for virtual vacationing. Why travel to the New England coast when you can book a room at the Yacht Club? Yearning for that easy island feeling? Pack your sarong and head to the Caribbean Beach resort. Longing for the adventure of the African savanna? Disney's answer is the Animal Kingdom Lodge, complete with real giraffes lunching on trees outside your window. Disney does a magnificent job of capturing everything in cliché, and nowhere is their mastery of illusion and attention to detail more pronounced than at their resorts. Walk up to the Wilderness Lodge and you'll see towering pine trees and western wildflowers. (You won't, however, find dreadlocked locals selling ganja and good times on Disney's Caribbean Beach.) You may feel compelled to explain to your children that, no, Jamaica, Aruba, and Trinidad (fill in the blank) aren't exactly like this. But if you want to be totally immersed in Disney fantasy day and night, then go for it (and get your wallet out).

Universal Orlando plays the theme game, too, with three on-site resorts. Choose from an Italian seaside village, a rock-music bonanza, or a Polynesian island paradise—all run by the upscale Loews chain. If you plan to spend a good deal of time at the Universal theme parks (a good idea if you're a thrill junkie or are traveling with teens in tow), then consider staying on-site and saving yourself a bunch of time on the road, waiting in traffic. Guests staying at Universal Orlando resorts receive some nice privileges, too, such as Universal Express front-of-the-line access to selected attractions with their room keys. There's also complimentary transportation to and from all parks and on-site hotels via water shuttles.

To Sleep with the Mouse...or Not

Disney offers room rates ranging all the way from $79 to over $2,440 a night. In general, you'll pay more for Disney resort accommodations than for comparable rooms off-site (although they *do* offer the very real added advantage of "Extra Magic Hours" in one of their parks each day you're with them—see below). For example, a standard room (two queen-size beds and a daybed) at **Disney's Grand Floridian** runs $359 a night, while a similar-size room at **Disney's Yacht Club** and **Beach Club** resorts runs about $305. Ouch. Compare that to a standard room at International Drive's **Doubletree Castle,** replete with jeweled chairs, pointy headboards, and its own cast of castle characters, for about $120 to $215. Small studio villas at **Disney's BoardWalk Inn** feature a scant 359 square feet (not a lot of room), a microwave oven, mini-refrigerator, coffeemaker, and wet bar, and will cost you about $305 to $475 a night; compare that to the **Staybridge Suites** in Lake Buena Vista and International Drive, each offering a large, two-bedroom suite with full kitchen and living area, for about $239 a night. A better deal are Disney's "moderate" or "value-priced" options, such as the **All-Star resorts, Pop Century, Port Orleans, Coronado Springs,** and **Caribbean Beach,** all of which range from $79 to $215 per night. About $250 a night will get a standard room at the **Animal Kingdom Lodge,** complete with exotic animals on view, or at the Wilderness Lodge, where you get to gaze at a geyser. An economical option for campers is Disney's **Fort Wilderness Resort & Campground.** It's a help to know that Disney's resorts are clustered around each of its theme parks. If you plan on spending most of your time at one particular park, you'll save commuting time if you stay at a resort nearby. Here's how they're bunched: **Magic Kingdom**–area resorts are the **Contemporary, Grand Floridian Resort & Spa, Polynesian, Wilderness Lodge, Fort Wilderness,** and **Shades of Green** (open to military members and their families only). **Epcot**-area resorts are **Caribbean Beach, BoardWalk Inn, BoardWalk Villas, Yacht Club, Beach Club, Beach Club Villas,** and **Swan** and **Dolphin.** Area resorts for the **Animal Kingdom** are **Coronado Springs, All-Star Sports, All-Star Music, All-Star Movies,** and the **Animal Kingdom Lodge. Pop Century** is closest to **Disney's Wide World of Sports. Downtown Disney** resorts include the **Saratoga Springs Resort & Spa, Port Orleans Resort,** and **Old Key West.**

Let's take a look at the Disney resorts' list of privileges/ enticements. Service? Yes, you can count on that. Convenience? Usually, but not always. Getting around Disney quickly and efficiently requires the savvy maneuvering of a New York cabbie in rush hour. Depending on where you stay in the World, your return trip could take up to a half-hour—even longer—on crowded buses, boats, and monorails. After standing in line all day at the park, plan on standing in line again to catch your ride home. You'll hear of a number of other "advantages" for staying at a Disney resort. Let's take a look at them:

- **The Disney resort ID card,** allowing you to charge meals and purchases to your room. But surprise! Your regular credit card works just as well. Another upside: If you spring for souvenirs in the park, you can get them delivered right to your hotel room (delivery can take a day or two though). But for those prices, delivery should be included anyway.
- **Use of all Disney recreational facilities,** including golf, rental bikes, boat rentals, and watersports. Of course, they all cost extra, even for resort guests, and

are often available to non-Disney day guests as well, sometimes for the same price. Disney guests do, however, get preferred tee times.

- **Advance dining reservations,** up to 180 days in advance. Surprise again. Anyone can call Tel 407/WDW-DINE to secure Advance Reservation arrangements (see the Dining chapter). Besides, do you know anyone who plans meals that far in advance? ("Yes, honey, I think that 3 months from now, on April 20, I'll be in the mood for sushi.") If your Disney vacation just wouldn't be complete without catching the Hoop-Dee-Doo Musical Revue dinner show, a character breakfast at Cinderella's Royal Table, or your heart is absolutely set on dinner at Victoria & Albert's (three of Disney's most popular dinner spots), call ahead; see chapter 2, Dining, for a little advice in the reservation wars. Otherwise, just plan on making reservations at the restaurant of your choice when you get to town; it shouldn't be a problem. With any luck, the starry-eyed couple who made reservations 2 months ago are now history, and you'll get their corner table at Victoria & Albert's. I have noticed, however, that Disney resort guests almost always get into even solidly booked restaurants—more so than when not a guest.
- **Enter parks early, leave late.** This is a real benefit. Disney's "Extra Magic Hours" allow resort guests into a different park an hour earlier than the general mobs each morning, or alternatively, allow resort guests to stay an hour later than the hoi polloi. If you're organized about it, this can help you avoid some of the bigger lines. Call Disney (Tel 407/824-4321) as soon as you arrive (or ask at the guest-services desk at your resort) to find out which park has early entry for the days you'll be in town.
- **Guaranteed park entry.** When the parking lots are full, Disney resort guests can still get in using park transportation. Think twice about whether this is a good thing or not—do you really want to enter the Magic Kingdom when the sign says FULL? Sounds like a good day to stay at the pool.
- **"Free" transportation.** Disney resort guests get access to the **Walt Disney World Transportation System,**

Rumor Mill: Magic a Little Bit More Your Way

For years, most guides advised you to avoid Disney's "Dream Vacation" packages like the plague—the packages were inflexibly built to include (and charge for) all kinds of amenities your average person would never use. You either got too few park admissions or too many, or you were allowed to enter as many parks as you wanted for an insanely brief window of time. And to add financial insult to injury, the packages often cost more than if you'd booked each component individually. However, with the 2005 debut of "Magic Your Way" packages, Disney at last offers a range of options you might actually get to use, at a sliding scale of discounts in the "more you buy, the more you save" vein. Now you can book the number of hotel nights you want, and then, a la carte, buy the number and kind of park admission tickets you want as well. There's also a dining plan that grants you a certain number of meals per day. Of course, if you insist on blowing a wad of cash, feel free to indulge in the Magic Your Way Premium or Platinum plans, which resurrect the old-fashioned ginormous per diems in exchange for granting you every Disney privilege you could ever want, and then some. Check out www.waltdisneyworld.com for current Magic Your Way details and prices.

which includes monorail trains, ferryboats, launches, and motorcoach shuttles to all areas in the World. This can be a benefit if you plan to hop from one area to another during the day: Say you want to spend a few hours in the morning at the Magic Kingdom, have lunch at Disney–MGM, and then hop over to Epcot for the afternoon. (Are you nuts?!? This is supposed to be a vacation.) Free transit is also an advantage if you plan to exit and return to the park during the day (a good idea, as it lets you take a nap, swim in the pool, and return refreshed). There's only one problem: Let's say you're staying at a primo Disney resort but decide to take in another Orlando attraction (as you should).... Just try to get a Disney World bus driver to drop you off at Universal Studios. No way, José. Most non-Disney hotels in the area do offer free shuttle service to the major attractions, including Disney World and Universal Studios, while others charge a nominal fee. Should you prefer using your own wheels, Disney resort guests get free parking at the theme parks (which leaves you with an extra $9 to put toward those new Mickey ears!).

- **Discount Passes.** Disney is very good at never giving away something for nothing, so don't expect red-carpet admission into the theme parks just because you're forking over for a Disney room. However, they've gotten a little more relaxed about how their upgrades and add-ons can be sold, allowing you to pick and choose what you buy to go with your hotel reservation. How much you save depends entirely on what you're willing to pony up initially—are you ready to make it worth Mickey's while to treat you nice, big spender?

The Lowdown

Only in Orlando... Welcome to total-immersion vacationing. Here, you'll not only spend your days in fantasyland but your nights, too. Take your pick: Are you in the mood for a timber-framed Western lodge, Southwestern hacienda, seaside inn, beach cottage, Caribbean island abode, classic Victorian resort, Southern manor on the bayou—or how about a room that overlooks an African savanna? They don't call it the World for nothing. And Disney doesn't have the lock on themed lodging, either. Orlando-area resorts outside Disney World compete with their own faux settings and over-the-top designs. You can't spend the night at Cinderella Castle in the Magic Kingdom, but if you really want to play in a palace, book a room at **The Doubletree Castle,** a frivolous, all glitter-and-gold fortress on International Drive. In the spacious rooms, you'll find upholstered chairs painted purple, with pointy backs, all studded with multicolored stones, plus thrones, headboards, jeweled mirrors, hand-set mosaics of kings, queens, and jesters, and stuffed mystical castle creatures peering around the corners. Even the swimming pool has a fountain and a regal hot tub. Kitschy? Sure; but it is so gloriously over the top, you won't care. Besides, rooms are bright and spacious, the location is great (although the traffic is horrendous), and the price is right. You'll pay twice as much at a comparably themed Disney resort. For a cinematic experience, guests at the **Sheraton Studio City** get to travel back in time as they are transported to the "homes" of Hollywood stars, complete with period furnishings, costumed hosts, vintage movies, free popcorn, and more. (The Marilyn Monroe rooms sport zebra-striped shower curtains and oversize, colorful makeup mirrors.)

Tropical delights... It's hot and sultry; so what if there's not a sea in sight? Tropical-themed resorts are big in Orlando. At the **Caribe Royale All-Suites Resort,** you'll find a variety of suites and villas, all sitting on a 30-acre parcel of giant palm trees and colorful foliage. Actually, there's not much more to it than the giant pink facade that says "Caribbean," but you could do a lot worse for the money, and the "all-adult" third tower is a definite plus for those without kids. **Disney's Polynesian Resort** has always been one of their most popular, and it's definitely got some things going for it. The lobby hits the mark with trickling waters, South Pacific foliage, island music, and thatched things all about. Be prepared to drop a load here ($315–$600 per night). I like the **Disney's Caribbean Beach Resort** better, for less than half the price. This lively and colorful resort sits on a 42-acre lake, surrounded by 200 acres; it also features one of Disney's best pools. You'll find lots of water activities on site, too. On the downside, it sprawls, and getting from one end of the resort to the other can take a while. Over at Universal Orlando, the **Royal Pacific Resort** is Asian/South Pacific in design (its orchid garden is sublime), though less overtly themed than Disney's Polynesian. Part palm trees, part bamboo, the resort is elegant, yet moderately priced—and it gets my top vote in this category.

Out of Africa... Here's your chance to stay in a South African game reserve without a passport and hours spent on a plane (not to mention those nasty vaccinations for who knows what). All you have to do is book a room at Disney's **Animal Kingdom Lodge.** The impressive lobby features hand-carved furnishings, a mud fireplace, and stunning views of a 33-acre savanna. You'll find lots of other carvings as well, along with rich jewel-tones, low lighting, and thatched huts, all done very tastefully. (Peter Dominick, of Disney's Wilderness Lodge fame, had his hand in this property, too.) Catch sightings of animals and exotic birds from the lodge's large picture windows or the rooms' balconies (some 100 grazers and 130 birds live on the property's private reserve), and forget for a moment that you really are in Orlando. Of course, this mind-over-body transportation will cost you; rooms here are at Disney's deluxe side of the scale, costing $250 and up a night.

In the meantime, another option is to follow the leopard carpeting to the front lobby of the **Sheraton Safari Resort.** This out-of-Africa-themed hotel includes fine furnishings, a lush courtyard, and a kid-approved pool. (And nothing spells video relaxation like in-room PlayStations.) There are no exotic animals roaming outside, but the prices are tamer ($150–$219 per night for rooms and small suites).

La Dolce Vita... The luscious **Portofino Bay Hotel** at Universal Orlando conjures up images of an idyllic Italian fishing village. Never mind that you're mere seconds away from cavorting with Spider-Man and the Incredible Hulk; once here, you'll be enchanted. This Loews Hotel property—which comes complete with imported Italian cypress and olive trees, elaborate *trompe l'oeil* paintings created by artists from Portofino, Italy (the real one), a harbor dotted with fishing boats, and extra-comfy beds in the guest rooms—was Universal's first on-site hotel, and it's still a beauty. Families will like the main pool area, complete with water slide; adults will enjoy the quiet second pool hidden back by the bocce court. I like its elegant style and proximity to Universal's parks and CityWalk. Mandara, a deluxe, full-service European-style spa, is located on the premises. Book a massage and life will suddenly start looking sweeter.

Disney's forest fantasies... Nestled on the shores of Bay Lake, **Disney's Wilderness Lodge** is a tribute to early-20th-century national-park lodges, and it's one of Disney's best-executed themes. Okay, maybe it's not the sweeping view you'd get if you were looking out the window of the Old Faithful Lodge in Yellowstone, but the hotel lobby elicits more than a few oohs and ahhs: It features a seven-story pine-beamed great hall with an 80-foot quarry-stone fireplace, a giant, carved totem pole, magnificent tepeelike chandeliers, and carved wooden bears, goats, and eagles peering at you from all directions. Bubbling hot springs start in the lobby and cascade outdoors into the pool. In true Disney let's-take-it-over-the-top fashion, an erupting geyser completes the scene. The rooms are spacious, in Disney terms, done up in Western-style furnishings with plaid bedspreads and buffalo-print sheets, and the surroundings of woods and water give the resort a quiet, secluded feeling. Is that sagebrush we smell?

You won't even know you're in Orlando... Check in to the **Hyatt Regency Grand Cypress** and you may not even make it to the amusement parks. This 1,500-acre megaresort is a sports-minded hedonist's wet dream: a grand pool with grottoes and waterfalls, plus a 21-acre lake, 45 holes of championship golf, lush grounds, an equestrian center, tennis courts, racquetball.... Need we say more? This place is deluxe, inside and out. Rooms are decorated in soft, tropical hues, and the public areas—the lobby, hallways, restaurants, and outside gardens and walkways—are filled with sunlight and top-notch art and sculpture. The hotel has five restaurants, including Hemingway's, an upscale Key West–style eatery overlooking a free-form swimming pool, waterfalls, and gardens. Also in the get-all-your-needs-met-under-one-roof category is the gigantic **Orlando World Center Marriott,** a 200-acre resortopolis surrounded by tropical foliage, golf fairways, and cascading waterfalls. It boasts one of the largest meeting facilities in the country, so you'll be surrounded by suits and badges. Never mind; they'll all be in meetings while you splash in the gigantic freshwater pool, complete with waterfalls and a water slide (of course), or soak in one of the secluded spas. The building itself—a towering cement structure with a 12-story atrium lobby and glass elevator—is not terribly unique, but the oversize rooms have classy pastel-and-floral-draped furnishings, and the grounds are luscious. Finally, you *definitely* won't feel like you're in Orlando at the **Celebration Hotel** in the Disney-created town of Celebration. In fact, walking the streets in this made-to-be-perfect real town (you can actually buy a house here, if you promise to keep your lawn mowed, the kids' toys inside, laundry off the line, and your sidewalks rolled up after dark, among other things that I can only imagine) is like being stuck in *Pleasantville.* The town, of course, is perfect: perfect little upscale shops, perfect little restaurants, perfect little park on the water, perfect little coffee shop, and so on, and so on. The town center is not actually owned by Disney anymore, but the Celebration Hotel, located there, is quite nice and provides a fabulous escape from the theme park frenzy. The place is a flashback to old Florida, when the pace was slower and the scale much smaller. The four-star boutique hotel borders the lake (what else?) and features an understated clapboard and stucco design, a brick courtyard entrance, and a quiet, elegantly casual atmosphere. (Think Ernest Hemingway, not Jimmy Buffett.)

Two recent additions to the resort skyline of Orlando can be found at the luxury development of **Grande Lakes,** just east of SeaWorld. The **JW Marriott,** the taller of the two resorts, reflects a Spanish style and is the pinnacle of Marriott luxury. The neighboring **Ritz-Carlton** lives up to the luxury resort chain's reputation—reminiscent of an Italian palazzo, it's posh with a capital "P." Both properties sit side by side, sharing a Greg Norman–designed championship golf course, a 24,000-square-foot, winding, lazy-river pool, and a 40,000-square-foot spa. You'll choke on the prices ($299–$890) but not on smoke (both hotels are smoke-free).

Hiding from Mickey... You'll find no cutesy mouse-ear topiaries, gushing geysers, or water-sprouting dragons at the **Saratoga Resort Villas.** This oasis, located just 4 miles from the entrance to Disney World off the busy U.S. 192 strip, doesn't look like much from the road, but it's perfect for folks who can't stand another moment of Disneyness. The beautifully furnished one-, two-, and three-bedroom villas come with a full kitchen, two full bathrooms, and bilevel floor plan and run $125 to $199 a night. The 15-acre resort includes a boardwalk that winds through the property.

The **Gaylord Palms** is themed, true, but not in any Disney fashion. Located across I-4 from the Downtown Disney area, the resort occupies just over 4 acres, including an attached conference center. An atrium offers an overview of the state of Florida that spans the width of the resort and includes replicas of famous Florida landmarks, including Castillo de San Marcos, Key West's Mallory Square, the bell tower from Flagler College, and the Everglades. The rooms, however, which start at $199 a night, are pure elegance, decorated in rich colors themed to different Florida locations. Add to this luxury touches such as an on-site full-service branch of the legendary Canyon Ranch spa, and free bottles of juice and water daily, and the resort is a great way to be close to the theme parks but not immersed in them.

Grand gambles... Reeking of class and elegance, Disney's **Grand Floridian Resort & Spa** makes a great first impression: A stately white Victorian-style hotel with a red-shingled roof and a zillion balconies, it sits facing the Seven Seas Lagoon. The lobby is all chandeliers, arched windows, and gold birdcages. High tea is served at 3pm (raise that pinkie, now). But the prize here is getting one of the coveted lagoon-view rooms that face the Magic Kingdom. These rooms are few and never guaranteed (and the others are nice, but not worth the hefty price), so you're taking a gamble on the $359-to-$940 price tag.

Disney's **BoardWalk Inn** and **BoardWalk Villas** take the 1930s Atlantic-seaboard scene to the max. The bustling seaside illusion takes place outdoors: Disney's G-rated, golly-gee clubs, street performers, shops, and restaurants are clustered along a lakefront boardwalk. In other words, let the good times roll, and roll, and roll...after a day's worth of fun, fun, fun at the parks, you may not get the quiet you need to recharge. The smallish, inn-style rooms will set you back a whopping $305 to $825 a night, and the larger BoardWalk villas break the bank—we're talking $305 to $2,020 (for the two-bedroom Presidential Suite). You're better off renting a room elsewhere and visiting the BoardWalk for an evening.

Disney's Contemporary Resort was one of the first two resorts to open when the park did in 1971. Based on Walt's idea of a futuristic hotel, the resort's A-frame allows the monorail to run right through it (which makes the resort noisier than most). The two Garden wings (constructed years later) are not convenient to anything, and rooms in the Tower will set you back $355 and up per night. If you can luck into one of the rooms with a balcony overlooking Seven Seas Lagoon, you'll have memory-making views of both Magic Kingdom's nightly fireworks and the nightly Electrical Water Pageant. And I do mean luck, because while you can request such a room, Disney will not guarantee you'll get it, even if you pay the premium price. Still, if you can take the financial pounding, it's worth a try. After a massive update and renovation, rooms at the Contemporary are now among the nicest at Disney World.

When you want to see and be seen... Disney's Grand Floridian Resort & Spa attracts those who request the best and most expensive place to stay at the World (Oprah's stayed here!). When money is no object, or, perhaps, more accurately, when money *is* the object, the Grand Floridian is the hotel of choice. It tries to be gracious and elegant—in that Disney faux-style way—with lots of chandeliers, arched windows, and lavish decor. Cutesy shops have been replaced with high-end boutiques, and a Mickey mannequin sports top-of-the-line resort wear in the obligatory Disney store on premises. Disney's **Yacht Club** and **Beach Club** are also celebrity favorites. If it's rock stars you're looking for, head over to the **Hard Rock Hotel.** Want some names? How about Aerosmith's Steven Tyler, *NSYNC, and Cheap Trick? Most bands playing the Hard Rock Live venue stay here, drawn to this perfect blend of funk and function. Jam-packed with rock-'n'-roll memorabilia, it's a hit with adults and kids, alike. You'll relish the swimming pool (one of Orlando's largest), with its piped-in underwater music. Five on-site restaurants and lounges, and its close location to the parks—only a short walk from your front door—make it even better. Celebs looking for a more low-key experience, such as Steven Spielberg, often book one of the suites at Universal's **Portofino Bay.**

When you come to your senses... Families or groups on a budget should consider the **Suites at Old Town** on U.S. 192 in Kissimmee. Though this property does have regular rooms, the suites are the main reason to stay here. Get twice the space of a normal hotel room for the same price and a kitchen area to boot. Located next to Old Town, there's plenty to do without driving anywhere, but the property also offers free shuttles to the Disney parks.

Deals at Disney... The lively **Caribbean Beach,** one of the Epcot resort-area hotels, was first to enter Disney's moderate category, and it's still a bargain with rooms starting at $139 a night. The price point draws a lot of families, so expect it to be a bit on the noisy and active side. Rent a paddleboat and join the fun. Also considered a "moderate," Disney's version of New Orleans, the **Port Orleans Resort's French Quarter** section ($139–$215 a night) lacks the Big Easy's 24-hour jazz-club-hopping, while the legendary New Orleans ladies of the evening have been replaced by squeaky-clean bell captains, and you'll never have to flash any body part to get beads. Still, it has lots of wrought-iron railings, picturesque courtyards, and a kid-popular pool—climb up a sea serpent's back and drop out of its mouth into the water. The rooms are lighter than they used to be but still seem small; romance is best found strolling along the cobblestone streets and the meandering river walk. The adjoining **Riverside** section, with its old–Southern Mississippi theme, is priced similarly. However some of its rooms offer an additional child-size trundle bed, making it a great value for a family of five.

Feel like sacrificing yourself on a 46-foot mock Mayan pyramid complete with a water slide rushing down its "ceremonial" stone steps? It's possible at Disney's "moderate" **Coronado Springs Resort.** Of course, Disney's depiction of the Southwest can be a bit clichéd and sterile, but the resort's price tag (rooms start at $139 a night) and obsessive attention to detail make this a good deal. Disney Imagineers set out to transport guests to a combination of the American Southwest and the Mexican Riviera with Mickey Mouse–shaped cactus landscaping, a 15-acre man-made lagoon, and the aforementioned Mayan Temple pool area. You can choose between the lively, brightly colored casitas (my favorite), the quirky beach cabanas, and the earthy, Western-styled ranchos. The lobby and the resort's large food market are built around "La Fuente de las Palomas," a "spring-fed" fountain bubbling up from a Spanish urn. The ranchos and cabanas are closest to the Mayan pool and the casitas are closest to the food market/main building. And yes, Mickey wears a sombrero here. Pick up yours in the gift shop.

But to truly grab the lowest prices for Disney accommodations, one must be willing to find their inner child and let it come out to play. Otherwise you may find the decor of the **All-Star Sports, All-Star Music, All-Star Movies,** and **Pop Century Resort** resorts too hard on the senses and even too much to take. There's nothing subtle about Disney's entries into the lower-price lodging market (also known as "value resorts"). Suffice it to say, kids will love the larger-than-life themes. The All-Star Sports resort has giant surfboards, taller-than-the-building football helmets, and stairwells in the shape of soda cans. Things are just as wacky at the All-Star Music resort: Get ready for three-story-tall cowboy boots, a guitar-shaped pool, and a walk-through, neon-lit jukebox. The All-Star Movies resort will appeal to die-hard fans of Disney's animated movies as it features, among other things, a 35-foot-tall Buzz Lightyear from *Toy Story,* the towering bodies of Pongo and Perdita from *101 Dalmatians,* and Mickey the Sorcerer from *Fantasia.*

The Pop Century resort is probably the value resort with the broadest appeal, as the different sections are themed according to the pop culture of each decade from the 1950s to the 1990s. The '50s buildings offer a three-story-tall jukebox, bowling alley pool, and dancers at the hop. The '60s buildings, with their yo-yo stairwells, are all about Flower Power (and are closest to the main building/food court). The '70s buildings have disco music piped in the courtyard that features a huge foosball court and a three-story-tall Big Wheel. The '80s are hard to miss with the Rubik's Cube stairwells, and the '90s has only one building featuring cellphone stairwells and a three-story laptop computer. Note that the icons decorating their facades and the outdoor layout may differ slightly, but the four value resorts are basically clones: Each has a fast-food-style court, small and sparse rooms (think 1950s budget motel dressed up in Mickey garb), and even tinier bathrooms. Clearly, Disney wants to inspire an overdeveloped sense of togetherness in its guests. The resorts are also set off in their own little section of the World (probably so they won't frighten off guests with fatter wallets), and transportation to the parks via Disney's crowded buses is often time consuming. But hey, what do you want for $79 to $137 a night?

If you picked up arms for Uncle Sam, even Disney will give you a discount, specifically at its **Shades of Green Resort,** a spot reserved for active and retired military personnel and their families. It's the best bargain on Disney soil, though room rates are based on military rank (the scale begins at $76 per night). All the large rooms offer TVs with wireless keyboards (access to the Internet is offered for a fee), balconies or patios, and pool or golf-course (there are three of them) views.

Where to go to get away from kids... The best answer is someplace else, preferably out of state. This is Disney World, folks, where kids rule and parents pool all their resources to 1) pay for the adventure and 2) keep their cool while doing so. If the tiny bundles of noise and energy really do drive you up the wall, book a room at the quiet and elegant **Peabody Orlando Hotel.** Parents with young ones feel instantly out of place when they walk into what is in fact a very gracious lobby, full of beautiful art, subtle tones, and hushed voices. Spend an afternoon at the Peabody Athletic Club (classes, machines, personal fitness trainers, tennis courts, and a lap pool are all available), and then treat yourself to an intimate dinner at the sophisticated Dux restaurant, on the premises (see the Dining chapter). If you must, there's also daily bus transportation to all the theme parks. The **Caribe Royale All-Suites Resort** sections off one of its three accommodation towers for "adults only." This means that while you may still have to deal with kids at the pool, they won't be running up and down your hallway all day. If you want to stay on WDW property, the **Coronado Springs Resort**'s moderate pricing may appeal to families, but the convention center on its premises means a bunch of business travelers make it their home base and give it a slightly quieter edge.

The much pricier **Walt Disney World Dolphin** and **Walt Disney World Swan** hotels aren't actually owned by Disney (they're owned by Starwood Hotels), so the Mickey theme is toned down a notch or two, and there are fewer kids in the house. Noted architect Michael Graves—yes, he of the silver-and-blue toasters at Target—designed these striking, over-the-top buildings with rooftops graced respectively by a five-story-high giant swan and a dolphin fish. The Dolphin is the more whimsical of the two (witness the circuslike tent and dolphin fountains in the lobby), though both hotels have had their themes scaled down thanks to a redesign (with Graves at the helm yet again). "Unique" is an understatement. Guest rooms at both properties have a palette of silver-blue and white, and they include Starwood signature items, such as the Westin Heavenly Bed and Heavenly Bath treatments. The two resorts face Crescent Lake and share a slice of sandy beach—one of the best places in the World to watch Epcot's nightly fireworks. ***Tip for canoodlers:*** The outside beach and pool area can be quite romantic at night.

For honeymooners and romantics... First, don't even think about **Disney's Polynesian Resort.** This is the top choice for honeymooners visiting Disney World, for no apparent reason. Only thing I can figure is that this resort sounds so romantic—a touch of the French Polynesian islands, warm breezes, thatched roofs. What you'll actually get is a nice enough room, but the resort itself is packed with diaper-clad crawlers and hot, harried parents. Watch out for the stroller traffic jams at the door. If you're willing to pay for the romantic atmosphere, you'll enjoy your stay more next door at the **Grand Floridian**—and since you're there, splurge (and I mean splurge) on a meal at the resort's small award-winning fine-dining restaurant, Victoria and Albert's.

The romance and lure of a national park lives on at **Disney's Wilderness Lodge.** So what if it's full of pretend hot springs and manufactured geysers—it's still one of Disney's best. The surrounding woods and somewhat secluded setting on Bay Lake Beach give a sense of privacy. Rent a bike and take a ride in the pines. The Wilderness is a great place to come home to—the towering wood-and-stone lobby is stunning. Wait until the sun starts to head for the other side of the world, then find a table for two at the small, upscale Hemingway's restaurant in the **Hyatt Regency Grand Cypress** resort. After a fine dinner, stroll the lush grounds and then pick a private spot at the giant grotto pool. Listen to the waterfalls, and sneak into one of the tucked-away spas. Nothing says romance more than an Italian villa on the water, so it should come as no surprise that Universal's **Portofino Bay Hotel** is a top romantic getaway. Request a room with a private balcony overlooking the harbor and share a bottle of wine while you watch the sun set over the water. The oversize bathtubs and showers also lend to the intimate mood.

Aquatic wonderlands... The Orlando area has to have the largest concentration of swimming pools per square mile in the world. Every hotel, motel, campground, and resort has at least one, and often five or six. Lots of these may be your basic, dip-your-feet-in models, but there are also plenty of the spare-no-expense, over-the-top examples sure to fulfill your wettest and wildest dreams. Among my favorites is Stormalong Bay, the free-flowing fantasy pool shared by the **Disney Yacht** and **Beach Club resorts.** In the middle of the 3-acre pool is a giant pirate ship; kids climb in and zip down the water slide. Meanwhile, adults can relax in the spas tucked away in rockscapes or enjoy the zero-entry sandy-bottom pool areas. For a tropical experience, Universal's **Royal Pacific Resort** offers up a zero-entry, 12,000-square-foot lagoon pool with its own beach and deck. Adults can seek serenity in the private cabanas and whirlpools. The pool at the **Hard Rock Hotel** gets my vote for best L.A.-hipster vibe, with a 240-foot slide, 12 underwater speakers, interactive fountains, private cabanas, and a sandy beach.

If you prefer languorous soaks in the sun and sensuous cool floats on the sparkling water, check out **Orlando World Center Marriott,** where guests have a choice of four pools: indoor, children's, sport, and the sprawling freshwater pool with its rock-framed waterfalls, four secluded spas, and fast-moving water slide. At the **Hyatt Regency Grand Cypress,** there's a stunning free-form pool with grottoes, cascading waterfalls, and a water slide, all surrounded by a maze of tropical foliage and meandering walkways. You'll find spas tucked away in corners and hidden under waterfalls. If you like the feel of sand between your toes, stroll over to the beach, where you can build your own castle, go sailing, or take a dip in the lake.

Pamper palaces... Another day of jostling among the sweating masses, waiting in line for Splash Mountain and the Incredible Hulk coaster?!! Don't stress out. Instead, take a break and book a few hours at the spa. Stay at **Disney's Grand Floridian Resort & Spa, Disney's Saratoga Springs Resort & Spa,** Universal's **Portofino Bay Hotel** and its Mandara Spa, or the **Gaylord Palms Resort,** with its prestigious Canyon Ranch SpaClub, and you'll have the luxury of a full-service spa on-site. If those aren't enough to ease your tension, try the huge tri-level spa complex shared by the new **JW Marriott** and **Ritz-Carlton** at **Grande Lakes.** The services and amenities at the **Buena Vista Palace** are also top-notch. All the spas discussed above offer the standard treatments, as well as signature services and special packages. Of course, you don't have to be a guest to partake of the resort spas—but oh, how much easier it is to pop in for a wonderful massage and foot rub when it's only two floors away. Even better—have them come to you in your room.

Simple and cheap... Grottoes, waterfalls, fake environments, doting bellcaps? Hell, you just want a clean room with two beds, a pool, and an ice machine nearby. And you want to pay a reasonable price (reasonable by tourist-town standards, anyway). No problem. For starters, you can't beat the **Microtel Inn and Suites,** a pleasant motel-style accommodation that always gets top marks with returning travelers on a budget. Who can argue with clean, bright rooms, a heated pool, snack bar, free continental breakfast, and free local calls (surprisingly a rarity in Orlando)—all for around $62 to $90 a night? Its convenient location, just off I-Drive, behind Wet 'n' Wild, is another plus. The rooms at the **Radisson Barcelo Hotel** on International Drive won't charm your pants off, but they're okay. Management has tried to spruce up the outdoor pool area with some trees and flowers, and you do get a refrigerator in the room and a restaurant on the premises. One great perk: Guests get free passes to the well-equipped YMCA Aquatic Center, located right behind the Radisson. Just down the street, the **Quality Inn Plaza,** located across from the Pointe Orlando shopping/entertainment complex, has some extra niceties. All rooms include a refrigerator, microwave, and coffeemaker, and outside there's a good-size pool. Throw in free breakfast and shuttles to the theme parks, and you've got a great deal for under $80 a night. The **Tropical Palms Fun Resort** in Kissimmee offers spacious, separate home-style accommodations that management's dubbed "FunSuites." These include two bedrooms, sleeping loft, a pullout sofa in the living area, and a full kitchen (enough room for you and seven pals) for $149 per night. In the chain department, clean hotel rooms, good pools, a free breakfast, free local calls, shuttles to main attractions, and a 100%-satisfaction guarantee mean you really can't go wrong with a **Hampton Inn.** You'll find many of them in the theme-park areas, but the best in terms of location is the Hampton Inn at Universal Studios on Windhover Drive.

And cheaper still... If you're really looking to spend microbucks, your best bets are the small, locally owned U.S. 192/Kissimmee motels. All of the following establishments charge less than $60 a night. **Magic Castle Inn & Suites,** near Disney World on U.S. 192, is a family-owned property offering a clean room at a budget price. They also offer a free continental breakfast and weekly rates that average out to around $35 a night. As one guest explained, "We get up early; we're gone all day. When we return, we take a dip in the pool and fall asleep. Why pay for a fancy place to stay?" Over by Universal, the **Days Inn Lakeside** is showing its age on the outside, but offers clean rooms, lakefront views, and a free shuttle to Universal Orlando. Rates are usually under $60 a night. For the ultracheap, only one hostel remains in the Orlando-theme-park areas: The **Palm Lakefront Resort & Hostel** in Kissimmee. Formerly a Hostelling International property, amenities include a lakefront, a beach, a pool, paddleboats, and private family rooms, as well as dorm rooms. Be aware that you may end up sharing a room with up to five strangers in exchange for the average rates of around $19. I'd personally rather coerce five friends to split a hotel room.

I want to be alone.... If privacy is what you seek in Orlando, you'll have to stay in your room and lock the door. Otherwise, no matter when or where, you'll be in a crowd. That said, there are a few spots that are more secluded than others. The **Hyatt Regency Grand Cypress** is big enough to let you remain incognito—it's quite possible to check in next to people you'll never see again until checkout time. While you're golfing, they're horseback riding. While you're playing tennis, they're at the driving range. While you're in one restaurant, they're in another. In fact, you could both be at the pool at the same time and not bump into one another—the resort is that big. The **JW Marriott** and **Ritz-Carlton** share a 500-acre complex over in the Grande Lakes development. Lose yourself in the 40,000-square-foot spa or play golf until you can't stand green anymore. **The Gaylord Palms Resort & Convention Center** takes privacy a step further, designing each room with individual doorbells and electronic DO NOT DISTURB signs.

Suite deals... Suite accommodations are a big deal in the Orlando area. No wonder: After battling the masses all day, the idea of waiting in line for dinner and then bunking down with your buddies in a tiny hotel room may not sound like your idea of a vacation. You want a place to sprawl out and relax, with a separate room for sleeping and a cold beer in the fridge. Even if you pay a little more for the room itself, just think of what you could save by purchasing snacks and meals from the grocery store instead of some overpriced restaurant (Orlando has plenty of those, too). The six-story, 350-room **Residence Inn SeaWorld International Center** is one of the newest all-suite properties on the block. Families, business travelers, and groups flock here, piling into the one- and two-bedroom suites (studios are also available). The under-$300-a-night price point for a two-bedroom suite is a bargain when you consider the extras: free shuttle to SeaWorld, Universal's theme parks, and Wet 'n' Wild; fully equipped kitchens; free hot breakfast buffet; pool (overrun by young tykes); sports courts; and more. If you're traveling with kids, they even have their own poolside bar that serves pizza and ice cream. At **Staybridge Suites,** you get a spacious living area, full kitchen, two bedrooms, and two bathrooms for less than you'd pay for a tiny room at the deluxe Disney properties and plush Orlando resorts. There's also a small pool and an on-premises restaurant and lounge, and you're within walking distance to about a hundred restaurants and shops. Free continental breakfast and free shuttles to Disney World and Orlando International Airport make this an even bigger deal.

You'll pay more at the **Buena Vista Suites** on World Center Drive, just a mile or so from Disney World, where rooms are smaller, the suites have only one bathroom, and there's a mini-kitchen setup (small fridge, microwave oven, and coffeemaker). On the other hand, the rooms were recently upgraded and the public areas are more deluxe; they include a large swimming pool, exercise room, and tennis courts. For a more tropical-flavored escape, try the neighboring **Caribe Royale All-Suites Resort.** It's all pink and green with lots of foliage, giant palm trees, and pretty flowers spread out on a 30-acre parcel just outside Disney World. Unfortunately, the high-rise buildings give it away—no, Dorothy, you're not in the Caribbean, either. Still, the suites offer a bit more space than a standard hotel room, plus kitchen facilities. They come in lots of variations; the standard package is living room plus bedroom, while the deluxe suite gives you a pullout couch in the living area. What the designers saved on the suites (they kept them pretty basic, with just enough room), they put into the public areas. The free-form swimming pool has a 75-foot water slide, whirlpools, and a poolside bar and grill, plus an adults-only sun deck.

Home away from home... What? No cartoon characters, no overdone themes, no giant water slides? The **Disney Vacation Club** (DVC for those in the know) is Disney's answer to timesharing. They've taken the already tricky concept and complicated it even further, so the ownership system is about as easy to understand as a computer manual. Disney rents out individual villas and suites when they aren't in use, so you don't have to pay the exorbitant buy-in costs. (Though you'll still pay a pretty penny—$299–$1,099 depending on the size of your unit.) Forget trying to get a place here during peak season; they're booked up for years to come. But if you go off-season, you might get lucky, so ask about it when you call Disney reservations. The DVC resorts offer the best of two worlds: a Disney property with a giant pool and lots of activities and amenities, and comfortable home-style accommodations, complete with kitchens. The suites are roomy, bright, and airy, with a choice of studios, one-bedrooms, two-bedrooms, and grand villas. Properties included in the Disney timeshares are the **Old Key West Resort,** the **Beach Club Villas,** the **BoardWalk Villas,** the **Wilderness Lodge Villas,** and the new **Saratoga Springs Resort & Spa.**

Fairways in the foreground... If your idea of the perfect vacation spot includes an 18-hole golf course outside your door and a pro on staff, start packing your clubs. The Orlando area has a number of top-ranked golf resorts. Only minutes from Disney is **Arnold Palmer's Bay Hill Club and Lodge,** consistently ranked one of the top courses in the country. If you have that obsessive, gotta-golf-every-day passion, you'll fit right in at Bay Hill. The lodge-style rooms at the resort are modest, but nobody notices. They come for Palmer's renowned golf academy, in hopes of shaving off a few strokes from their score, and for the demanding play on 27 championship holes. Nongolfing partners will not have to pray for rain when they decide to stay at the **Hyatt Regency Grand Cypress**—there's plenty to keep everyone busy at this opulent, anything-your-little-heart-desires resort. First, the golf course: a

Nicklaus-designed championship layout, inspired by Scotland's classic St. Andrews links, with lots of vistas and heathered fairways. Second, the golf school: one of the best, with state-of-the-art teaching techniques. Finally, the resort: one of the finest around, with sprawling grounds, a giant pool, fine restaurants, tasteful accommodations, and more activities than you'll be able to handle in one vacation. The sprawling **Grande Lakes** complex features a Greg Norman–designed par-72 course adjacent to the **Ritz-Carlton Orlando.** Extending the resort's unparalleled tradition of service onto the green, the innovative Caddie-Concierge Program—the first of its kind at any golf resort in Central Florida—assigns each group a knowledgeable, professional attendant to enhance the golf experience and take care of the guest's needs while on the course. In the same class is the **Orlando World Center Marriott,** a spectacular high-rise hotel with six restaurants, eight tennis courts, and expansive, free-flowing pools with slides and spas. Did we mention golf? Marriott's Golf Club is situated on 130 acres, just off Disney's doorstep. Improve your game at John Jacob's School of Golf, which was once named the "Golf School of Choice" by *Golf Magazine.* The club also offers practice and driving ranges, private or group clinics, and one of the best pro shops in the country. Of course, **Disney World's** no Mickey Mouse operation (well, you know what I mean) when it comes to golf. There are five championship courses on WDW property—Eagle Pines, Palm, Magnolia, Osprey Ridge, and Lake Buena Vista—offering a total of 99 holes, as well as three pro shops and 15 pros on hand. (See the Getting Outside chapter for more info.) Stay at any Disney resort and you'll receive preferred tee times. ***Tee tip:*** If you plan to go golfing more than park-hopping, look into one of Disney's Magic Your Way packages. These come in a variety of price ranges and configurations, and they can include a choice of Disney accommodations, park admissions, dining, golf, transportation—you name it.

Condo-mania... Condos and rental homes are often the cheapest way to go for large groups in Orlando. It's possible to rent a two- or three-bedroom condo or house with a community pool for $100 to $150 a night, though you can certainly spend more if you want even more space and amenities (even within a given property, there's usually a wide range of price options). The word about these bargains has been slow to get out, but this type of lodging is definitely catching on. The disadvantage is that it feels like, well, a home, instead of a resort—the maid service is usually minimal—and if you crave action, you'll hate it, as it's pretty dead on the premises. Spending all your waking hours at the attractions (that's why you came here, isn't it?) might help. **All Star Vacation Homes** (Tel 407/997-0733 or 888/249-1779; www.allstarvacationhomes.com) offers a large selection of villas, town houses, and elegant single-family homes in Kissimmee, all within a few minutes of Disney World. Spacious living quarters, fully equipped kitchens, washers and dryers, air-conditioning, a community pool, a clubhouse, and rec areas are often part of the package. For more condominium info, ask for the Orlando/Orange County Convention and Visitors Bureau's free Planning Kit. It lists several other condo and vacation-home rental agencies in the area.

Taking care of business... In addition to the hotels inside Walt Disney World proper, six off-Disney properties feature on-site meeting and convention facilities. **The Gaylord Palms Resort & Convention Center** is going after the upscale convention crowd in a big way. The massive convention center and exhibition and meeting spaces lure the big crowds, while on-site amenities and services try to keep everyone happy. Lush atriums filled with tropical plants, bogs, swamps, caves—even a replica of the *Castillo de San Marcos,* the oldest Spanish fort in America, and a "fountain of youth" complete the Florida theme. Resort restaurants are top-notch and you'll love the on-site Canyon Ranch SpaClub. The **Hyatt Regency Grand Cypress** is also a favorite among the working crowd—well, among those who are supposed to be working, anyway. It's tough to put the nose to the grindstone when you're surrounded by 1,500 acres of lush grounds, waterfalls, a massive swimming pool, world-class golf, an equestrian center, and more. But, hey, if the company's paying, why not? Meeting planners have 65,000 square feet of space to play with, including 7,000 square feet of prefunction space, 16,768 square feet of exhibition space, and 29 meeting rooms, all within walking distance of the golf club and villas. If your VIPs need to helicopter in, you can arrange landing clearance at the resort's helipad. Only a bit less sybaritic, with more than 200,000 square feet of meeting space, **Orlando World Center Marriott** ranks as one of the largest meeting resorts in Florida; it's a magnet for really big groups. The individual business traveler is provided for, too, with a complete business center—equipped with fax, copy machine, and IBM and Macintosh computers—and a full-service audiovisual production unit. Off-hours, the resort offers more recreational opportunities than you'll have time for: swimming, golf, a driving range, tennis courts, a health club, and, of course, all those Orlando/Disney attractions nearby. Bet you end up playing hooky. Not quite in the same class is the **Buena Vista Palace,** a 27-acre property near Downtown Disney, which features translation and secretarial services, fax, computers, and photocopying at its business center. The resort has 44 meeting rooms, a ballroom, and a conference/exhibit hall. This place looks all business—low ceilings, dark halls—until you get to the spa. Be sure to schedule a visit to this full-service nirvana for a massage, body wrap, facial, or a hydrotherapy treatment—way more fun than catching the bus to Disney World on your afternoon off. The prices are kinda high for the ho-hum rooms, but the outside swimming area and walkways are pleasant, and you'll get a good view of sunsets against the skyline (and, later, the nightly fireworks) from the lounge on the 27th floor. High-powered executives favor the posh, subdued **Peabody Orlando Hotel,** right across from the convention center. Its pale and plush surroundings are very soothing to come home to after a day on the convention floor, and buttoned-down types may well prefer such traditional decor to the tropical riot of most other Orlando lodgings. The high-rise **Renaissance Orlando Resort** is a major convention facility, catering more to business than pleasure, but it's near SeaWorld. It also features the world's largest atrium lobby, with a $600,000 tropical aviary and a pool of more than 200 rare Japanese koi.

Happy campers... Let's suppose your blood is already thin and you can handle the sweatbox conditions of Central Florida (and let's suppose the bugs don't bother you)—well, then, camping just may be the way to go. Or perhaps you have one of those traveling homes on wheels and just need a place to plug in. If so, you're in luck. Disney's **Fort Wilderness Resort & Campground** is downright plush by camping standards. More than 700 acres of woods surround the campground, where you'll find sites for tents and RVs. There are also a number of "wilderness cabins" for rent that accommodate up to six people, with separate living space, fully equipped kitchens, telephone, and daily housekeeping. Of course, prices have gone up, but call way ahead, because these spots fill up months in advance; campsites and hookups run about $39 to $92 a night, while wilderness cabins rent for $239 to $349. At this huge campground, you'll find snack bars, restaurants, bike and boat rentals, game rooms, horseback riding, nightly campfires, movies and entertainment, tennis, two swimming pools, and a small beach. Not exactly roughing it! You'll also have access to theme parks by boat or bus. The **Kissimmee KOA Kampground** features spaces for tents and RVs, including slide-outs. A pool, bicycle rentals, fishing, and high-speed Wi-Fi Internet access are available to guests. Value Kard holders get extra discounts, so it might be worth the $14 or so to join up. Then you can head for the theme parks with the money you saved on lodging. (A shuttle runs to Disney World, Universal Orlando, and SeaWorld.) However, be advised: Wilderness camping this ain't. It's more akin to pitching a tent in the parking lot at Wal-Mart.

Doggie digs... Can't bear to leave your four-legged treasure at home? No prob. You'll find lots of places where Fido is welcome in Orlando, including the **Seralago Hotel & Suites Main Gate East** and **Residence Inn SeaWorld International Center.** Disney resorts, except for the **Fort Wilderness Resort & Campground,** do not allow pets. On-site kennels are available, however, at Epcot, Magic Kingdom, Animal Kingdom, and MGM Studios. And overnight boarding is available at the Ticket and Transportation Center for Disney resort guests. Kennels for day use are also available at SeaWorld and Universal Orlando. The three on-site Universal hotels—**Portofino Bay Hotel, Hard Rock Hotel,** and the **Royal Pacific Resort**—are run by Loews, which means pets are not only welcome as guests but are pampered alongside their owners.

Map 2: Orlando Accommodations

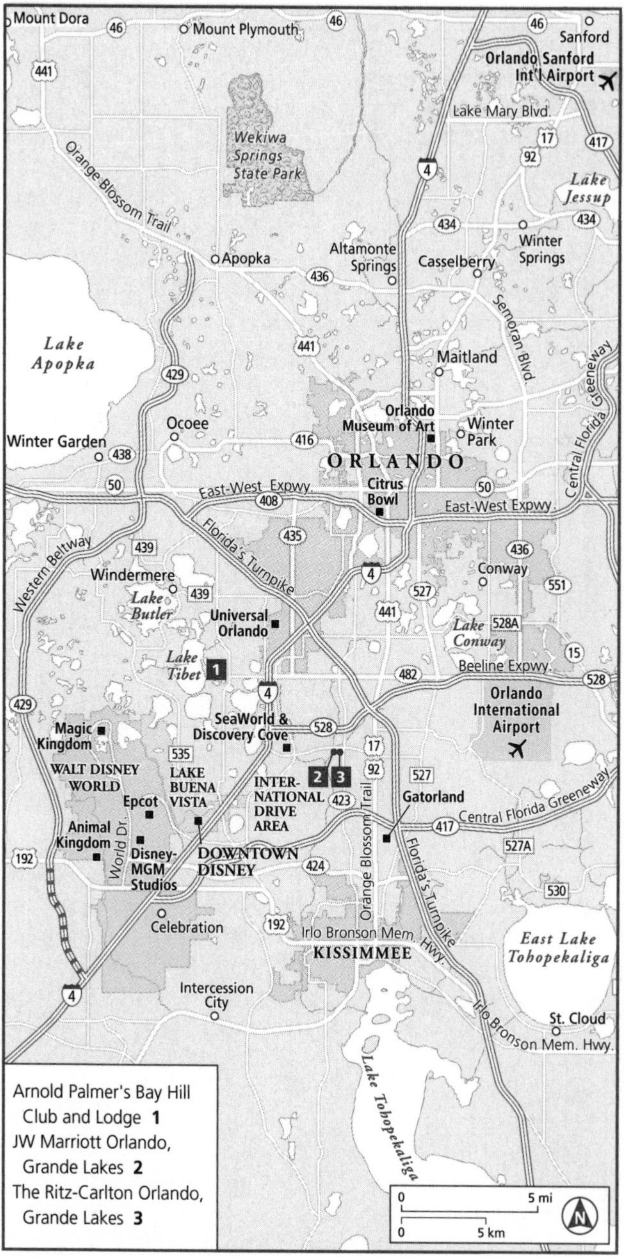

Map 3: WDW & Lake Buena Vista Accommodations

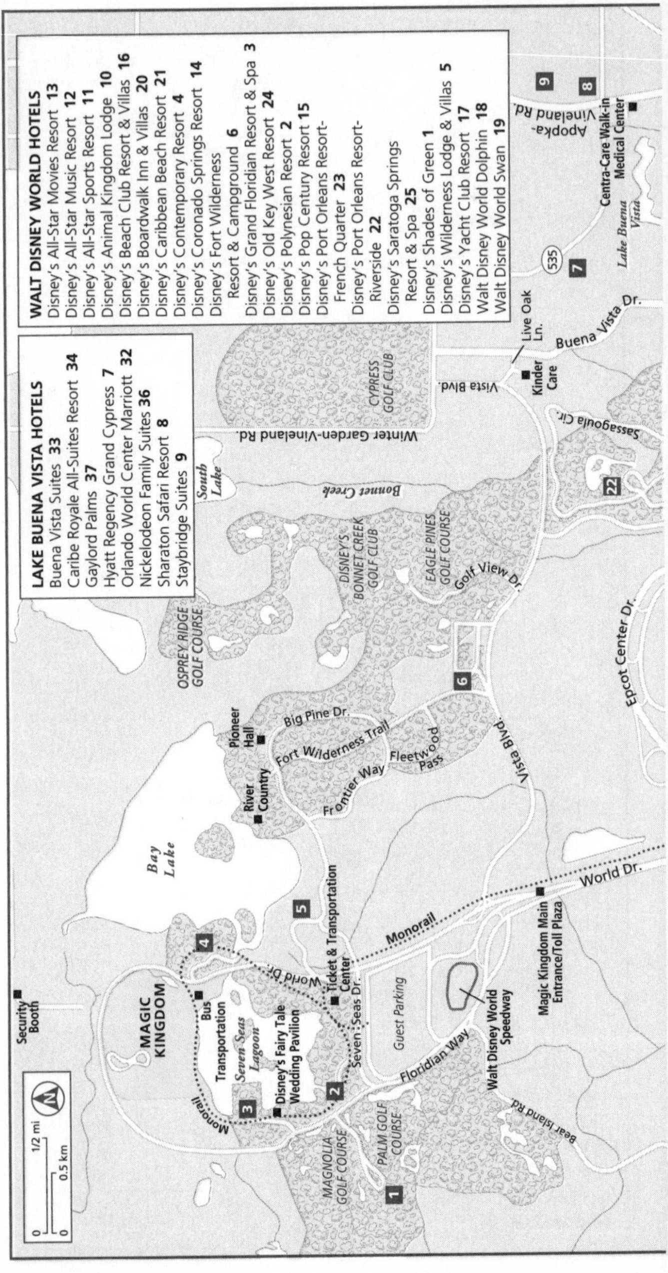

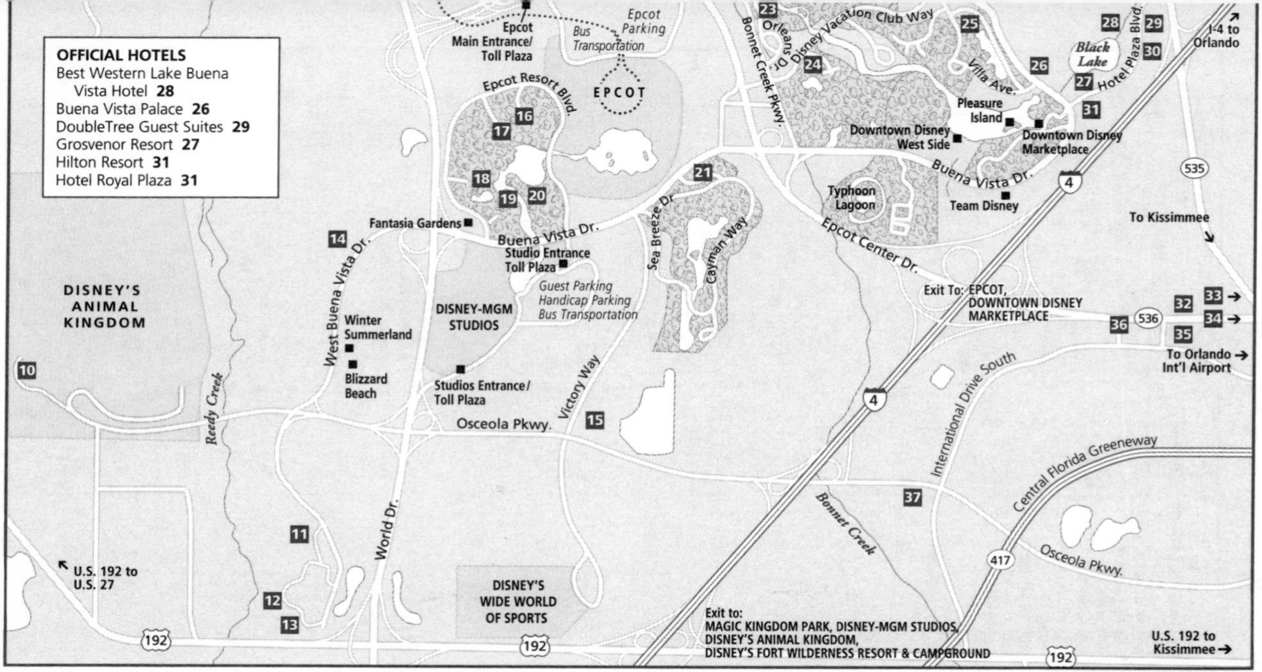
OFFICIAL HOTELS
Best Western Lake Buena Vista Hotel 28
Buena Vista Palace 26
DoubleTree Guest Suites 29
Grosvenor Resort 27
Hilton Resort 31
Hotel Royal Plaza 31
Epcot Main Entrance/Toll Plaza
Bus Transportation
Epcot Parking
EPCOT
Epcot Resort Blvd.
Fantasia Gardens
Buena Vista Dr.
Studio Entrance Toll Plaza
Guest Parking
Handicap Parking
Bus Transportation
DISNEY-MGM STUDIOS
Studios Entrance/Toll Plaza
West Buena Vista Dr.
Winter Summerland
Blizzard Beach
DISNEY'S ANIMAL KINGDOM
Reedy Creek
Osceola Pkwy.
Victory Way
Sea Breeze Dr.
Cayman Way
World Dr.
DISNEY'S WIDE WORLD OF SPORTS
U.S. 192 to U.S. 27
192
Bonnet Creek Pkwy.
Orleans Dr.
Disney Vacation Club Way
Villa Ave.
Pleasure Island
Downtown Disney West Side
Downtown Disney Marketplace
Black Lake
Hotel Plaza Blvd.
Typhoon Lagoon
Team Disney
Epcot Center Dr.
Exit To: EPCOT, DOWNTOWN DISNEY MARKETPLACE
I-4 to Orlando
535
To Kissimmee
536
To Orlando Int'l Airport
4
International Drive South
Central Florida Greeneway
Bonnet Creek
417
Exit to: MAGIC KINGDOM PARK, DISNEY-MGM STUDIOS, DISNEY'S ANIMAL KINGDOM, DISNEY'S FORT WILDERNESS RESORT & CAMPGROUND
U.S. 192 to Kissimmee

Map 4: Universal Orlando & International Drive–Area Accommodations

Days Inn Lakeside **7**
The DoubleTree Castle **10**
Hampton Inn at Universal Studios **1**
Hard Rock Hotel **3**
Microtel Inn and Suites **6**
The Peabody Orlando Hotel **12**
Portofino Bay Hotel **2**
Quality Inn Plaza **11**
Radisson Barcelo Hotel **8**
Renaissance Orlando Resort at SeaWorld **13**
Residence Inn SeaWorld International Center **14**
Royal Pacific Resort **4**
Sheraton Studio City **5**
Staybridge Suites **9**

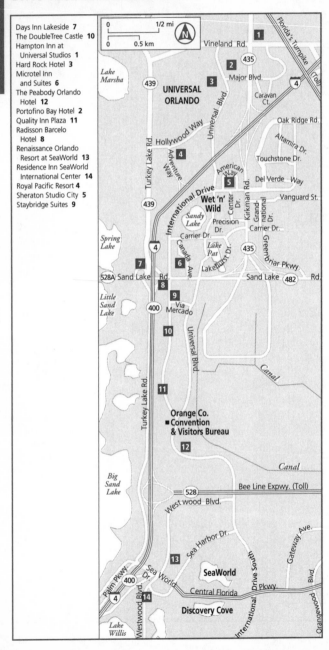

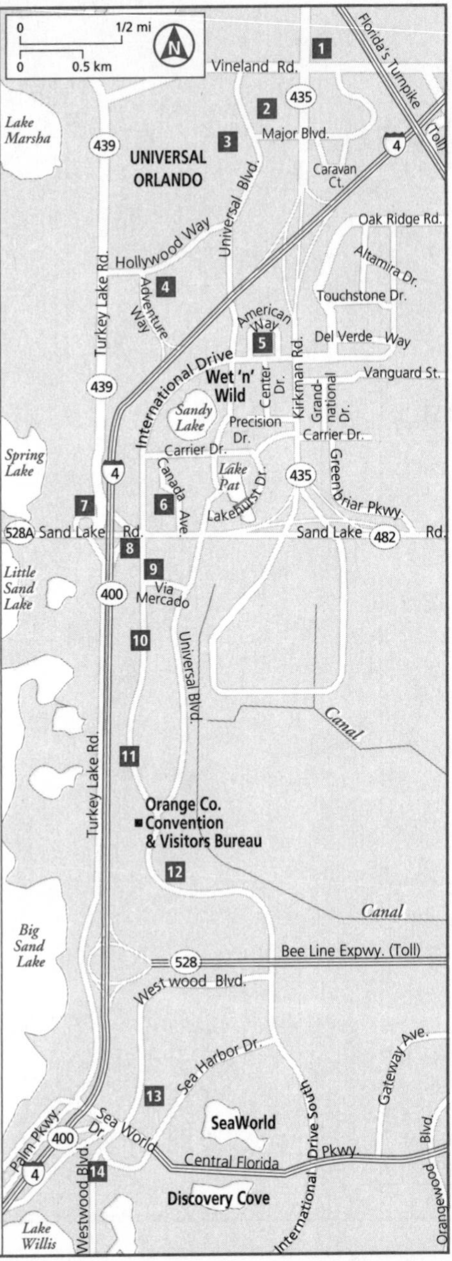

Map 5: U.S. 192/Kissimmee Accommodations

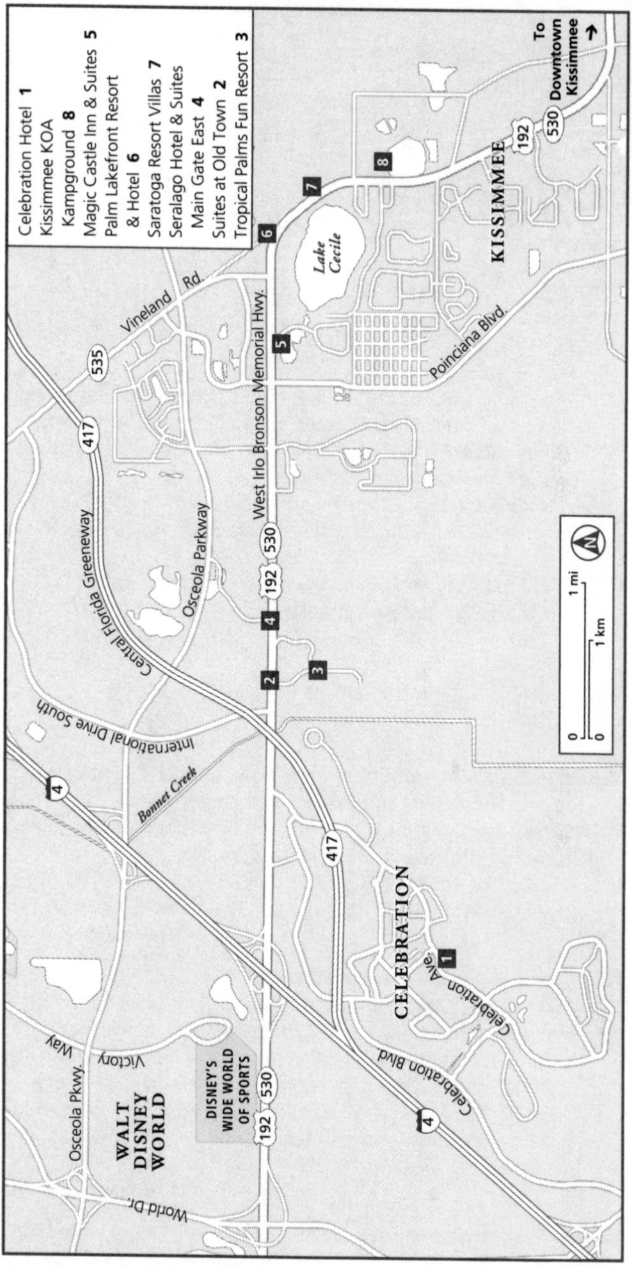

The Index

$$$$$	over $200
$$$$	$150–$200
$$$	$90–$149
$$	$50–$89
$	under $50

Price ratings are based on the lowest price quoted for a standard double room in high season, including taxes and charges. Unless otherwise noted, rooms have air-conditioning, phones, private bathrooms, and TVs.

Note: All hotels with names preceded by the word "Disney" are on Walt Disney World property, as are the Walt Disney World Swan and Dolphin.

The following abbreviations are used for credit cards:

AE	American Express
DC	Diners Club
DISC	Discover
MC	MasterCard
V	Visa

Arnold Palmer's Bay Hill Club and Lodge (p. 42) ORLANDO This country club/mini-resort is a favorite among golfers, who come to test their skill on the top-rated golf courses and to attend Palmer's Academy. Lots of packages available.... *Tel 407/876-2429 (toll-free 888/422-9445). Fax 407/876-1035. www.bayhill.com. 9000 Bay Hill Blvd. 70 rooms. AE, MC, V. $$$$$*

See Map 2 on p. 47.

Best Western Lake Buena Vista (p. 21) LAKE BUENA VISTA Located near Downtown Disney, this 18-story high-rise sits on a pretty lake, and many rooms offer great views of water and the World. But that's the only reason to consider staying here, as the staff is often rude and rooms are showing their age.... *Tel 407/828-2424 (toll-free 800/348-3765). Fax 407/828-8933. www.orlandoresorthotel.com. 2000 Hotel Plaza Blvd. 325 rooms. AE, DC, DISC, MC, V. $$$*

See Map 3 on p. 48.

Buena Vista Palace (p. 38) LAKE BUENA VISTA This 27-acre hotel is pleasant, offering a fabulous location and nice service but average rooms. The on-site full-service spa will cure any aches after a long day at the parks.... *Tel 407/827-3228 (toll-free 866/397-6516). Fax 407/827-6034. www.buenavistapalace.com. 1900 Buena Vista Dr. 1,012 rooms. AE, DC, DISC, MC, V. $$$$$*

See Map 3 on p. 48.

Buena Vista Suites (p. 41) LAKE BUENA VISTA This basic all-suite property offers accommodations with mini-kitchens at a decent price. A free breakfast buffet and shuttle to the Disney parks add to the value, but if you want something a little more upscale, try the Caribe Royale Resort next door.... *Tel 407/239-8588 (toll-free 800/537-7737). Fax 407/239-1401. www.bvsuites.com. 8203 World Center Dr. 279 suites. AE, DISC, MC, V. $$$$*

See Map 3 on p. 48.

Caribe Royale All-Suites Resort (p. 28) LAKE BUENA VISTA Lushly planted grounds give this high-rise suite property a slight Caribbean feel. Recent renovations include improvements to the lobby and a new fitness center. The 250,000-gallon free-form pool will inspire you to take a dip, and Tower III's "adults only" accommodations offer asylum from the kid parade.... *Tel 407/238-8000 (toll-free 800/823-8300). Fax 407/238-8050. www.cariberoyale.com. 8101 World Center Dr. 1,218 suites, 120 villas. AE, DC, DISC, MC, V. $$$$*

See Map 3 on p. 48.

Celebration Hotel (p. 30) CELEBRATION Elegant and lovely old Florida–style hotel, perfect for adults who want to get away from tourist central. Too bad it's in Disney's manufactured town of Celebration, which tries too hard to be the perfect Stepford version of small-town America.... *Tel 407/566-6000. Fax 407/566-1844. www.celebrationhotel.com. 700 Bloom St. 115 rooms. AE, DC, DISC, MC, V. $$$$$*

See Map 5 on p. 51.

Days Inn Lakeside (p. 40) INTERNATIONAL DRIVE Families flock to this hotel on the lake but the buildings are showing signs of wear and tear. The lakefront views and free shuttle to Universal make this budget property a little more attractive.... *Tel 407/351-1900 (toll-free 800/777-3297). Fax 407/352-2690. 7335 Sand Lake Rd. 695 rooms. AE, DC, DISC, MC, V. $$–$$$*

See Map 4 on p. 50.

Disney's All-Star Movies Resort (p. 34) WDW Giant-size characters from Disney movies adorn this budget-priced property. Loud and busy, but fun if you're a Disney movie fan and don't mind midget-size rooms.... *Tel 407/939-7000. Fax 407/939-7111. www.waltdisneyworld.com. 1991 W. Buena Vista Dr. 1,920 rooms. AE, DC, DISC, MC, V. $$–$$$*

See Map 3 on p. 48.

Disney's All-Star Music Resort (p. 34) WDW Themed to different musical styles, this kitschy value resort is a favorite with cheerleading groups. Avoid it like the plague if there's a competition going on.... *Tel 407/939-6000. Fax 407/939-7222. www.waltdisneyworld.com. 1801 W. Buena Vista Dr. 1,920 rooms. AE, DC, DISC, MC, V. $$–$$$*

See Map 3 on p. 48.

Disney's All-Star Sports Resort (p. 34) WDW Disney's salute to big-league sports can be crowded and noisy, especially when school sports competitions are being held at Disney's Wide World of Sports.... *Tel 407/939-5000. Fax 407/939-7333. www.waltdisneyworld.com. 1701 W. Buena Vista Dr. 1,920 rooms. AE, DC, DISC, MC, V. $$–$$$*

See Map 3 on p. 48.

Disney's Animal Kingdom Lodge (p. 28) WDW Nestled behind Animal Kingdom, this African-themed resort offers panoramic views of a 33-acre savanna brimming with birds and exotic animals. Close to the Disney hubbub, but removed enough to appeal to those not totally Disney-enamored.... *Tel 407/938-3000. Fax 407/938-4799. www.waltdisneyworld.com. 2901 Osceola Pkwy. 1,293 rooms. AE, DC, DISC, MC, V. $$$$$*

See Map 3 on p. 48.

Disney's Beach Club Resort (p. 33) WDW This is Disney's attempt to mimic Cape Cod's grand summer hotels circa 1870, and they do it well. The casual ambience is courtesy of wicker furniture, pastel colors, and seashell decor. Reasons to book here: Stormalong Bay, a great mini-water park, will cool you off, as will Beaches & Cream's ice cream concoctions. The short walk to Epcot is another plus.... *Tel 407/934-8000. Fax 407/934-3850. www.waltdisneyworld.com. 1800 Epcot Resorts Blvd. 583 rooms. AE, DC, DISC, MC, V. $$$$$*

See Map 3 on p. 48.

Disney's Beach Club Villas (p. 42) WDW The timeshare arm of the Beach Club, the Villas range from studios to two-bedroom arrangements. Often available for rentals, the villas are more expensive than regular rooms (but are sometimes available when the regular Beach Club is sold out, especially for longer stays).... *Tel 407/934-2175. Fax 407/934-3850. www.waltdisneyworld.com. 1800 Epcot Resorts Blvd. 280 rooms and suites. AE, DC, DISC, MC, V. $$$$$*

See Map 3 on p. 48.

Disney's BoardWalk Inn (p. 32) WDW Themed after the Eastern seaboard of the 1930s, it comes complete with an actual boardwalk filled with shops and clubs (Atlantic City back when it was still a beauty). Inn rooms seem a bit smaller than comparable resorts; water-view rooms can be noisy in the evenings. A short walk around the promenade brings you to Epcot.... *Tel 407/939-5100. Fax 407/939-5150. www.waltdisneyworld.com. 2101 N. Epcot Resorts Blvd. 378 rooms. AE, DC, DISC, MC, V. $$$$$*

See Map 3 on p. 48.

Disney's BoardWalk Villas (p. 32) WDW Part of the same complex as the BoardWalk Inn, these sometimes pricey accommodations (sold as timeshares, but also rented to visitors) range from small studios to three-bedroom villas.... *Tel 407/939-5100. Fax 407/939-5150. www.waltdisneyworld.com. 2101 N. Epcot Resorts Blvd. 532 villas. AE, DC, DISC, MC, V. $$$$$*

See Map 3 on p. 48.

Disney's Caribbean Beach Resort (p. 28) WDW Close to Epcot, this island-themed property is popular with families; activity and noise levels can be high. Six pools, a small beach, boat rentals, and a food court are spread out over more than 200 acres. Some rooms are a half-mile hike from the main building, so request accordingly.... *Tel 407/934-3400. Fax 407/934-3288. www.waltdisneyworld.com. 900 Cayman Way. 2,112 rooms. AE, DC, DISC, MC, V. $$$–$$$$*

See Map 3 on p. 48.

Disney's Contemporary Resort (p. 32) WDW The tower rooms of this A-frame building have views of the Magic Kingdom, Bay Lake, and/or Seven Seas Lagoon, but you won't know which you get until check-in. Avoid the garden-wing rooms, which are far from the monorail station and restaurants. Recent upgrades put it among Disney's top rooms.... *Tel 407/824-1000. Fax 407/824-3539. www.waltdisneyworld.com. 4600 N. World Dr. 1,053 rooms. AE, DC, DISC, MC, V. $$$$$*

See Map 3 on p. 48.

Disney's Coronado Springs Resort (p. 34) WDW Southwestern in theme, this resort is one of the best on WDW property, although the on-grounds convention center can make rooms hard to come by. The grounds include waterfalls, a swimming pool with giant pyramidal water slide, and a 15-acre lagoon. Request a casita room to get away from the noise by the pool.... *Tel 407/939-1000. Fax 407/939-1001. www.waltdisneyworld.com. 1000 W. Buena Vista Dr. 1,967 rooms. AE, DC, DISC, MC, V. $$$–$$$$*

See Map 3 on p. 48.

Disney's Fort Wilderness Resort & Campground (p. 46) WDW Accommodations at this 700-plus-acre Disney campground run the gamut from campsites and RV hookups to "Wilderness Cabins." Back-to-nature amenities include walking and biking trails, boating, fishing, horseback riding, swimming, campfires, and more. The Trails End restaurant offers one of Disney's best all-you-can-eat dining deals, but the wait for a bus can be infernal.... *Tel 407/824-2900. Fax 407/824-3508. www.waltdisneyworld.com. 4510 N. Fort Wilderness Trail. 788 campsites, 407 cabins. AE, DC, DISC, MC, V. $–$$$$$*

See Map 3 on p. 48.

Disney's Grand Floridian Resort & Spa (p. 32) WDW Extravagant, with a lavish turn-of-the-20th-century Victorian design, the resort's lobby alone may make your jaw drop. Several award-winning restaurants, a full-service spa, monorail access, and extraordinary detailing...but to truly justify the hefty price tag, a lagoon view is the only way to go.... *Tel 407/824-3000. Fax 407/824-3186. www.waltdisneyworld.com. 4401 Grand Floridian Way. 900 rooms. AE, DC, DISC, MC, V. $$$$$*

See Map 3 on p. 48.

Disney's Old Key West Resort (p. 42) WDW Sunny, large studios and villas, furnished in light woods and subtle island prints, are the hallmark of this Disney Vacation Club property. Accommodations come with fully equipped kitchens. Hop the water shuttle to Downtown Disney.... *Tel 407/827-7700. Fax 407/827-7710. www.waltdisneyworld.com. 1510 N. Cove Rd. 497 rooms. AE, DC, DISC, MC, V. $$$$$*

See Map 3 on p. 48.

Disney's Polynesian Resort (p. 28) WDW South Pacific in theme, this resort is popular with honeymooners...who should get as far away from it as they can. Too many kids means the nightly luau dinner is the only reason to come.... *Tel 407/824-2000. Fax 407/824-3174. www.waltdisneyworld.com. 1600 Seven Seas Dr. 853 rooms. AE, DC, DISC, MC, V. $$$$$*

See Map 3 on p. 48.

Disney's Pop Century Resort (p. 34) WDW Disney's newest inexpensive option showcases pop culture with staircases fashioned out of yo-yos and Rubik's Cubes, and a three-story-tall laptop computer—all masking the same basic rooms as the All-Stars.... *Tel 407/938-4000. Fax 407/938-4040. www.waltdisneyworld.com. 1050 Century Dr. 2,880 rooms. AE, DC, DISC, MC, V. $$–$$$*

See Map 3 on p. 48.

Disney's Port Orleans Resort–French Quarter (p. 33) WDW The Big Easy's French Quarter a la Disney. Wrought-iron railings, courtyards, and old-fashioned street lamps help make up for the modest rooms. You don't have to show any body parts here to get beads.... *Tel 407/934-5000. Fax 407/934-5353. www.waltdisneyworld.com. 2201 Orleans Dr. 1,008 rooms. AE, DC, DISC, MC, V. $$$–$$$$*

See Map 3 on p. 48.

Disney's Port Orleans Resort–Riverside (p. 34) WDW The Mississippi Delta and the Old South, ranging from plantation mansions to bayou cabins with simple but tasteful decor. One of Disney's better values, you get six swimming pools, boat and bike rentals, and a water shuttle to Downtown Disney.... *Tel 407/934-6000. Fax 407/934-5777. www.waltdisneyworld.com. 1251 Dixie Dr. 2,048 rooms. AE, DC, DISC, MC, V. $$$–$$$$*

See Map 3 on p. 48.

Disney's Saratoga Springs Resort & Spa (p. 38) WDW Inspired by 19th-century Saratoga Springs, a popular New York summer retreat, the resort's got Victorian-themed studios and villas with kitchens, a "natural springs" pool, and water shuttle access to Downtown Disney. But its main asset is the renowned full-service spa.... *Tel 407/934-7639. Fax 407/827-1151. www.waltdisneyworld.com. 1901 Buena Vista Dr. 552 rooms. AE, DC, DISC, MC, V. $$$$$*

See Map 3 on p. 48.

Disney's Shades of Green (p. 35) WDW Just west of the Polynesian, this resort is reserved for active and retired military personnel and their families; rates are determined by rank. Renovated and expanded in 2004, it's the best bargain at Disney, bar none.... *Tel 407/824-3600. Fax 407/824-3640. www.shadesofgreen.org. 1950 W. Magnolia Palm Dr. 599 rooms. AE, DC, DISC, MC, V. $$–$$$$$*

See Map 3 on p. 48.

Disney's Wilderness Lodge (p. 29) WDW You'll think you're in a ski lodge in the Rockies at this spectacular resort on Bay Lake. A favorite with families due to its proximity to the Magic Kingdom and availability of bunk beds in some rooms.... *Tel 407/824-3200. Fax 407/824-3232. www.waltdisneyworld.com. 901 Timberline Dr. 728 rooms. AE, DC, DISC, MC, V. $$$$$*

See Map 3 on p. 48.

Disney's Yacht Club Resort (p. 33) WDW Like its Siamese twin, the Beach Club (the resorts share all facilities), this resort's a Disney replica of turn-of-the-20th-century New England's sea coast. Posher than its sister, with nautical touches: brass fixtures, boats, dark woods. It's pricey, but not a bad place to drop anchor.... *Tel 407/934-7000. Fax 407/934-3450. www.waltdisneyworld.com. 1700 Epcot Resorts Blvd. 630 rooms. AE, DC, DISC, MC, V. $$$$$*

See Map 3 on p. 48.

The Doubletree Castle (p. 27) INTERNATIONAL DRIVE This towering purple and pink hotel makes for a fun place to stay, if you like this sort of thing. Inside, you'll find a whimsical decor (think jester colors and jewel-bedecked headboards), a backdrop of Renaissance music, and the chirping of crickets and birds. International Drive location, and a bargain in the theme category.... *Tel 407/345-1511 (toll-free 800/952-2785). Fax 407/248-8181. www.doubletreecastle.com. 8629 International Dr. 216 rooms. AE, DISC, MC, V. $$$*

See Map 4 on p. 50.

Doubletree Guest Suites in the Walt Disney Resort (p. 21) LAKE BUENA VISTA Located at the tail end of Hotel Plaza Boulevard from Downtown Disney, this hotel is the best value for families who still want to be on Disney property but not at a Disney resort. Two-room suites sleep up to six. Other amenities include a pool, tennis courts, a refrigerator/wet bar/microwave area in each room, complimentary shuttles to the Disney parks and Downtown Disney, and yummy chocolate-chip cookies upon check-in.... *Tel 407/934-1000 (toll-free 800/222-8733). Fax 407/934-1015. www.doubletree.com. 2305 Hotel Plaza Blvd. 229 suites. AE, DC, DISC, MC, V. $$$$*

See Map 3 on p. 48.

Gaylord Palms Resort & Convention Center (p. 31) LAKE BUENA VISTA This grand resort-style property a mile from Disney is a magnet for convention-going suits and their spouses. Its indoor atrium is themed to reflect the geography of the state from St. Augustine to Key West and the Everglades, complete with a fort, ship, and fountain of youth. A bit over the top but, hey—this is Orlando. The resort's four signature restaurants and the premium on-site Canyon Ranch SpaClub are a big plus.... *Tel 407/586-0315. Fax 407/586-0397. www.gaylordpalms.com. 6000 W. Osceola Pkwy. 1,406 rooms. AE, DC, DISC, MC, V. $$$$$*

See Map 3 on p. 48.

Grosvenor Resort (p. 21) LAKE BUENA VISTA Subtly British-themed complete with a Sherlock Holmes–inspired mystery dinner theater. A scaled-down Disney Character breakfast is available 3 days a week. Conveniently located next to the Downtown Disney entertainment complex.... *Tel 407/828-4444 (toll-free 800/624-4109). Fax 407/828-8192. www.grosvenorresort.com. 1850 Hotel Plaza Blvd. 626 rooms. AE, DC, DISC, MC, V. $$$–$$$$*

See Map 3 on p. 48.

Hampton Inn at Universal Studios (p. 39) INTERNATIONAL DRIVE Basic hotel rooms but with pools, free breakfast, local calls, shuttles to main attractions, and a 100% satisfaction guarantee, you really can't go wrong. In addition to this location, the chain has more than 10 properties in the Orlando area.... *Tel 407/351-6716 (toll-free 800/763-1100). Fax 407/363-1711. www.hamptoninn.com. 5621 Windhover Dr. 120 rooms. AE, DC, DISC, MC, V. $$$*

See Map 4 on p. 50.

Hard Rock Hotel (p. 33) UNIVERSAL ORLANDO This is a happening, AAA four-diamond hot spot in the Universal Studios Orlando resort area. Impressive rock-'n'-roll memorabilia throughout; outside is a giant pool with a sand beach, water slide, and piped-in underwater music. Walk to Islands of Adventure and Universal Studios parks or take the complimentary water shuttle. A Loews hotel, so it also has that chain's benefits.... *Tel 407/503-7625 (toll-free 800/235-6937). Fax 407/503-7625. www.loewshotels.com/hotels/orlando_hard_rock. 5800 Universal Blvd. 650 rooms. AE, DC, DISC, MC, V. $$$$$*

See Map 4 on p. 50.

Hilton in the Walt Disney World Resort (p. 21) LAKE BUENA VISTA It's a Hilton; what more can we say? Expect to pay more for its location near the Downtown Disney entertainment area.... *Tel 407/827-4000 (toll-free 800/782-4414). Fax 407/827-3805. www.hilton.com. 1751 Hotel Plaza Blvd. 814 rooms. AE, DC, DISC, MC, V. $$$$*

See Map 3 on p. 48.

Hotel Royal Plaza (p. 21) LAKE BUENA VISTA Some of the best deals amongst the Downtown Disney hotels can be found at this property. Every room has a sleeper sofa and coffeemaker.... *Tel 407/828-2828 (toll-free 800/248-7890). Fax 407/827-6338. www.royalplaza.com. 1905 Hotel Plaza Blvd. 394 rooms. AE, DC, DISC, MC, V. $$$$*

See Map 3 on p. 48.

Hyatt Regency Grand Cypress (p. 30) LAKE BUENA VISTA This self-contained 1,500-acre megaresort definitely ups the wow factor. A half-acre swimming pool, a private lake, an equestrian center, 45 holes of Jack Nicklaus–designed golf, a 21-acre lake, and a kids' program are among the many amenities. Minutes from Disney.... *Tel 407/239-1234 (toll-free 800/239-3800). Fax 407/239-3800. www.grandcypress.hyatt.com. 1 Grand Cypress Blvd. 750 rooms. AE, DC, DISC, MC, V. $$$$$*

See Map 3 on p. 48.

JW Marriott Orlando, Grande Lakes (p. 31) ORLANDO Luxury resort situated on 500 acres with lush, tropical landscaping at the Grande Lakes development minutes east of SeaWorld. Shares amenities with the neighboring Ritz-Carlton, including a Greg Norman–designed golf course and a 40,000-square-foot spa.... *Tel 407/206-2300 (toll-free 800/228-9290). Fax 407/206-2301. www.grandelakes.com. 4040 Central Florida Pkwy. 1,064 rooms. AE, DC, DISC, MC, V. $$$$$*

See Map 2 on p. 47.

Kissimmee KOA Kampground (p. 46) KISSIMMEE This recently renovated campground features spaces for tents and RVs, including slide-outs. Pool, bicycle rentals, fishing, and Wi-Fi Internet access are also available. Value Kard holders get extra discounts. More primitive than rustic.... *Tel 407/396-2400 (toll-free 800/562-7791). www.koa.com/where/fl/09329. 2644 Happy Camper Place. 200 sites. AE, DISC, MC, V. $–$$*

See Map 5 on p. 51.

Magic Castle Inn & Suites (p. 39) KISSIMMEE A clean budget-priced family-run motel with a pool minutes from Disney in Kissimmee. Free continental breakfast and local calls. Weekly rates available; ask about the Internet special.... *Tel 407/396-2212 (toll-free 800/446-5669). www.magicorlando.com. 5055 W. Irlo Bronson Memorial Hwy. (U.S. 192). 107 rooms. AE, MC, V. $*

See Map 5 on p. 51.

Microtel Inn and Suites (p. 39) INTERNATIONAL DRIVE This property is centrally located just off International Drive behind Wet 'n' Wild and offers clean, basic rooms and suites at a budget price and even throws in free breakfast and local calls.... *Tel 407/226-9887 (toll-free 800/457-0077). Fax 407/226-9877. www.microtelsuitesorlando.com. 7531 Canada Ave. 128 rooms. AE, DC, DISC, MC, V. $$*

See Map 4 on p. 50.

Nickelodeon Family Suites by Holiday Inn (p. 22) LAKE BUENA VISTA This top-notch place for families sports the only Nickelodeon character appearances outside of Universal Studios. Conveniently located on the doorstep to Disney World.... *Tel 407/387-5437 (toll-free 866/462-6425). www.nickhotel.com. 14500 Continental Gateway. 800 suites. AE, DC, DISC, MC, V. $$$$*

See Map 3 on p. 48.

Orlando World Center Marriott (p. 30) LAKE BUENA VISTA One of the top places to stay in Orlando. You'll love the grotto swimming pool with waterfalls and hidden spas, plus the 200-acre golf course. Upper floors facing towards Disney have great views of nightly fireworks.... *Tel 407/239-4200 (toll-free 800/621-0638). Fax 407/238-8777. www.marriottworldcenter.com. 8701 World Center Dr. 2,000 rooms. AE, DC, DISC, MC, V. $$$$$*

See Map 3 on p. 48.

Palm Lakefront Resort & Hostel (p. 40) KISSIMMEE This lakefront property on Lake Cecile offers dorm-style rooms (separate women's and men's quarters), up to six to a room; private family rooms are also available. Bare-bones basic accommodations with a price to match. Minutes from Disney World.... *Tel 407/396-1759. Fax 407/396-1598. www.orlandohostels.com. 4840 W. Irlo Bronson Hwy. (U.S. 192). 9 dorm rooms and 34 private rooms. MC, V. $–$$*

See Map 5 on p. 51.

The Peabody Orlando Hotel (p. 36) INTERNATIONAL DRIVE This gracious and elegant hotel across from the Convention Center is made for those wanting to get away from Disney madness and other people's kids. Its I-Drive location is close to the action without being smothered by it. Home to the famous Peabody Ducks and the award-winning Dux restaurant.... *Tel 407/352-4000 (toll-free 800/732-2639). Fax 407/351-0073. www.peabodyorlando.com. 9801 International Dr. 891 rooms. AE, DC, DISC, MC, V. $$$$$*

See Map 4 on p. 50.

Portofino Bay Hotel (p. 29) UNIVERSAL ORLANDO Universal Orlando's first on-site resort hotel and its most deluxe. This lush and lovely Italian-themed hotel features imported paintings and plantings, butlers, water-shuttle, and a full-service spa. The only Universal property with two pool areas and a bocce court. Ask for a room with a balcony overlooking the water.... *Tel 407/503-1000 (toll-free 888/273-1311). www.loewshotels.com/hotels/orlando_portofino_bay. 5601 Universal Blvd. 750 rooms. AE, DC, DISC, MC, V. $$$$$*

See Map 4 on p. 50.

Quality Inn Plaza (p. 39) INTERNATIONAL DRIVE Simple rooms, pool, restaurant, and lounge on premises, shuttle service to attractions. All rooms include refrigerator, microwave, and coffeemaker. Across from Pointe Orlando.... *Tel 407/996-8585 (toll-free 800/999-8585). Fax 407/996-6839. www.qualityinn-orlando.com. 9000 International Dr. 1,020 rooms. AE, DC, DISC, MC, V. $$*

See Map 4 on p. 50.

Radisson Barcelo Hotel (p. 39) INTERNATIONAL DRIVE This hotel on International Drive has a good location and free admission to the YMCA Aquatic Center next door. Tower rooms also have microwaves.... *Tel 407/345-0505 (toll-free 800/333-3333). Fax 407/352-5894. www.orlando-hotelbarcelo.com. 8444 International Dr. 300 rooms. AE, DC, DISC, MC, V. $$–$$$$*

See Map 4 on p. 50.

Renaissance Orlando Resort at SeaWorld (p. 45) INTERNATIONAL DRIVE This high-rise upscale Marriott hotel, located directly across from SeaWorld, has large rooms, four on-site restaurants, an adjacent golf course, swimming pool, and fitness center.... *Tel 407/351-5555 (toll-free 800/327-6677). Fax 407/351-9991. www.marriott.com. 6677 Sea Harbor Dr. 842 rooms. AE, DC, DISC, MC, V. $$$$$*

See Map 4 on p. 50.

Residence Inn SeaWorld International Center (p. 41) INTERNATIONAL DRIVE What's to say? You'll get the usual room decor in this all-suite property near SeaWorld. Complimentary breakfast buffet is included.... *Tel 407/313-3600 (toll-free 800/331-3131). Fax 407/313-3611. www.residenceinnseaworld.com. 11000 Westwood Blvd. 350 suites. AE, DC, DISC, MC, V. $$$*

See Map 4 on p. 50.

The Ritz-Carlton Orlando, Grande Lakes (p. 31) ORLANDO Über-luxury resort situated on 500 acres with lush, tropical landscaping just east of SeaWorld. Shares amenities with the neighboring JW Marriott, including a Greg Norman–designed golf course and a 40,000-square-foot spa. Minutes from SeaWorld.... *Tel 407/206-2400 (toll-free 800/241-3333). Fax 407/206-2401. www.grandelakes.com. 4012 Central Florida Pkwy. 584 rooms. AE, DC, DISC, MC, V. $$$$$*

See Map 2 on p. 47.

Royal Pacific Resort (p. 28) UNIVERSAL ORLANDO This South Pacific/Asian–themed resort is a favorite of families with its zero-entry pool, weekly luau, and kids' activities. Emeril's Polynesian restaurant, Tchoup Chop, is also on the property.... *Tel 407/503-3000 (toll-free 800/235-6937). www.loewshotels.com/hotels/orlando_royal_pacific. 6300 Hollywood Way. 1,050 rooms. AE, DC, DISC, MC, V. $$$$$*

See Map 4 on p. 50.

Saratoga Resort Villas (p. 31) KISSIMMEE Located just east of the intersection of 192 and 535 in Kissimmee, this resort may not look like much from the road. But tucked inside are two- and three-bedroom bi-level villas with full kitchens and two full bathrooms—all at reasonable prices. Complimentary shuttle to Disney.... *Tel 407/397-0555 (toll-free 800/222-8733). Fax 407/397-1968. www.saratogaresortvillas.com. 4787 W. Irlo Bronson Hwy. (U.S. 192). 150 villas. AE, DC, DISC, MC, V. $$$*

See Map 5 on p. 51.

Seralago Hotel & Suites Main Gate East (p. 46) KISSIMMEE Comfortable rooms, kitchenettes, a kids' program, including Kid-Suites, a pool, and a shuttle to Disney. Families will also appreciate the kids-eat-free program.... *Tel 407/396-4488 (toll-free 800/366-5437). Fax 407/396-8915. www.seralagohotel.com. 5678 W. Irlo Bronson Hwy. (U.S. 192). 614 rooms. AE, DC, DISC, MC, V. $$$*

See Map 5 on p. 51.

Sheraton Safari Resort (p. 29) LAKE BUENA VISTA Can't afford Disney's Animal Kingdom Lodge? This fanciful hotel gives the African-safari motif full play as well, with leopard-spotted carpeting, woodcarvings, African prints, a python water slide, and Olympic-size pool. You can't beat the location either (there are lots of restaurants and shops nearby).... *Tel 407/239-0444 (toll-free 800/645-7666). Fax 407/239-1778. www.sheratonsafari.com. 12205 Apopka-Vineland Rd. 489 rooms. AE, DC, DISC, MC, V. $$$$*

See Map 3 on p. 48.

Sheraton Studio City (p. 27) INTERNATIONAL DRIVE Can't miss this 21-story towering tower of steel topped by a rooftop globe. The property offers Art Deco decor and a movie-star theme. Good location if you're doing the Universal parks.... *Tel 407/351-2100 (toll-free 800/327-1366). Fax 407/352-8028. www.sheratonstudiocity.com. 5905 International Dr. 301 rooms. AE, DC, DISC, MC, V. $$$*

See Map 4 on p. 50.

Staybridge Suites (p. 41) INTERNATIONAL DRIVE/LAKE BUENA VISTA This all-suite hotel chain hosts lots of value-minded vacationers at its International Drive location. Modest furnishings, full-size kitchens, and more-than-adequate facilities make it a bargain. Near the Disney parks.... *International Drive: Tel 407/352/2400 (toll-free 877/238-8889); fax 407/352-4631; 8480 International Dr.; 146 suites. Lake Buena Vista: Tel 407/238-0777 (toll-free 877/238-8889); fax 407/238-2640; 8751 Suiteside Dr.; 150 suites. www.staybridge.com. AE, DC, DISC, MC, V. $$$$-$$$$$*

See Map 4 on p. 50.

See Map 3 on p. 48.

Suites at Old Town (p. 33) KISSIMMEE Ignore the regular rooms—the suites are the main reason to stay here. Get twice the space of a normal hotel room for the same price, and a kitchen area to boot. Free shuttles to the Disney parks add to the appeal.... *Tel 407/396-7900 (toll-free 800/327-9126). Fax 407/396-1789. www.suitesatoldtown.com. 5820 W. Irlo Bronson Hwy. (U.S. 192). 603 rooms. AE, DISC, MC, V. $$-$$$*

See Map 5 on p. 51.

Tropical Palms Fun Resort (p. 39) KISSIMMEE If you're traveling in a motor home, trailer, or pop-up, you'll find lots of inexpensive hookups here. Or, if the camping life isn't your thing, stay in one of their spacious two-bedroom cottages. It's in the middle of the U.S. 192 strip.... *Tel 407/396-4595 (toll-free 800/647-2567). Fax 407/396-8938. www.tropicalpalms.com. 2650 Holiday Trail. 144 rooms. AE, DISC, MC, V. $$$*

See Map 5 on p. 51.

Walt Disney World Dolphin (p. 36) WDW If you don't want to put up the bucks to stay here, at least come by for a peek at the Michael Graves design. Spacious rooms sport whimsical touches, and the outdoor pool area is great. Water shuttle to Epcot and Disney–MGM.... *Tel 407/934-4000 (toll-free 800/227-1500). www.swandolphin.com. Fax 407/934-4710. 1500 Epcot Resorts Blvd. 1,510 rooms. AE, DC, DISC, MC, V. $$$$$*

See Map 3 on p. 48.

Walt Disney World Swan (p. 36) WDW This high-priced Disney property screams to be noticed. The Swan shares the sandy beachside plaza with the Dolphin (see above). Water shuttle to Epcot and Disney–MGM.... *Tel 407/934-3000 (toll-free 800/227-1500). Fax 407/934-4710. www.swandolphin.com. 1200 Epcot Resorts Blvd. 758 rooms. AE, DC, DISC, MC, V. $$$$$*

See Map 3 on p. 48.

D I N

I N G

2

Basic Stuff

It's hard not to find a restaurant in Orlando that caters to whatever you may be craving at the moment. The hard part is agreeing on a single choice. From cheap drive-thrus to eateries run by celebrity chefs, just deciding where you want to eat can take up a good portion of your day. Throw in the concept of working within your budget and your head may start spinning faster than Linda Blair's in *The Exorcist.* And you thought deciding on a place to stay was hard.

Orlando's tourist strips boast more fast-food outlets and major chain eateries than you could ever possibly imagine, much less want to eat at. As America's top tourist destination, it's only natural that Orlando is a proving ground for the nation's fast-food giants. Dying to test the latest culinary inspiration from America's major McFood chains? Pull into any drive-thru. And where but Orlando would you expect to find the world's largest McDonald's?

Suffice it to say that homey little one-of-a-kind eateries are as endangered as now-plentiful alligators once were. Still, for those diners who bother to sleuth 'em out, the local haunts that have survived the fast-food onslaught are gems indeed. Example: **Kim Wu,** an Orlando favorite, has offered great traditional Chinese cuisine for more than 20 years and rivals any other Asian restaurant in town.

If you're itching to ditch the tourist scene and dine where the locals do, head downtown, also home to the club scene for Orlando's 20-something set (see the Nightlife & Entertainment chapter). The Dr. Phillips area of Sand Lake, just west of I-Drive, has no less than 10 fine-dining experiences in a two-block section of the road. Plus, good eats crop up in places where you'd least expect them; upscale mall Pointe*Orlando houses two better-than-average options (**Dan Marino's Town Tavern** and **Lulu's Bait Shack**). Then again, it also has a Hooters.

But don't think it's going to be easy to leave the parks just to eat. Disney and Universal have gone to great lengths setting up "dining and entertainment zones" specifically designed to keep you and your money within their grasp. At Disney the big deal is the Downtown Disney complex. Universal's two parks are set up so that you *have* to walk through CityWalk just to reach your car. SeaWorld got wise to the idea and built its Waterfront area so that most guests will walk through the complex, but it's the only one of Orlando's big three that requires theme-park admission to access any of its restaurants.

Dining at any of the Downtown Disney or CityWalk restaurants is not just about the choice of the cuisine—you must also choose a theme. New Orleans? Rock 'n' roll? Hollywood? The list literally goes on and on. These are definitely not the places you want to eat if you absolutely cannot stand noise or crowds. But these zones do allow you to embark on a culinary adventure tour; sample Emeril Lagasse one night, Wolfgang Puck the next. Or their recipes, anyway.

Make it out of the park and past the dining complexes and you still have more choices waiting for you at your hotel if you're staying at any of the Disney or Universal on-site resorts. Most upscale resorts such as the Peabody Orlando (home of top-rated **Dux**) or the Gaylord Palms offer highly regarded restaurants, as well.

Dining Disney

Not too long ago, Disney was hardly considered a bastion of fine dining (with the exception of a few restaurants). The last 10 years have seen a conscious effort by the Mouse to improve Disney's menu choices. Where once all you swam through was a sea of burgers and chicken fingers, now you'll find the occasional oasis of hummus, salads, and wraps. That's the good news. The bad news is that you'll pay handsomely for it. Walt Disney World sells about 10 million burgers and 9 million hot dogs each year. Add fries (a mere 8.5 million pounds of them) and a Coke and you've just dropped about $12. Want to take a load off your feet and enjoy a table-service dinner? For dinner for two, including tax and tip, look for a bill of $50 or more (sometimes, a lot more). Of course, it's not just the food you're paying for...it's the ambience as well (dining code speak for "you've got theme"). Enjoy your fajitas in the shadow of an active volcano, your steak in a cozy cellar. Get chefs who whip up your dinner with great fanfare while you watch. Waiters who dance the Hokey Pokey. Tables shaped like mouse ears. A dining room designed to resemble a drive-in movie. It boggles the mind.

For the biggest variety of choices in a single park, get thee to Epcot, where, for the price of admission, you get the privilege of dropping still more cash at the restaurants in the World Showcase, a round-the-world pastiche of pavilions representing France, Germany, Mexico, China, Norway, Canada, the United Kingdom, Italy, Japan, Morocco, and the good ol' U.S. of A. (No poor or war-torn nations need apply.) Sure, Epcot has rides and exhibits and such, but some people come for the food and the Disneyesque appeal of visiting scads of foreign countries without so much as a tetanus shot. (You can even buy little passports that they'll stamp at each "country.") Take your time strolling around Epcot's re-created villages to fantasize where you'll eat next. You'll notice that the architecture is painstakingly authentic, and the young servers are actually from the countries they represent. If dining "around the world" sounds good to you, visit Epcot when they bring in even more international cuisine options to the World Showcase during the 6-week **International Food and Wine Festival** from October 1 to mid-November. Most samples are $1 to $5 apiece.

Regarding Reservations

In true Disney fashion, Mickeyville's take on reservations is completely different than you'll find anywhere else. Normally a reservation is a guaranteed seating time. At Disney you'll hear it referred to as an "Advance Reservation" (formerly known as "Priority Seatings"). What this means is that instead of getting a guaranteed table time, Disney only guarantees you the next available table for your party size *after* the time specified in the "reservation" (provided you show up 5 min. early to let them know you're there). Even then, you still might end up waiting 15 to 30 minutes for a table; if you show up and they aren't ready, you may get this *Star Trek*–looking beeper device that will flash you (with lights...this is Disney!) when your table is ready, so you can wander around instead of lingering in line. Regardless, note that absolutely no tables are ever allocated for walk-ins—sauntering up to a busy restaurant with no Advance Reservation can mean an hour-plus wait.

Most restaurants and character meals can be reserved 180 days in advance, including the hottest ticket in town: breakfast or lunch at **Cinderella's Royal Table.** That meal quite literally gets filled up with reservations mere moments after a particular seating's 180-day window opens up. Operators are absolutely standing by, but most of them will be telling you, "Sorry, we're full." Exceptions to the 180-day rule include **Bistro de Paris** (dinner only, 30 days in advance); **Wolfgang Puck Cafe** (60 days); **Fulton's Crab House, House of Blues, Portobello Yacht Club,** and the Chef's Table at **Victoria & Albert's** (90 days); and the **Hoop-Dee-Doo Musical Revue** (a whopping 730 days in advance). Be sure to check the cancellation policies, as you'll also be required to pay in full at time of reservation for

Cinderella's Royal Table, the Hoop-Dee-Doo Review, and that swanky Chef's Table at Victoria & Albert's.

If you need help with calculating your Advance Reservation availability windows, visit the non-Disney website, **Planning Strategy Calculator** (www.pscalculator.net), which lets you punch in your date of dining and shows you the available reservations windows. Once you've figured out all the numbers (still easier than a tax return, but not by much), call Tel 407/WDW-DINE (939-3463) to make your Advance Reservation.

Scary as all this sounds, you'll only face serious wait times at peak seasons and the hottest venues. Otherwise, walk-up waits will be reasonable. And if you arrive at Disney without preexisting plans, you can hedge your bets by visiting **Guest Services** desks upon entering each park or at your Disney resort and have them make the Advance Reservation right then. Every little bit helps.

How to Dress

Think casual. You're on vacation and most tourist-area restaurants understand that. In most places, it's acceptable to dine in a tank top and shorts if you so choose. Even in Orlando, though, it's considered tacky to show up in beachwear at any of the upscale restaurants. And don't let the heat fool you; even when it's 90°F (32°C) and sweltering outdoors, it can be sweater weather inside, thanks to overzealous air-conditioning. (And during the winter, when temps can occasionally sink into the 40s [single digits Celsius], those tank tops and shorts will have you sporting goose bumps.)

Saving Money

It may look impossible, but you can save money if you choose to dine at a theme park. You just have to know the tricks. Eat your biggest meal at lunch, when some restaurants serve slightly smaller portions of dinner menu items, usually for a substantially lower price. Consider splitting an appetizer and entree rather than ordering two separate entrees. You won't go hungry—many table-service portions are big enough to share. At the counter-service restaurants, order from the kids' menu. You'll often get a small burger/chicken/hot dog, fries, and small soda for around $4 to $6. Disney doesn't actually condone this, but who's to say your kids aren't sitting down at a table instead of in line with you (even if you don't have any kids at all).

THE GREAT MUG DEBATE

All Disney resorts offer their guests the opportunity to buy mugs emblazoned with the resort's logo for $20. After the initial purchase, all nonalcoholic beverages at the resort's quick-service (also known as counter-service) restaurants are free. The price may seem steep, but if you consider that most sodas cost $2–$3 individually and you take into account how much you'd drink during your stay, it's actually a good deal. Plus, you get a useful souvenir to take home. The mugs must be used at the resort in which they were purchased—you can't use an All-Star mug to get soda at the Grand Floridian. But the Big Debate in Mugville is whether or not you can use them for subsequent visits. To make my publisher (and his lawyers) happy, I will say that official Disney policy states the mug can only be used for free refills during the visit in which you purchased said mug. If you visit again later, you must buy a new mug. That said, unless Disney redesigns its mugs, there's no way anyone will be able to tell that you didn't purchase a particular resort mug during a particular stay. So you know the rules—it's up to you whether you're comfortable bending them.

Annual-pass holders at all the major theme parks receive discounts of 10% at select restaurants. A Florida resident? Disney offers a dining program that offers even more savings...for an annual fee, of course.

Clear Channel, which operates several radio stations in Orlando, offers $50 certificates to many of CityWalk's restaurants for only $25 at its **half-price dining site** (halfprice.cc orlando.com). Unfortunately, you can only order one at a time, so you get hit with a fee of almost $4 for each certificate, but when all is said and done, you're still saving over $20.

You can win dining certificates for many Orlando restaurants via auction at **IBidUSA** (www.ibidusa.com) or **Restaurant.com** (www.restaurant.com).

The **Entertainment Book** (www.entertainment.com) offers two-for-one dining deals at many Orlando restaurants. Or just stop at any tourist booth on I-Drive or U.S. 192 and grab handfuls of the free booklets that offer dining coupons.

The Lowdown

Cheap eats... After a day or two of sticker shock at Disney, a meal or two at a Denny's or Shoney's will start to look damn good. The city's many ethnic joints are also good for a cheap bite. **Cafe Annie,** downtown, offers Greek and

Middle Eastern classics for under $6, while **Tijuana Flats** serves up a two-handed stuffed burrito and 12-station hot-sauce bar that will peel layers off the roof of your mouth for $7 to $9. Just north of Universal on Kirkman, tucked away in a little shopping center, you'll find **Kim Wu,** which offers dining specials that include a soup, egg roll, entree, and tea for as low as $7. On the tourist track, **Café Tu Tu Tango,** a funky little artists' loft on I-Drive, only offers a tapas menu, but get a couple of the appetizer-size dishes and pass them around for a fun meal that costs under $10 a person. Don't dismiss happy hours for cheap eats—many restaurant chains in the tourist areas (T.G.I. Fridays, Chevy's, Chili's) offer late-afternoon deals on appetizers and drink specials in the bar area.

Best deals at Disney? The smoked turkey legs sold at little stands around the Magic Kingdom. I don't want to know the genetic mutations that went into producing turkeys big enough to have drumsticks this size, but there's more than enough to share for less than 6 bucks. ***FYI:*** You'll also find some of these gobblers at Islands of Adventure, inside the **Enchanted Oak Tavern & Alchemy Bar,** where you can enjoy a medieval atmosphere along with your turkey leg.

When you'd rather not slip 'em a Mickey... If you or your kids are too cool to be enthralled by a mute grown-up in a mouse suit, one of O-Town's sports-themed eateries may do the trick. Basketball fans should try **NBA City,** at CityWalk. Here, homage is paid to hoopsters, plus you can play interactive, sports-themed games. This is one of my least favorite theme restaurants, though, simply because the food is bland and the service is indifferent. And lest you think Disney hasn't got game, there's the **All-Star Cafe Orlando** at Disney's Wide World of Sports complex. Here, you'll sit in baseball-mitt-shaped booths surrounded by enough memorabilia to fill Yankee Stadium. Don't want to trek all the way out there? You'll find a similar atmosphere at the **ESPN Club** over at Disney's BoardWalk resort. Like watching drivers make left turns all day at high speeds? You have a choice between CityWalk's **NASCAR Cafe** and **Race Rock** over on I-Drive. At all of the above, count on huge video screens blaring live-action games and Memorable Moments in sports. Keep in mind, however, that food is not the main attraction at any of these restaurants; it's all basically glorified pub grub.

It's only rock 'n' roll, but I like it.... If music is more your scene, head to the **Hard Rock Cafe** at CityWalk. I know, you've been there, done that, but this *is* the world's largest Hard Rock. Elvis, they say, has left the building, but his pink Caddy perches precariously over the bar. Other noteworthy options at CityWalk: **Bob Marley—A Tribute to Freedom,** with a Jamaican menu and nightly live reggae music; **Latin Quarter,** with a menu culled from 21 Latin American nations served to the loud beat of a live band nightly; or, for Parrotheads, **Jimmy Buffett's Margaritaville** (though this place has the most expensive cheeseburger at CityWalk). Pop on over to **The Kitchen,** on the lower level of the Hard Rock Hotel, for a rock-'n'-roll bistro with great food and even better service. Upon informing my waiter I was heading out to the theme parks, I received a soda to go and a free bottle of Evian. For a post-IMAX-movie bite at Pointe*Orlando, there's always **Johnny Rockets,** which offers kid-friendly grub such as chili-cheese fries, good 'n' greasy hamburgers, and malted milkshakes in a 1950s-soda-shop setting.

Where to go if someone else is paying... You've really arrived when an Orlandoan invites you to **Manuel's on the 28th,** boasting the loftiest views in the city, from the 28th floor of downtown's Bank of America Building. Owner Manuel Garcia trumped the old Arthur's 27 restaurant (in the Buena Vista Palace) by setting *his* place one floor higher. Here, altitude is everything, although the food often rises to tantalizing heights, too, offering the likes of miso-marinated Chilean sea bass with seaweed salad, or five peppercorn Angus filet with smoked gouda potatoes. The tab can easily run to $180 for two. If you're paying, suggest **Pebbles,** also operated by Manuel Garcia. Less flash, to be sure, but reliably good food and decidedly down-to-earth prices.

Best place to take your lover... Planning to pop the question? Hedge your bets at **Victoria & Albert's** at Disney's Grand Floridian Resort & Spa, where every conceivable romantic cliché is trotted out—all *you* have to do is show up with a no-limit credit card. A harpist or violinist will set the proper mood, as will fresh flowers, Royal Doulton china, personalized menus, and a seven-course feast featuring luxe-'n'-lusty choices such as caviar and roast pheasant. This is considered the most romantic, intimate venue at Disney, so the servers—always named, duh, Victoria and Albert—are well versed in the art of hide-the-ring-in-the-Grand-Marnier-soufflé, or whatever ploy you choose. A little less expensive but still romantic is the **Bice Ristorante** at the Portofino Bay Hotel at Universal. Enjoy delicious Milanese Italian specialties with a view of the harbor.

Best place to take your mother... Treat Mum to a proper teatime in a setting straight out of *The Great Gatsby* (by way of Mickey). High tea at the **Garden View Lounge** at Disney's Grand Floridian Resort & Spa is extremely mom-worthy; fill a plate with fresh-baked scones and Devonshire cream, top it off with a little dollop of English trifle, pour yourselves a spot of lemon verbena tea, and settle in for a chat. Teatime treats are offered daily from 2 to 4:30pm. The cost of the grand version ($25 per person) is a tad steep, but the real deal at London's Claridges is twice that price, so this actually translates into that Holy of Holies—a (relative) Disney bargain.

As seen on TV... Over the last few years, the species known as "celebrity chef" has been migrating to Orlando with increasing frequency. Wolfgang Puck was the first to arrive, when his self-monikered **Wolfgang Puck Cafe** opened in Downtown Disney. Funny thing is, he no longer owns the Orlando locations that bear his name, but the menu still offers some of his recipes. Emeril Lagasse, of New Orleans and Food Network fame, is giving Puck some competition in the Superstar Chef category with not one, but two eateries. **Emeril's Restaurant Orlando** at CityWalk serves Creole and Cajun cuisine, while **Emeril's Tchoup Chop** offers up Polynesian-inspired dishes at the Royal Pacific Hotel. **Todd English's bluezoo** serves innovative seafood in an unusually vibrant setting at the Walt Disney World Dolphin. Over at restaurant row near I-Drive, award-winning Hawaiian chef Roy Yamaguchi offers Euro-Asian cuisine at **Roy's.** All of these restaurants offer great meals, but don't forget to bring a full (very full) wallet.

Local foodie havens... Local chefs rave about **Le Coq au Vin** on South Orange Avenue. Don't be misled by the shambled exterior: It's French with a Cajun kick, minus the attitude. If it were located on Disney property, they'd charge twice as much. Speaking of which, try the **California Grill** at the Contemporary Resort, considered by WDW brass to be the best eats at Disney. The chefs have won a wall's worth of awards—among them, "Top Meal in America" by *USA Today.* The view of the Magic Kingdom isn't so bad either.

Honey, I ditched the kids.... You don't have kids and don't want to be surrounded by other people's poorly behaved offspring either. While I can't promise that *nobody* will brazenly smuggle a colicky tot into one of these restaurants, your odds of avoiding kids are better than average at **Fulton's Crab House,** on the lagoon at Disney's Pleasure Island, and at the **Samba Room,** a local favorite on Dr. Philip's Restaurant Row. Like its namesake, San Francisco's Fulton Street Fish Market, Fulton's offers fresh fish, flown in from all over the world, and house specialties such as mustard-crusted trout. You'll never go wrong with Fulton's "crab experience," a crab combo platter with Alaskan king, Dungeness, and snow crab (even tastier when there are no kids around to go, "Ewww...yuck!"). The Samba Room offers Latin fusion cuisine, a cigar lounge, and a live band on the weekends. It's a great place to enjoy a delicious meal before kicking up your heels on the dance floor. Another place where the kids are few and far between is Disney's Celebration. If you can get past the eerie perfection of this Disney-created "small town," you'll find **Columbia Restaurant,** an outpost of the famous Cuban place in Tampa's Ybor City that claims to be Florida's oldest restaurant. Afterward, you can take a horse-and-carriage ride, or stroll around the lake.

Vegging out... Even Disney World has gotten the message that not everyone devours animal flesh. Many of its buffet meals offer more than one vegetarian option besides salad. Meanwhile, at **Cosmic Ray's Starlight Cafe** (Magic Kingdom), guests can order a variety of freshly tossed salads and veggie burgers, along with the typical burgers and fries. The **ABC Commissary** at Disney–MGM Studios offers healthy, meatless selections such as tabbouleh wraps and vegetarian Asian noodles, or just grab an apple or banana from the **Anaheim Produce** stand by the Tower of Terror. Away from the theme parks, head north on Orange Avenue, just past downtown, where you'll find the **White Wolf Cafe.** This bohemian restaurant isn't totally vegetarian, but the vegetarian plate with black-bean hummus and mango-nut tabbouleh is to die for.

World Showcase winners... Where else but Disney could you walk a mere mile and sample the cuisine of 11 nations? In theory, anyway. Most of the food at World Showcase aims for authenticity—and is pretty good, if not exactly cutting-edge. (With one exception; read on.) Forgot to make a reservation with **WDW Dining** (Tel 407/939-3463)—shame on you for being spontaneous!—and feeling hunger pangs? Try the underrated **Restaurant Marrakesh** in the Morocco pavilion. Since the average American isn't familiar with Moroccan cuisine, people stay away in droves. Their loss: The dishes are mildly spiced, quite tasty, and inexpensive (for Epcot) to boot. Plus, the chef was personally recommended by no less than King Hassan II. Try the Taste of Morocco feast for two, the tasty platter of veggie couscous, and a Florida-meets-Morocco dish, tagine of grouper, where the fish is poached in a flavorful mix of lemon and vegetables. Kids can order more familiar hamburgers or chicken tenders. The Moroccan-palace setting is a stunner, and Moroccan musicians and bejeweled belly dancers add an exotic element. Most foodies take direct aim at Epcot France, where three famous owner-chefs lend their gastronomic éclat to Disney dining. Culinary artistes Paul Bocuse, Roger Vergé, and Gaston Lenotre developed the menu, trained the chefs, and drop in on a regular basis to supervise the kitchen at **Chefs de France.** The place has an authentic brasserie feel, and you won't be disappointed with the classic cuisine. And ooh-la-la! That pastry cart! Nice as this is, skip it, and go where the real action is, upstairs to **Bistro de Paris.** Surprise: The Three Chefs have lent their magic touch to this less-expensive eatery as well, and seemed to have had a bit more fun with the menu. Call it country French with an edge.

Do drink the water—or better yet, the Dos Equis—and treat yourself to a meal at Epcot's Mexico. It's twilight time again (and again and again) at the **San Angel Inn,** set along the boat-ride route of El Rio de Tiempo (the River of Time), a man-made indoor river. Even at high noon it's deliciously cool here. Some quibbles: The tables are too close together and it's almost too dark to see your food, but mostly this one rates high. The chicken with spicy mole (chocolate-infused) sauce is soul-satisfying, especially when paired with an ice-cold *cerveza.* Across the "street," the **Cantina de San Angel,** an outdoor cafe overlooking the World Showcase Lagoon, serves the best cheap eats at Epcot—burritos, tostadas, tacos, and the like. A decent place to escape the heat and hoist a pint is the **Rose & Crown Pub and Dining Room** at Epcot's United Kingdom. This clubby spot is positively brill ("brilliant," in Brit-speak) by Epcot standards. The atmosphere's too smoke-free (like all Disney restaurants) to be wholly authentic, but that doesn't stop expatriate Englishmen from flocking here. It has outdoor waterfront tables, and a menu that relies on pub standards such as cottage pie and the runaway bestseller, fish-and-chips. And, by the looks of things at the elbow-to-elbow bar, the ales, lagers, and stouts are a big draw—you can even ask to have them served authentically, at room temperature. This pub is always crowded, especially at night during the Illumi-Nations Reflections of Earth show, as this is the only full-service restaurant on Epcot's World Showcase Lagoon.

World Showcase losers... After two tries, I still have yet to be impressed by the Italy pavilion's **L'Originale Alfredo Di Roma Ristorante.** Yeah, I know, it's based on the original Roma ristorante where fettuccine Alfredo was born, but the food's heavy, worn, and overpriced, and you can get better Italian elsewhere in Orlando. It's hard to whistle "Yankee Doodle Dandy" when you realize that the American pavilion's sole dining spot is the **Liberty Inn,** a counter-service burger-and-hot-dog joint. Considering the number of regional specialties the U.S. has to offer (Boston clam chowder, Philly cheese-steak sandwiches, and so on), to sum up our cuisine with a burger is...well, un-American.

Best place to escape at Epcot... It's 90°F (32°C) in the shade (or it would be, if there *were* any shade), you've stood on the pavement with approximately 20,000 other sweaty souls to hear the Mariache Cobre and the Drums of Matsuriza (still ringing in your ears).... Where to make it all go away? Sneak away to the **Matsunoma Lounge,** on the second floor of the Mitsukoshi Department Store in Japan, where they've got a sake martini (vodka or gin) with your name on it. Passable sushi, too. You can also get away from it all in the deliciously dungeonlike **Le Cellier Steakhouse** in Canada, where an ice-cold Canadian microbrew never tasted so good and the steak is acceptably fleshy.

Epcot for hearty eaters... If the gang is hot, tired, and famished, consider one of Epcot's all-you-can-eat buffets. **Restaurant Akershus,** at the Norway pavilion, probably scares people off, thanks to Norway's reputation for creamed-herring cuisine. To counter this, Epcot has installed smiling Norsk gals with peaches-and-cream complexions to beckon you inside this medieval-fortress-style dining room. The food isn't so bad if you like hearty fare: lots of salads and deli, plenty of fresh fish, macaroni-and-cheese with ham, meatballs in gravy. And, yes, herring. Every day is Oktoberfest at Germany's **Biergarten,** with all that implies: polka dancing, accordions, and lederhosen. If that sounds enticing, get in line for the all-you-can-eat buffet. It's not all sausage, spaetzle, and sauerkraut; the groaning buffet table also has roasted chicken and lots of salads, all uncomplicated and pretty uncontroversial grub. I suspect many guests are drawn by the 33-ounce steins of bier. Not the wurst place to spend an hour or two.

Quick bites at Universal Orlando... Universal probably figures its CityWalk restaurants will look really good to you after a day on the fast-food track. But what if you're so hungry you don't want to have to leave the park? Over on the Universal Studios Florida side, if you're going to eat at any of the counter-service restaurants, make it **Mel's Drive-In,** a replica of the hangout in *American Graffiti,* complete with red Naugahyde stools at the counter and a vintage car parked out front (Harrison Ford not included). Mel's features burger baskets and wonderful, frosty shakes. So busy will you be at Islands of Adventure, what with waiting in line for Spider-Man and the Hulk coaster, you won't want to waste precious minutes eating. Just as well.

While the restaurants fit in perfectly with the themed Islands—could there be a place cuter than the **Green Eggs & Ham Cafe** at Seuss Landing?—the cuisine at each is usually the basic burger or chicken offerings (or green scrambled eggs—don't worry, it's only food coloring). Try the **Comic Strip Cafe,** which offers a more diverse menu, including Chinese and Mexican choices. Sword and sorcery fans will want to stop for a bite at the **Enchanted Oak Tavern & Alchemy Bar,** located in the Lost Continent. Look for the enormous gnarled oak tree at the entrance. The interior resembles a medieval pub where you can gnaw a giant turkey drumstick (wonder where they got that idea?) and hoist a pint. ***Tip:*** This is a great place to duck into while the more adventurous (or suicidal) in your party are in line for the Dueling Dragons coaster across the way. You'll have an hour to yourself, one of the few times you'll be grateful for long lines at the attractions.

Ragin' Cajun... New Orleans has a surprising culinary presence in Orlando with four separate eateries. **Emeril's Restaurant Orlando** at CityWalk is an upscale take on Creole cuisine. The "Bam!" guy from *Emeril Live* shows he's no flash in the pan—his signature Louisiana oyster stew and succulent "mudbug" (crayfish) creations are excellent eats. Book your table at least a month in advance or you may not get in. If you can't get into Emeril's, go drown your sorrows at **Pat O'Brien's Orlando,** a replica of the legendary New Orleans bar, where they don't stint on the firepower (or the alcohol). Everybody orders a big ol' Hurricane to wash down the spicy Cajun catfish fillets. An older crowd grooves to the dueling boogie-woogie pianists when the sun sets. You'll find the shack that holds the

Go Out of Your Way for Good Thai

Tucked in an unexpected piney nook off Universal Boulevard (though well south of Universal Orlando itself), ***Siam Orchid*** *represents the best choice for fairly authentic Thai food anywhere near the tourist and resort areas. It's a little pricey, but you won't regret the expense if you're a fan of pad Thai or any of the stellar rice, curry, or noodle dishes on the menu. They'll spice it up or down to your taste, but order a bunch of dishes so everyone can sample at will. And you absolutely must end with the homemade coconut ice cream, which is almost worth a visit all by itself.*

House of Blues (okay, it's really more Mississippi Delta than Big Easy) over at Downtown Disney. Not only is the food first-rate, but you'll sometimes be serenaded by nationally known blues artists as you enjoy your dinner. Need to get away from the theme-park atmosphere for your Cajun fix? **Lulu's Bait Shack** at the Pointe*Orlando complex on I-Drive features items such as jambalaya at prices in the single digits.

Dining with character, Disney-style... If you have small fries in tow, you'll be Mom and Dad of the Year if you treat 'em to a Disney Character Dining Experience (Disney's caps, not ours). If you're an adult worshipper of all things Disney, this is a religious pilgrimage of the first order. Meals are generally buffet-style, and every character, it is promised, stops at each table. (Imagine the psychic damage of being ignored by Eeyore! Yikes!) Character meals are held at the theme parks and at WDW hotel restaurants. ***Note:*** You'll be required to pay park admission, in addition to your meal tab, at theme-park restaurants. You don't have to be a Disney resort guest to partake in a character meal at a resort. The lineup of who's where may change, so be sure to reconfirm when you call to make your Advance Reservation with **WDW Dining** (Tel 407/939-3463).

Here's a quick rundown of who's currently appearing on the Disney celebrity dining circuit, as not every character appears at every location. Be absolutely sure to call ahead and confirm the character lineup, inasmuch as Disney is willing to confirm anything. These rosters were current at press time, but last-minute changes or substitutions are not uncommon. ***In the Magic Kingdom:*** Cinderella and the Fairy Godmother (and occasionally Belle, Jasmine, and Snow White) at **Cinderella's Royal Table** in Cinderella Castle for breakfast ($32 adults, $22 kids) and lunch ($34/$23)—remember, this is the hardest one to get an Advance Reservation for. Winnie the Pooh, Eeyore, Piglet, and Tigger join you for breakfast ($19 adults, $11 kids), lunch ($21/$12), and dinner ($28/$13) at **Crystal Palace** (no wonder he's a "tubby little cubby"). Chip 'n' Dale, Minnie, and Pluto dine at **Liberty Tree Tavern** in Liberty Square for family-style dinner; the cost is $28 for adults, $13 for kids, plus park admission.

At Epcot: Norway's **Restaurant Akershus** is where you'll find the "Princess Storybook Breakfast." The princess lineup varies, but you'll usually find Belle, Jasmine, Snow White, and Sleeping Beauty ($23 adults, $13 kids). Join Mickey and friends at the **Garden Grill Restaurant** in The Land for lunch ($21 adults, $12 kids) or dinner ($28/$13), plus park admission. ***At Disney's Animal Kingdom:*** The A list (Mickey, Goofy, Donald, Pluto) turns up in safari gear at Donald's Breakfastosaurus buffet at **Restaurantosaurus** in Dinoland U.S.A. The cost is $19 for adults, $11 for kids, plus theme-park admission.

In the resorts: Goofy and friends table-hop during breakfast ($19 adults, $11 kids) at the **Cape May Café** in **Disney's Beach Club Resort.** Mickey, Chip 'n' Dale, and Goofy turn on the charm at **Chef Mickey's Buffet, Disney's Contemporary Resort,** at breakfast ($19/$11) and dinner ($28/$13). Mary Poppins and Alice in Wonderland are occasionally joined by Pooh and Tigger at **1900 Park Fare,** Disney's **Grand Floridian Resort & Spa,** for breakfast ($19/$11). At dinnertime, Cinderella and friends show up here for a prime-rib buffet ($29/$14). Join Lilo & Stich and pals for the **Best Friends Breakfast** at **'Ohana,** at Disney's **Polynesian Resort.** The cost is $19 for adults, $11 for kids. Two words for this...Tonga Toast! See the Accommodations chapter for the lowdown on all of Disney's resorts.

A whale of a meal... SeaWorld offers two options for those who want to dine with its mascot, Shamu. Early risers can enjoy the "Shamu and Crew Character Breakfast" at the **Seafire Inn,** joined by Shamu and other SeaWorld characters ($15 adults, $9.95 kids, plus park admission). In the evening, enjoy the show provided by real killer whales at "Dine with Shamu" ($37/$19, plus park admission), held in a side alcove of the big **Shamu Stadium.** During the dinner buffet (with several delicious choices), trainers talk about working with their large friends as the whales perform tricks and pose for photos. The show is a lot of fun, and, as an added bonus—even alcoholic beverages are complimentary with the meal. Be sure to request a table by the water if you go, and don't forget your camera.

Under the boardwalk... Can there be a place more Disney than **Flying Fish Café?** It's worth a trip to Disney's BoardWalk (Atlantic City minus the sin) to check out this lively spot with a Ferris-wheel motif and bustling show kitchen (open for dinner only). All this and a dessert called the Flying Fish Chocolate Collection. It's a carnival ride, all right, and some diners will need an Alka-Seltzer chaser at the end of the evening. The menu lives up to the atmosphere here, relying mostly on seafood and seasonal fruits and vegetables. Try the signature dish, potato-wrapped red snapper with leek fondue and red-wine butter, and just try to get away without at least sampling that chocolate collection.

What do tapas have to do with Atlantic City? I give up. But that didn't stop Disney from plunking down a Mediterranean restaurant called **Spoodles** in the middle of their so-called Jersey coast. Tapas, as everybody must know by now, are small nibbles ordered for sharing or sampling. Disney's added some full-size entrees for more finicky eaters: lemon chicken, oak-fired salmon, and steak. Here, too, there's an open kitchen.

Where the wild things are... At Disney's Animal Kingdom Lodge, the *Out of Africa* theme extends to the restaurants. At **Jiko—The Cooking Place,** they offer ever-so-slightly exotic, South African–inspired cuisine, while **Boma—Flavors of Africa** features a wood-burning grill and food stations. You'll find the latter hard to resist; that woodsy aroma infiltrates the entire lodge. Diners wander around, gander at the open kitchen, and choose among curries, chutneys, grilled fish and meats, stews, and veggies. The breakfast buffet at Boma is wonderful as well and offers interesting options—try the pap-and-quinoa porridge—alongside the usual breakfast standards. And then there's **Artist Point,** the signature high-end restaurant at Disney's Wilderness Lodge—a dazzling version of a turn-of-the-20th-century national-park lodge. You'll either love it or hate it. The restaurant offers an uneven menu it calls "Pacific-Northwest-inspired." The salmon is delicious, but the quality of the rest of the dishes depends on the chef on duty. Better to camp out at the lodge's family-friendly **Whispering Canyon Cafe,** where you can gaze at the slash pines outside and enjoy the woodsy aroma of the meats roasting inside. But forget the whispering concept; this one's got something of a cowboy theme, a folksy attitude, and a jovial din.

Chowing down at Downtown Disney... Lest anyone dare sneak off the Disney property to spend money at a non-Disney nightclub or eatery, WDW created **Downtown Disney,** an entertainment-and-restaurant zone. To make the place hip, they've enlisted some serious star power. Gloria Estefan and husband Emilio created **Bongos Cuban Cafe,** a Latin-themed restaurant/nightclub at Downtown Disney West Side. Granted, the food is no better than what you'd get at other Cuban restaurants in town—in fact, some of it is downright horrible—but the room is lively (dig the bongo seats at the bar and that Desi Arnaz impersonator!) and the live salsa bands encourage a party atmosphere (but forget about conversation). **Wolfgang Puck Cafe** was Florida's first restaurant by the big-name West Coast chef. Skip the upstairs, formalish dining room; instead, opt for an interesting pasta concoction or one of Puck's famous pizzas. The sushi bar gets high marks, too.

Praise the Lord and pass the pork chops. At **House of Blues,** created by Dan Aykroyd, Jim Belushi, and Aerosmith, grub, gospel, and blues are an inspired mix. This restaurant/concert hall boasts a menu indebted to the Mississippi Delta and cooked with more spice and gumption than you'd expect. Think jambalaya with dirty rice, étouffée, and—a must—bread pudding with whiskey sauce. The musical acts—all top-flight—run the gamut from blues to jazz, R&B to fusion, Sammy Hagar to Fiona Apple. The House of Blues Sunday gospel brunch, with all-you-can-eat vittles, is a can't-miss event—so much so, that they had to add a second showtime to accommodate everyone. Reservations aren't accepted for the dining room but are recommended for the gospel brunch. On the other side of Downtown Disney is **Earl of Sandwich** (the famous edible was invented by said earl in 1762 when he was too busy playing cards to eat a real meal—I wouldn't toss in a royal flush for a four-course affair either). This eatery (owned in part by one of the earl's descendants) offers a great selection of sandwiches, wraps, and salads for those looking for a light meal at a decent price.

Where's the beef?... The Orlando area has several choices (most of them of the chain variety) for committed carnivores. Among the poshest (and the most manly man steakhouse in town) is **Morton's of Chicago,** a member of the venerable chain on Restaurant Row, boasting generous, expensive cuts of meat and an atmosphere that screams power dining. Purists will appreciate **Charley's Steak House,** where the steaks are aged 4 to 6 weeks, then cooked in a wood-fired pit over 1,100°F (592°C) heat. (Reportedly, they got the method from the Seminole Indians—who knew Indians beat cowboys in the meat-grilling department?) Perhaps all you need with your hunk of beef is a good scotch, but, for the record, Charley's also has an outstanding wine list. Upscaled sports bar **Dan Marino's Town Tavern** at Pointe*Orlando leans more toward pub than club, but they still sling serious steaks and ribs there. The **Ruth's Chris Steak House** chain established one of its upscale joints practically next door to Morton's, featuring melt-in-your-mouth beef and fresh seafood. **The Palm** at the Hard Rock Hotel not only features great steaks but a chance to ogle the occasional celebrity diner. Sail right on past the overpriced, so-so **Yachtsman's Steakhouse** at Disney's Yacht Club Resort, with its glassed-in butcher shop (haven't they carried that "behind the scenes" stuff a little too far?), and walk over to **Le Cellier** in Epcot's Canada for one of the better steaks you'll find under $30. If you want real carnivorous bliss, though, you have to hit **Shula's Steak House** at the **Dolphin** hotel, where you'll thank the gods that cows were made so tasty. Most of the steaks will set you back about $40—unless you go for the gusto with the $75 48-ounce porterhouse—but it's some of the best meat money you'll ever spend.

Fishing for compliments... If you want an ocean, you'll need to drive more than an hour; but when you can't do Florida without getting in some grouper, red snapper, or other "catch of the day," the fish fly out of the open kitchen at the **Flying Fish Café** at Disney's BoardWalk resort. The **California Grill** at Disney's Contemporary Resort also displays some skill with the gilled, though grilled pork tenderloin is the top-selling item on the menu. You think *you* brought a lot of luggage to Orlando? **Fulton's Crab House** flies in tons of fish daily from all over the world. Like its namesake, San Francisco's Fulton Street Fish Market, this restaurant has a waterfront location, housed in an 1800s paddleboat on the lagoon at Pleasure Island. House specialties include chargrilled Gulf shrimp, salmon, Alaskan halibut, and Australian lobster tails, but you'll never go wrong with Fulton's "crab and lobster experience for two," a combination platter with Alaskan king and snow crab, and 1¼ pounds of lobster. Another place to spend your hard-earned clams: Epcot's **Coral Reef Restaurant,** which features a huge floor-to-ceiling, 5.6-million-gallon saltwater aquarium—you can go eye-to-eye with a 500-pound grouper while eating a less-lucky member of the same species. Subdued lighting and classical music (Handel's *Water Music,* among other aquatic choices) adds to the intriguing undersea feel. Unfortunately—especially considering the price tag—most of the excitement takes place in the aquarium rather than on your plate. If you want a similar ambience at a lower price, **Sharks Underwater Grill** at SeaWorld, where you dine on Floribbean cuisine with a view of 50 menacing denizens of the deep, is a good choice. There's no fishy view, but at the Walt Disney World Dolphin, Todd English offers innovative seafood dishes and a raw bar that won't put a dent in your wallet at **Todd English's bluezoo.** Over at the Gaylord Palms, you'll feel like you're in Key West as you nosh on crab cakes, conch fritters, and oysters on the half shell, while on an actual boat at **Sunset Sam's Fish Camp.** That's right...a boat...on a lagoon...inside a hotel. Only in Orlando.

Viva Italia... The Loews hotel group went to great lengths to replicate their namesake Italian port city at the Portofino Bay Hotel at Universal Orlando. Makes sense that they'd aim for the same authenticity in the kitchen. And, *mama mia!* (Or should we say, Mama Della!), do they ever. **Mama Della** herself presides over the restaurant of the same name, decorated in homey style with mismatched chairs and china. Get your family-style cannoli and cacciatore here, served in big bowls. A local newspaper recently named this one the "Best Italian" in Orlando. Perhaps that's why Mama is occasionally prone to burst into song. Portofino Bay Hotel's splurgey option, **Bice Ristorante,** features Milanese specialties such as penne with smoked duck breast, braised veal-shank *osso buco,* and other savory options. Ask for a table on the outdoor terrace and you'll be transported to the Italian Riviera. I-Drive's **Bergamo's** has an authentic southern-Italian menu and a waitstaff inclined to hop up to the piano and belt out show tunes, Italian love songs, and operatic arias—it seems totally appropriate that Bergamo's offers a dish called pasta alla Norma (named for Verdi's opera). Don't miss the white-bean, fennel, and radicchio salad, a tangy blend of assertive flavors. For an entirely different feel—one more New England than Naples—there's the **Portobello Yacht Club** at Downtown Disney's Pleasure Island. Photos of classic sailing yachts adorn the walls of this expansive lagoon-side restaurant, where a long mahogany bar is the centerpiece. Brick-oven pizzas are a light choice here, but they're nothing special; Portobello does a lot better with northern-Italian-influenced pasta dishes such as *spaghettini alla portobello* (pasta with pieces of Alaskan king crab, scallops, shrimp, and clams in light olive oil, wine, and herbs). Portobello leans toward the creative side of Italian, and offers several low-fat choices, which sets it apart from much of the competition. And once you've had a virtuous low-fat meal, you can blow it away with the signature dessert: *paradiso al cioccolato*—a rich layer cake with chocolate ganache, toffee pieces, and caramel sauce. This place can be noisy and crowded, so show up late (it stays open till 1:30am most nights) or come for lunch, when prices are lower and crowds are sparser.

Magic Kingdom grub... Disney is upgrading its food-service offerings, but you'd never know it at the Magic Kingdom. Until Tinkerbell sprinkles a little more pixie dust on 'em, you'll do best to steer clear of the sit-down restaurants here. While they're not horrible, they're just average and expensive. Adopt the strategy developed by Magic Kingdom veterans: Eat a big breakfast, then hit the pushcarts and snack as necessary. The street vendors here even sell fresh fruit these days, not to mention awesome popcorn. It might be tempting to "eat in the castle" at **Cinderella's Royal Table,** as it's the only way to actually get inside Cinderella Castle, but this is a feat of planning and endurance you should only attempt if you have kids (or "adults") that insist; see the Dining chapter for tips. If the hunger pangs strike and you just know a bucket of popcorn will be laughed off by your stomach, there are a few counter-service joints worth stopping at. Over in Tomorrowland, **Cosmic Ray's** has been serving up the best variety of any of Disney's serve-yourself restaurants. Different stations are set up for burgers, chicken, sandwiches, soup, and salad (even kosher meals!). You can choose to eat outside on the terrace facing the castle or inside with an animatronic band that entertains a la Chuck E. Cheese's. If you're stuck on the other side of the park, mosey on over to **Pecos Bill Café,** where in addition to being able to substitute a side of carrots for the fries in the burger baskets, the fixin's bar has gourmet items such as mushrooms and onions. Add some lettuce and tomato and you've got yourself a free side salad. Just up the back hallway from Pecos Bill's (or across from Pirates of the Caribbean if you're wandering around outside), you'll find **El Pirata y el Perico,** which offers up two huge, overflowing tacos for less than $5. *¡Olé!*

Dining Hollywood-style at Disney–MGM... Dining at this park is like traveling through a time warp to the 1950s. It's all Mom, meatloaf, and drive-in movies. You'll feel as if you've landed in a vintage TV sitcom at **50's Prime Time Cafe,** where the decor runs to Formica and knickknacks, and Beaver Cleaver is forever ageless on the black-and-white Philco. This concept seemed a little fresher before Nick at Nite introduced a new generation to Rob and Laura Petrie, but it's still cute. The food is just what you'd expect: pot roast, meatloaf with gravy (the mega-seller here), and chicken potpie, and it's not bad. Indulge your inner child and squeal on your dining companions if they don't eat their vegetables—your "Aunt" (or "Uncle" or whatever family member your server is playing) will be sure to properly scold them. Way cooler, and more appropriate to the movie-mad theme of Disney–MGM, is the **Sci-Fi Dine-In Theater Restaurant,** a tribute to the glory days of the drive-in movie. You'll sit in a faux 1955 convertible (your "carhop" will supply popcorn) and watch B sci-fi movie trailers and vintage drive-in commercials on a giant screen, under fiber-optic twinkling stars. Kind of puts one in the mood to cop a...meal. Lunch menus are heavy on the burgers/sandwich items, while dinner offers more gourmet fare. Skip the stale fries and ask for a different side. Shakes are mediocre, but tell your server you're sharing and you'll get two separate glasses with almost twice the shake for the price of one. The **Hollywood Brown Derby** has a classic "Hollywood power lunch" feel and celebrity caricatures on the walls, but I find it a bit overpriced for the experience. Lunch here is a much better deal than dinner.

A Fantasmic Deal

If you're planning to stay for the Fantasmic show at Disney–MGM, consider booking the ***Fantasmic Dinner Package*** *when calling for your Advance Reservation. For a set price (it varies according to the restaurant you choose), you get dinner and a pass that allows you to bypass the normal 2-hour wait for the nightly show. Currently this package is offered with the* ***Hollywood Brown Derby, Mama Melrose's Ristorante Italiano,*** *and* ***Hollywood & Vine.***

On the other side of the park, **Mama Melrose's Ristorante Italiano** offers traditional Italian menu choices such as penne alla vodka, but the brick-oven pizza is always a good, and filling, choice. Try the gooey four-cheese pizza, topped with asiago, mozzarella, provolone, and Gorgonzola. With hardwood floors, red-and-white-checked tablecloths, and hanging chianti bottles, it's your classic trattoria movie set, and the smell of the hickory-wood-burning oven will drive you crazy if you're really hungry. For hearty eaters, the buffet dinner at **Hollywood & Vine** is the best choice. Here you'll enjoy salads, vegetarian dishes, seafood, and carved oven-roasted meats, along with a dessert bar and nonalcoholic beverages. The price is steep compared to most buffets, but if you're hungry, it's worth the price. And for those with food allergies, the individual ingredients labels next to each dish are a lifesaver.

Toasting the town... Strange as it may sound (or not—all Disney, all the time could lead a few people to drink), some people visit Epcot for the sheer pleasure of "drinking around the World." Where else can you enjoy a Bass ale in Britain, a sake in Japan, and a glass of champagne in France—all within the span of an hour? But there are a few other notable purveyors of potent potables in WDW. The **Tune-In Lounge,** just off the main lobby of the **50's Prime Time Cafe,** offers a quiet place to escape the hectic crowds at Disney–MGM Studios. For a little added kitsch, ask for a light-up ice cube. Over at Disney's BoardWalk resort, you'll find the only microbrewery on Disney World property. The **Big River Grille and Brewing Works** offers several varieties of liquid hops, all brewed on-premises—get a sampler to try them all. But forget about having a drink at the Magic Kingdom. The Disney head honchos probably recognized that the visual overload in this park could lead to overindulgence, so it's completely dry—you won't find a drop of alcohol anywhere.

A pie by any other name... No matter how you like your pizza done, there are probably more pizza places in the theme-park areas than any other type of restaurant. Among the best values is **Ci Ci's Pizza,** which offers 16 different kinds of pizza on its buffet, along with salad and dessert. It's not the world's best pizza, but it's tasty, filling, and priced at $4 for all you can eat. Craving deep-dish Chicago-style pizza? I haven't found any better than the ones served by **Giordano's,** which has two locations near Disney. Don't over-order—a small will easily feed two to three people. Do, however, skip the pasta, which tastes more like store-bought frozen than freshly homemade. Staying in the I-Drive/Universal Orlando area? Give a call to **Broadway Pizzeria,** which will not only deliver delicious New York–style pizzas, Italian pasta dishes, and subs to your hotel, but will do it until 4am on the weekends for those who have the post-clubbing munchies.

We all scream for ice cream.... Central Florida's only **Ghirardelli Soda Fountain and Chocolate Shop,** a branch of the famous San Francisco institution, is located in the Downtown Disney Marketplace. For the ice cream addict, there's nothing like this renowned chocolate company's hot-fudge sundae. Try it over the toasted-almond ice cream for a real treat. Your whole gang has a sweet tooth? Get your taste buds over to **Beaches and Cream Soda Shop,** nestled by the pool at Disney's Yacht and Beach Club resorts, and order the Kitchen Sink. This concoction of vanilla, chocolate, strawberry, coffee, and mint chocolate-chip ice cream is smothered in every topping they have and served in a mock chrome sink. It'll either cure you or kill you of any craving for sugar. I tried it once with three friends and couldn't even look at ice cream for weeks.

Map 6: Orlando Dining

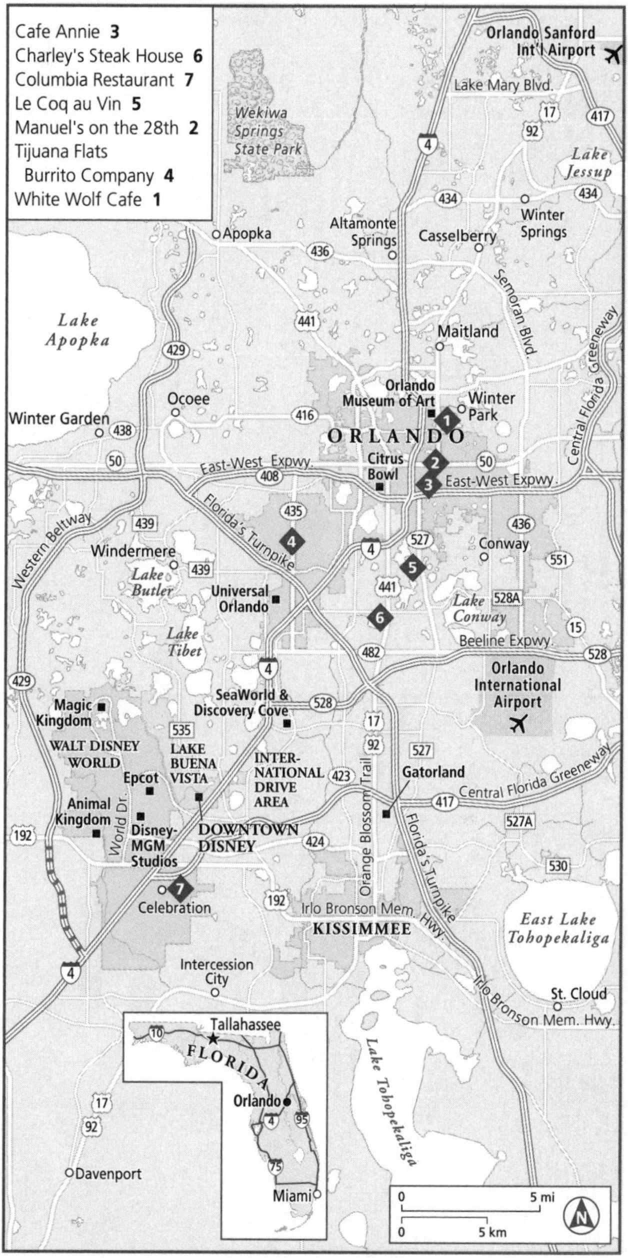

Map 7: WDW & Lake Buena Vista Dining

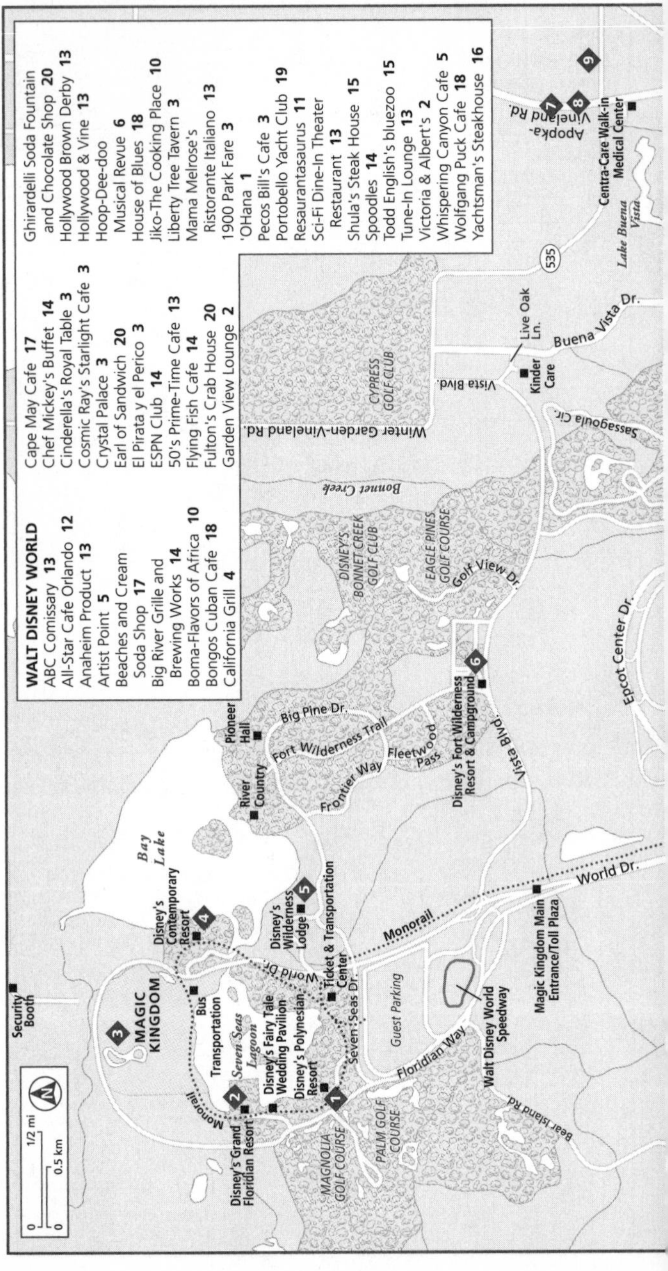
WALT DISNEY WORLD
ABC Comissary 13
All-Star Cafe Orlando 12
Anaheim Product 13
Artist Point 5
Beaches and Cream Soda Shop 17
Big River Grille and Brewing Works 14
Boma-Flavors of Africa 10
Bongos Cuban Cafe 18
California Grill 4
Cape May Cafe 17
Chef Mickey's Buffet 14
Cinderella's Royal Table 3
Cosmic Ray's Starlight Cafe 3
Crystal Palace 3
Earl of Sandwich 20
El Pirata y el Perico 3
ESPN Club 14
50's Prime-Time Cafe 13
Flying Fish Cafe 14
Fulton's Crab House 20
Garden View Lounge 2
Ghirardelli Soda Fountain and Chocolate Shop 20
Hollywood Brown Derby 13
Hollywood & Vine 13
Hoop-Dee-doo Musical Revue 6
House of Blues 18
Jiko-The Cooking Place 10
Liberty Tree Tavern 3
Mama Melrose's Ristorante Italiano 13
1900 Park Fare 3
'OHana 1
Pecos Bill's Cafe 3
Portobello Yacht Club 19
Resaurantasaurus 11
Sci-Fi Dine-In Theater Restaurant 13
Shula's Steak House 15
Spoodles 14
Todd English's bluezoo 15
Tune-In Lounge 13
Victoria & Albert's 2
Whispering Canyon Cafe 5
Wolfgang Puck Cafe 18
Yachtsman's Steakhouse 16
0 1/2 mi
0 0.5 km
N
Security Booth
MAGIC KINGDOM
Bus Transportation
Seven Seas Lagoon
Disney's Grand Floridian Resort
Disney's Fairy Tale Wedding Pavilion
Disney's Polynesian Resort
Disney's Contemporary Resort
Bay Lake
Disney's Wilderness Lodge
Ticket & Transportation Center
Monorail
World Dr.
Seven Seas Dr.
Guest Parking
Floridian Way
Walt Disney World Speedway
Magic Kingdom Main Entrance/Toll Plaza
MAGNOLIA GOLF COURSE
PALM GOLF COURSE
Bear Island Rd.
River Country
Pioneer Hall
Big Pine Dr.
Fort Wilderness Trail
Frontier Way
Fleetwood Pass
Disney's Fort Wilderness Resort & Campground
Vista Blvd.
DISNEY'S BONNET CREEK GOLF CLUB
EAGLE PINES GOLF COURSE
Golf View Dr.
Epcot Center Dr.
Bonnet Creek
Winter Garden-Vineland Rd.
CYPRESS GOLF CLUB
Kinder Care
Live Oak Ln.
Buena Vista Dr.
Sassagoula Cir.
535
Lake Buena Vista
Centra-Care Walk-in Medical Center
Apopka-Vineland Rd.

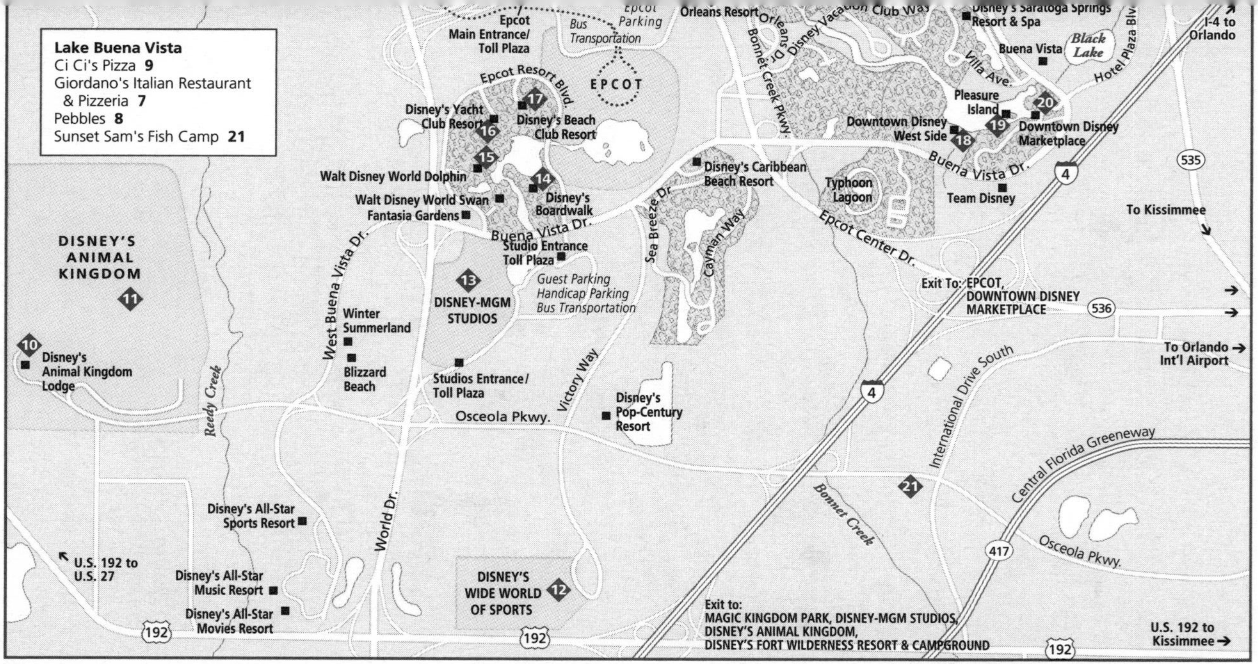
Lake Buena Vista
Ci Ci's Pizza 9
Giordano's Italian Restaurant & Pizzeria 7
Pebbles 8
Sunset Sam's Fish Camp 21
Epcot Main Entrance/ Toll Plaza
Bus Transportation
Epcot Parking
EPCOT
Epcot Resort Blvd.
Disney's Yacht Club Resort
Disney's Beach Club Resort
Walt Disney World Dolphin
Walt Disney World Swan
Disney's Boardwalk
Fantasia Gardens
Buena Vista Dr.
Studio Entrance Toll Plaza
Guest Parking
Handicap Parking
Bus Transportation
DISNEY'S ANIMAL KINGDOM
West Buena Vista Dr.
DISNEY-MGM STUDIOS
Winter Summerland
Blizzard Beach
Disney's Animal Kingdom Lodge
Reedy Creek
Studios Entrance/ Toll Plaza
Victory Way
Osceola Pkwy.
Disney's Pop-Century Resort
Sea Breeze Dr.
Cayman Way
Disney's Caribbean Beach Resort
Orleans Resort
Orleans Dr.
Bonnet Creek Pkwy.
Disney Vacation Club Way
Disney's Saratoga Springs Resort & Spa
Buena Vista
Black Lake
Hotel Plaza Blvd.
Villa Ave.
Pleasure Island
Downtown Disney West Side
Downtown Disney Marketplace
Typhoon Lagoon
Team Disney
Epcot Center Dr.
I-4 to Orlando
535
To Kissimmee
Exit To: EPCOT, DOWNTOWN DISNEY MARKETPLACE
536
To Orlando Int'l Airport
International Drive South
Central Florida Greeneway
Bonnet Creek
417
Osceola Pkwy.
Disney's All-Star Sports Resort
World Dr.
U.S. 192 to U.S. 27
Disney's All-Star Music Resort
Disney's All-Star Movies Resort
DISNEY'S WIDE WORLD OF SPORTS
192
Exit to: MAGIC KINGDOM PARK, DISNEY-MGM STUDIOS, DISNEY'S ANIMAL KINGDOM, DISNEY'S FORT WILDERNESS RESORT & CAMPGROUND
U.S. 192 to Kissimmee

Map 8: Epcot Dining

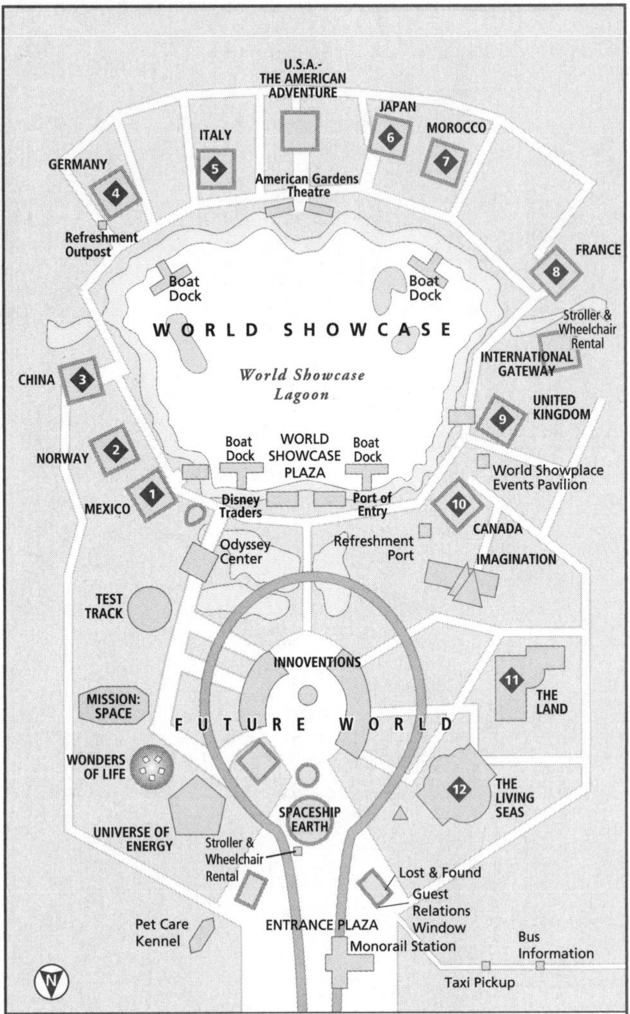

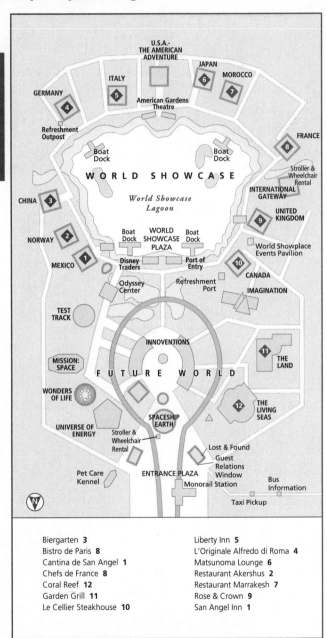

Biergarten **3**
Bistro de Paris **8**
Cantina de San Angel **1**
Chefs de France **8**
Coral Reef **12**
Garden Grill **11**
Le Cellier Steakhouse **10**
Liberty Inn **5**
L'Originale Alfredo di Roma **4**
Matsunoma Lounge **6**
Restaurant Akershus **2**
Restaurant Marrakesh **7**
Rose & Crown **9**
San Angel Inn **1**

Map 9: Universal Orlando & International Drive–Area Dining

Bergamos **14**
Bice Ristorante **2**
Bob Marley–A Tribute To Freedom **5**
Broadway Pizzeria **8**
Cafe Tu Tu Tango **15**
Comic Strip Cafe **16**
Dan Marino's Town Tavern **17**
Dux **18**
Emeril's Restaurant Orlando **5**
Emeril's Tchoup Chop **7**
Enchanted Oak Tavern and Alchemy Bar **6**
Green Eggs & Ham Cafe **6**
Hard Rock Cafe **5**
Jimmy's Buffet's Margaritaville **5**
Johnny Rockets **17**
Kim Wu **1**
The Kitchen **3**
Latin Quarter **5**
Lu Lu's Bait Shack **17**
Mama Della's Ristorante **2**
Mel's Drive-In **4**
Morton's of Chicago **10**
NASCAR Cafe Orlando **5**
NBA City **5**
The Palm **3**
Pat O'Brien's Orlando **5**
Race Rock **16**
Roy's **9**
Ruth's Chris Steak House **11**
Samba Room **12**
Seafire Inn **19**
Shamu Stadium **19**
Sharks Underwater Grill **19**
Siam Orchid **13**

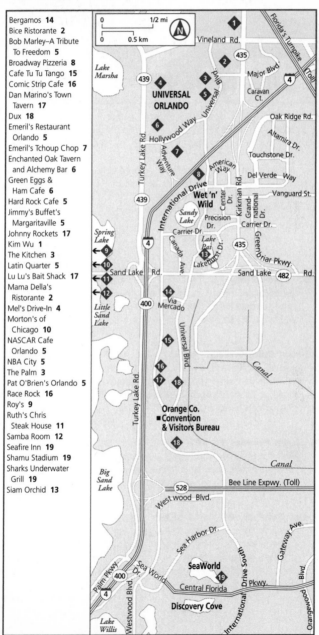

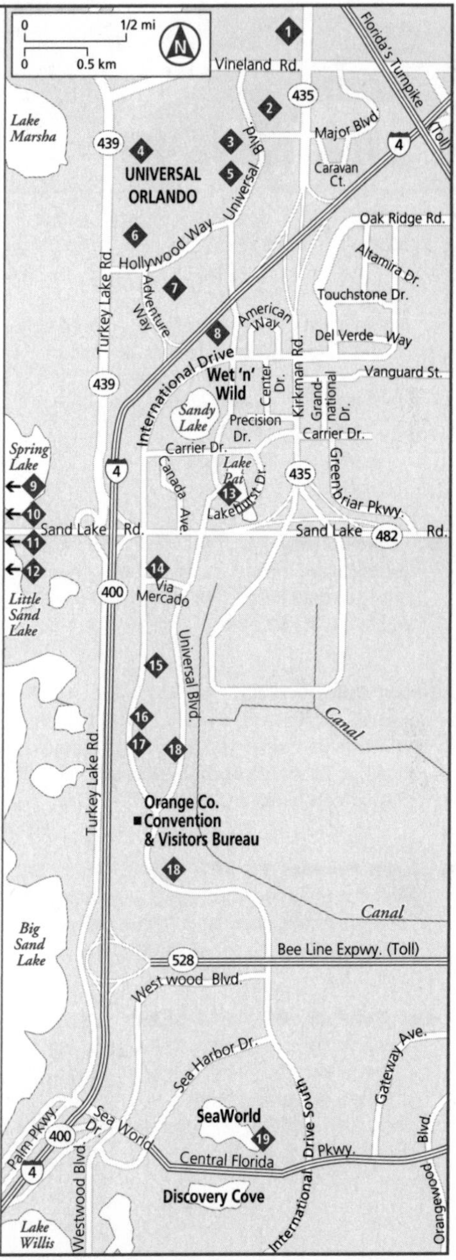

The Index

$$$$	over $25
$$$	$15–$25
$$	$7–$14
$	under $7

Prices given are per person for entrees only.

The following abbreviations are used for credit cards:

AE	American Express
DC	Diners Club
DISC	Discover
MC	MasterCard
V	Visa

ABC Commissary (p. 74) WDW *AMERICAN* The healthier-than-average fare makes up for the lack of ambience at this counter-service restaurant.... *Tel 407/WDW-DINE. Disney–MGM Studios. AE, DC, DISC, MC, V. $*

See Map 7 on p. 90.

All-Star Cafe Orlando (p. 71) WDW *AMERICAN* This celebrity-owned sports cafe, complete with baseball-mitt-shaped booths, is worth a visit if you're a major sports fan, but is no slam dunk.... *Tel 407/827-8326. Disney's Wide World of Sports, 6910 S. Victory Way. AE, DC, DISC, MC, V. $$–$$$*

See Map 7 on p. 90.

Anaheim Produce (p. 75) WDW *SNACKS* Set up like a produce stand with various fruits and vegetables; one of the most inexpensive snack options at Disney, with most items 99¢ to $3.... *Disney–MGM Studios. No credit cards. $*

See Map 7 on p. 90.

Artist Point (p. 81) WDW *SEAFOOD/STEAKS* This Pacific Northwest–themed restaurant has a great location in the Wilderness Lodge, but the food is hit or miss.... *Tel 407/WDW-DINE. Disney's Wilderness Lodge, 901 W. Timberline Dr., on the southwest shore of Bay Lake just east of the Magic Kingdom. AE, DC, DISC, MC, V. $–$$$$*

See Map 7 on p. 90.

Beaches and Cream Soda Shop (p. 88) WDW *ICE CREAM* Slip into this cool, old-fashioned soda shop for a Milky Way sundae, a fudge "mudslide," or a thick malted. Better yet, grab a few friends and attack the Kitchen Sink.... *Tel 407/WDW-DINE. Disney's Beach Club Resort, 1800 Epcot Resorts Blvd., off Buena Vista Dr. AE, DC, DISC, MC, V. $-$$*

See Map 7 on p. 90.

Bergamo's (p. 84) INTERNATIONAL DRIVE *ITALIAN* The menu and wine list span several regions of Italy; the singing servers throw in Italian ballads, show tunes, and opera. Dinner is served after 5pm nightly; music starts at 7pm. (Note that the owners plan to move Bergamo's to the Festival Bay Mall in October 2006.)... *Tel 407/352-3805. www.bergamos.com. The Mercado, 8445 International Dr. Reservations recommended. AE, DC, DISC, MC, V. $$$-$$$$*

See Map 9 on p. 93.

Bice Ristorante (p. 73) UNIVERSAL ORLANDO *ITALIAN* This high-end restaurant boasts views of Portofino Bay's "harbor," and regional specialties like veal Milanese.... *Tel 407/503-1415. www.biceorlando.com. Portofino Bay Hotel, 5601 Universal Studios Blvd. Reservations recommended. AE, DC, DISC, MC, V. $$$-$$$$*

See Map 9 on p. 93.

Biergarten (p. 77) WDW *GERMAN* Accordion playing, lederhosen, hearty fare—and, of course, beer—reign supreme at this German banquet hall. Go for the entertainment; pass on the food.... *Tel 407/WDW-DINE. Epcot. Advance Reservation recommended. AE, DC, DISC, MC, V. $$-$$$*

See Map 8 on p. 92.

Big River Grille and Brewing Works (p. 87) WDW *SEAFOOD/STEAKS* Skip the average food, but do try the brew sampler.... *Tel 407/WDW-DINE. Disney's BoardWalk, 2101 N. Epcot Resorts Blvd., off Buena Vista Dr. AE, DC, DISC, MC, V. $-$$$*

See Map 7 on p. 90.

Bistro de Paris (p. 75) WDW *FRENCH* Don't let the name fool you: Le Bistro is a bit more upscale than its downstairs Epcot neighbor, Chefs de France.... *Tel 407/WDW-DINE. Epcot. Advance Reservation recommended. AE, DC, DISC, MC, V. $$-$$$$*

See Map 8 on p. 92.

Bob Marley—A Tribute to Freedom (p. 72) UNIVERSAL ORLANDO *JAMAICAN* A re-creation of the King of Reggae's home in Kingston, Jamaica, with lush greenery and authentic eats/drinks such as roasted plantains, Jamaican beef patties, and Red Stripe Beer.... *Tel 407/224-3663. CityWalk. AE, DISC, MC, V. $$-$$$*

See Map 9 on p. 93.

Boma—Flavors of Africa (p. 81) WDW *AFRICAN* Follow your nose to the wood-burning grill, and check out what's hot at this African-influenced eatery. Experience exotic dishes alongside more familiar ones at the breakfast and dinner buffets.... *Tel 407/WDW-DINE. Disney's Animal Kingdom Lodge, 2901 Osceola Pkwy. AE, DC, DISC, MC, V. $$–$$$$*

See Map 7 on p. 90.

Bongos Cuban Cafe (p. 82) WDW *CUBAN* Disney goes Cuban, enhanced by the star-power of celeb-owner Gloria Estefan. The food's average, but the setting's better, especially when there are live bands.... *Tel 407/828-0999. www.bongoscubancafe.com. Downtown Disney West Side. AE, DC, DISC, MC, V. $–$$$$*

See Map 7 on p. 90.

Broadway Pizzeria (p. 88) INTERNATIONAL DRIVE *PIZZA* Great NYC-style pizzas, pasta, and subs. Delivers until 4am Thursday through Saturday.... *Tel 407/351-8989. 6807 Visitors Circle. AE, MC, V. $$*

See Map 9 on p. 93.

Cafe Annie (p. 70) DOWNTOWN ORLANDO *MEDITERRANEAN* A local downtown favorite. Serves tasty Greek/Mediterranean/Middle Eastern dishes cafeteria-style.... *Tel 407/420-4041. 131 N. Orange Ave. MC, V. $$–$$$*

See Map 6 on p. 89.

Café Tu Tu Tango (p. 71) INTERNATIONAL DRIVE *TAPAS* This funky little artists' loft serves a super tapas menu. Worth visiting just for the atmosphere.... *Tel 407/248-2222. www.cafetututango.com. 8625 International Dr. AE, DC, DISC, MC, V. $–$$*

See Map 9 on p. 93.

California Grill (p. 74) WDW *WEST COAST* Disney goes hip with this stylish restaurant atop the Contemporary Resort. The menu is tweaked regularly according to what's fresh at the market.... *Tel 407/WDW-DINE. Disney's Contemporary Resort, 4600 N. World Dr. Advance Reservation recommended. AE, DC, DISC, MC, V. $$–$$$$*

See Map 7 on p. 90.

Cantina de San Angel (p. 76) WDW *MEXICAN* Quick, grab one of the umbrella tables and a Mexican fast-food lunch. Or come for dinner and a margarita and watch the nightly IllumiNations laser show. Arrive early: Other people have caught on to this strategy.... *Tel 407/WDW-DINE. Epcot. AE, DC, DISC, MC, V. $$*

See Map 8 on p. 90.

Cape May Café (p. 80) WDW *SEAFOOD* Offers a character breakfast in the morning and a clambake in the evening.... *Tel 407/WDW-DINE. Disney's Beach Club Resort, 1800 Epcot Resorts Blvd. Advance Reservation essential. AE, DC, DISC, MC, V. $$–$$$$*

See Map 7 on p. 90.

Charley's Steak House (p. 83) ORLANDO *STEAKS* A bastion of big beef, award-winning Charley's serves flavorful, well-aged Western steaks and has an outstanding wine list.... *Tel 407/851-7130. 6107 S. Orange Blossom Trail. Reservations recommended. AE, MC, V. $$–$$$$*

See Map 6 on p. 89.

Chef Mickey's Buffet (p. 80) WDW *AMERICAN/CHARACTER MEAL* Join the world's favorite rodent as he whips up character breakfast and dinner buffets at Disney's Contemporary Resort.... *Tel 407/WDW-DINE. Disney's Contemporary Resort, 4600 N. World Dr. Advance Reservation essential. AE, DC, DISC, MC, V. $$–$$$$*

See Map 7 on p. 90.

Chefs de France (p. 75) WDW *FRENCH* Foodies make this restaurant their first priority at Epcot. The bill of fare features dishes created by three top French chefs—Paul Bocuse, Roger Vergé, and Gaston Lenotre—at their own restaurants in Paris and Lyons.... *Tel 407/WDW-DINE. Epcot. Advance Reservation recommended. AE, DC, DISC, MC, V. $$–$$$$*

See Map 8 on p. 92.

Ci Ci's Pizza (p. 88) CITYWIDE *PIZZA* Offers 16 varieties of pizza, plus salad and dessert in an all-you-can-eat buffet for only $4.... *Tel 407/238-7711. www.cicispizza.com. Lake Buena Vista: 8586 Palm Pkwy. AE, DC, DISC, MC, V. Call for other locations. $–$$*

See Map 7 on p. 90.

Cinderella's Royal Table (p. 79) WDW *AMERICAN/CHARACTER MEAL* Dining here is the only way to get inside Cinderella Castle at the Magic Kingdom, but getting a reservation for this character breakfast or lunch may prove more elusive than finding a fit for the glass slipper.... *Tel 407/WDW-DINE. Magic Kingdom. Advance Reservation essential. AE, DC, DISC, MC, V. $$$–$$$$*

See Map 7 on p. 90.

Columbia Restaurant (p. 74) CELEBRATION *CUBAN* Direct from Tampa's Ybor City, this spin-off of Florida's oldest fine-dining restaurant ironically resides in Disney's homage to gingerbread Americana. Try the paella and the irresistible Cuban bread.... *Tel 407/566-1505. www.columbiarestaurant.com. 649 Front St. AE, DC, DISC, MC, V. $–$$*

See Map 6 on p. 89.

Comic Strip Cafe (p. 78) UNIVERSAL ORLANDO *AMERICAN* Got a group of picky eaters? This counter-service restaurant offers Mexican, Chinese, American, and Italian menus.... *Tel 407/363-8000. Islands of Adventure. AE, DC, DISC, MC, V. $–$$*

See Map 9 on p. 93.

Coral Reef Restaurant (p. 84) WDW *SEAFOOD* A favorite among seafood lovers at Epcot, though you may find it a bit off-putting to eat seafood while watching its buddies swim by behind the glass wall.... *Tel 407/WDW-DINE. Epcot. Advance Reservation recommended. AE, DC, DISC, MC, V. $–$$$$*

See Map 8 on p. 92.

Cosmic Ray's Starlight Cafe (p. 74) WDW *AMERICAN* One of the largest and most diverse menus of all the Disney fast-food joints: beef, chicken, vegetarian—even kosher. Kids will enjoy the animatronic band; adults will think they've stepped into an alternate-reality Chuck E. Cheese's.... *Tel 407/WDW-DINE. Magic Kingdom. AE, DC, DISC, MC, V. $$*

See Map 7 on p. 90.

Crystal Palace (p. 79) WDW *AMERICAN/CHARACTER MEAL* Offers character buffet-style meals throughout the day. You'll usually find some of the Hundred Acre inhabitants here, including Pooh and Tigger.... *Tel 407/WDW-DINE. Magic Kingdom. Advance Reservation recommended. AE, DC, DISC, MC, V. $$–$$$$*

See Map 7 on p. 90.

Dan Marino's Town Tavern (p. 83) INTERNATIONAL DRIVE *STEAKS* Don't count on seeing owner Marino (although they say he does occasionally pop in). The big draws here are steaks and ribs, oak-grilled in the open kitchen, and the big TVs behind the football-shaped bar. Think gourmet sports pub.... *Tel 407/363-1013. www.danmarinosrestaurant.com. Pointe*Orlando, 9101 International Dr. AE, MC. $$–$$$*

See Map 9 on p. 93.

Dux (p. 67) INTERNATIONAL DRIVE *CONTINENTAL* A seasonally changing menu offers a creative international mix of ingredients, though, most definitely, not duck.... *Tel 407/352-4000. The Peabody Hotel, 9801 International Dr. Reservations recommended. AE, DC, DISC, MC, V. $$$–$$$$*

See Map 9 on p. 93.

Earl of Sandwich (p. 82) WDW *SANDWICHES* This Downtown Disney eatery has an actual royal pedigree, plus a good variety of gourmet deli sandwiches, salads, and wraps.... *Tel 407/WDW-DINE. Downtown Disney Marketplace. AE, DC, DISC, MC, V. $*

See Map 7 on p. 90.

El Pirata y el Perico (p. 86) WDW *MEXICAN* Offers tacos, nachos, and other Mexican staples.... *Tel 407/WDW-DINE. Magic Kingdom. AE, DC, DISC, MC, V. $–$$$*

See Map 7 on p. 90.

Emeril's Restaurant Orlando (p. 73) UNIVERSAL ORLANDO *CAJUN/CREOLE* Hotshot chef Emeril Lagasse created this culinary cousin of his New Orleans restaurant, but I've only seen him once bustling around the open kitchen. The menu is heavy on Cajun and Creole-inspired dishes.... *Tel 407/224-2424. www.emerils.com. CityWalk. Reservations essential. AE, DISC, MC, V. $$-$$$$*

See Map 9 on p. 93.

Emeril's Tchoup Chop (p. 73) UNIVERSAL ORLANDO *POLYNESIAN* Emeril's second Orlando restaurant lets you enjoy Polynesian-inspired dishes in an absolutely gorgeous lagoon-side setting. Go for lunch, when the same dishes are served in slightly smaller portions at a significantly reduced price.... *Tel 407/503-2467. www.emerils.com. Royal Pacific Resort, 6300 Hollywood Way. Reservations essential. AE, DISC, MC, V. $$-$$$$*

See Map 9 on p. 93.

Enchanted Oak Tavern & Alchemy Bar (p. 71) UNIVERSAL ORLANDO *AMERICAN* A cool example of Universal's playful approach to theme-park dining. Sit inside a giant faux oak tree, dig into some hickory-smoked chicken and a Dragon Scale Ale, and wait for Merlin to appear.... *Tel 407/363-8000. Islands of Adventure. AE, DISC, MC, V. $$*

See Map 9 on p. 93.

ESPN Club (p. 71) WDW *AMERICAN* Sports restaurant that offers the usual burgers and pub fare, an arcade, and every sports event known to mankind on the TVs.... *Tel 407/WDW-DINE. Disney's BoardWalk, 2101 N. Epcot Resorts Blvd., off Buena Vista Dr. AE, DC, DISC, MC, V. $–$$$*

See Map 7 on p. 90.

50's Prime Time Cafe (p. 86) WDW *AMERICAN* The decor is sit-com-kitchen-pastel Formica and chrome. Eat your meal off sectioned TV dinner platters while your "Aunt" admonishes you to eat your vegetables. Great atmosphere, decent food.... *Tel 407/WDW-DINE. Disney–MGM Studios. Advance Reservation recommended. AE, DC, DISC, MC, V. $–$$$*

See Map 7 on p. 90.

Flying Fish Café (p. 80) WDW *SEAFOOD* Lively, carnival-like setting and creative cuisine (don't skip the chocolate collection for dessert) make this one worth a visit.... *Tel 407/WDW-DINE. Disney's BoardWalk, 2101 N. Epcot Resorts Blvd., off Buena Vista Dr. Advance Reservation recommended. AE, DC, DISC, MC, V. $–$$$$*

See Map 7 on p. 90.

Fulton's Crab House (p. 74) WDW *SEAFOOD* This West Coast transplant is right at home on the Buena Vista Lagoon. Navigate the lengthy menu till you find your favorite shellfish.... *Tel 407/934-2628. www.fultonscrabhouse.com. Downtown Disney Marketplace. Advance Reservation recommended. AE, DC, DISC, MC, V. $-$$$$*

See Map 7 on p. 90.

Garden Grill Restaurant (p. 80) WDW *AMERICAN* The fare runs to family-style American meals and big platters of chicken, ribs, and fish. And yes, those cucumbers really do look like Mickey Mouse.... *Tel 407/WDW-DINE. Epcot. Advance Reservation recommended. AE, DC, DISC, MC, V. $$-$$$$*

See Map 8 on p. 92.

Garden View Lounge (p. 73) WDW *AFTERNOON TEA* This sunlit spot overlooking formal gardens offers daily high tea—scones, jam tarts, those cunning little sandwiches, even strawberries and champagne.... *Tel 407/WDW-DINE. Grand Floridian Resort & Spa, 4401 Floridian Way. AE, DC, DISC, MC, V. $$-$$$*

See Map 7 on p. 90.

Ghirardelli Soda Fountain and Chocolate Shop (p. 88) WDW *ICE CREAM* It's loaded with chocolate goodness and delicious treats. Try a hot-fudge sundae with the toasted-almond ice cream. Yum!... *Tel 407/WDW-DINE. Downtown Disney Marketplace. AE, DC, DISC, MC, V. $*

See Map 7 on p. 90.

Giordano's Italian Restaurant & Pizzeria (p. 88) LAKE BUENA VISTA *ITALIAN/PIZZA* Forget the rest of the menu, it's the deep-dish Chicago-style pizza that you want here.... *Tel 407/239-8900. www.giordanos.com. 12151 S. Apopka-Vineland Rd.; and other locations throughout Orlando. AE, DC, MC, V. $-$$$*

See Map 7 on p. 90.

Green Eggs & Ham Cafe (p. 78) UNIVERSAL ORLANDO *AMERICAN* At this green ham-shaped cafe, you can get real green eggs and ham or a normal-hued breakfast. Cute as can be.... *Tel 407/363-8000. Islands of Adventure. AE, DISC, MC, V. $-$$*

See Map 9 on p. 93.

Hard Rock Cafe (p. 72) UNIVERSAL ORLANDO *AMERICAN* The world's largest Hard Rock Cafe serves fun atmosphere and good food; the Twisted Mac 'n' Cheese is a favorite. Consider the "All-Access Pass," which gets you a $20 dining credit and jump-the-line privileges at this always busy spot.... *Tel 407/351-7625. www.hardrockcafe.com. CityWalk. AE, MC, V. $$-$$$*

See Map 9 on p. 93.

Hollywood & Vine (p. 87) WDW *AMERICAN* No characters to speak of, but you can still enjoy the hearty all-you-can-eat buffet.... *Tel 407/WDW-DINE. Disney–MGM Studios. AE, DC, DISC, MC, V. $$–$$$*

See Map 7 on p. 90.

Hollywood Brown Derby (p. 86) WDW *AMERICAN* A replica of the original Brown Derby in California, where movie stars went to see and be seen. Great decor, but overpriced—you can find better deals elsewhere in the park.... *Tel 407/WDW-DINE. Disney–MGM Studios. Advance Reservation recommended. AE, DC, DISC, MC, V. $–$$$$*

See Map 7 on p. 90.

Hoop-Dee-Doo Musical Revue (p. 68) WDW *AMERICAN/ CHARACTER MEAL* The most popular dinner show at Walt Disney World. It's corny, it's country; it's so cute it'll make your teeth hurt. Vittles include ribs, fried chicken, and corn on the cob.... *Tel 407/WDW-DINE. Three shows nightly at Pioneer Hall. Fort Wilderness Resort & Campground, 3520 N. Fort Wilderness Trail. Advance Reservation required. AE, DC, DISC, MC, V. $$$$*

See Map 7 on p. 90.

House of Blues (p. 79) WDW *SOUTHERN* Terrific music and delicious Southern comfort food (with a contemporary slant) make this house one you'll want to hang out in. The Sunday Gospel Brunch is not to be missed.... *Tel 407/934-2583. www.hob.com. Downtown Disney West Side, Walt Disney World. AE, DC, DISC, MC, V. $–$$$ (meals), $$$–$$$$ (gospel brunch)*

See Map 7 on p. 90.

Jiko—The Cooking Place (p. 81) WDW *AFRICAN* The signature restaurant (translation: most expensive) at Disney's Animal Kingdom Lodge features semi-exotic cuisine like fish steamed in banana leaves and fire-roasted sweet corn soup. If you have an adventurous palette, it's well worth the trip.... *Tel 407/WDW-DINE. Disney's Animal Kingdom Lodge, 2901 Osceola Pkwy. AE, DC, DISC, MC, V. $–$$$$*

See Map 7 on p. 90.

Jimmy's Buffett's Margaritaville (p. 72) UNIVERSAL ORLANDO *AMERICAN* Wasting away again is right. You could wait forever for a Cheeseburger in Paradise because it's that busy. Why, I don't know. Count on lots of families, Parrotheads, an erupting volcano (of margarita mix) when the blender needs refilling, and Floribbean cuisine. After 9pm, the venue offers live music, but the entertainment is hit or miss.... *Tel 407/224-2155. www.margaritavilleorlando.com. CityWalk. AE, DISC, MC, V. $$–$$$*

See Map 9 on p. 93.

Johnny Rockets (p. 72) INTERNATIONAL DRIVE *AMERICAN* Yes, it's part of a national chain, but you can't beat the nostalgia of dropping a nickel in the booth's jukebox as you sip a freshly made chocolate malt.... *Tel 407/903-0762. www.johnnyrockets.com. Pointe*Orlando, 9101 International Dr. AE, DC, DISC, MC, V. $$-$$$*

See Map 9 on p. 93.

Kim Wu (p. 71) INTERNATIONAL DRIVE *CHINESE* Here's traditional Chinese food done right. Flavorful, excellent presentation, and most entrees under $10. An Orlando favorite for more than 20 years; owner Tom Yuen works the floor nightly greeting guests like family.... *Tel 407/93-0752. Kirkman Shoppes, 4904 S. Kirkman Rd. AE, DISC, MC, V. $–$$*

See Map 9 on p. 93.

The Kitchen (p. 72) UNIVERSAL ORLANDO *AMERICAN* This great rock-'n'-roll bistro serves up everything from sandwiches to steak; try the Texas chili for a real bite. A separate kids' area with movies will keep little ones away while you eat.... *Tel 407/503-3463. Hard Rock Hotel, 5000 Universal Blvd. Reservations recommended. AE, DISC, MC, V. $$–$$$$*

See Map 9 on p. 93.

Latin Quarter (p. 72) UNIVERSAL ORLANDO *LATIN* Somehow, the shortish menu claims to represent 21 Latin nations. Look for black beans and rice, and plantains and flan, all spiced up with live music and impromptu salsa lessons.... *Tel 407/363-5922. CityWalk. AE, DISC, MC, V. $–$$$*

See Map 9 on p. 93.

Le Cellier Steakhouse (p. 83) WDW *STEAKS* Among the better steaks you'll find for under $30. Do try the regional Canadian microbrews and the Canadian cheddar cheese soup. The cellar decor isn't too kitschy either. Beauty, eh?... *Tel 407/WDW-DINE. Epcot. Advance Reservation recommended. AE, DC, DISC, MC, V. $–$$$$*

See Map 8 on p. 92.

Le Coq au Vin (p. 74) ORLANDO *FRENCH* Get past the worn country-inn exterior and you'll find a menu of rustic French food and not a smidgen of snobbery. In-the-know locals and area chefs dine here frequently.... *Tel 407/851-6980. 4800 S. Orange Ave., Orlando. AE, DISC, MC, V. $$–$$$$*

See Map 6 on p. 89.

Liberty Inn (p. 76) WDW *AMERICAN* Epcot's American pavilion's restaurant serves the usual hamburgers and hot dogs. This is the best they could come up with as an example of American cuisine?... *Tel 407/WDW–DINE. Epcot. AE, DC, DISC, MC, V. $–$$*

See Map 8 on p. 92.

Liberty Tree Tavern (p. 79) WDW *AMERICAN/CHARACTER MEAL* Disney dining goes patriotic at this faux colonial cafe. Lunch menu is a la carte while the nightly character dinners are buffet-style.... *Tel 407/WDW-DINE. Magic Kingdom. Advance Reservation recommended. AE, DC, DISC, MC, V. $$–$$$$*

See Map 7 on p. 90.

L'Originale Alfredo di Roma Ristorante (p. 76) WDW *ITALIAN* Heavy food, overly fussy decor, and strolling opera singers. You can find a better Italian dining experience elsewhere in Orlando.... *Tel 407/WDW-DINE. Epcot. Advance Reservation recommended. AE, DC, DISC, MC, V. $–$$$$*

See Map 8 on p. 92.

Lulu's Bait Shack (p. 79) INTERNATIONAL DRIVE *CAJUN/CREOLE* Step inside the bayou shack on the third floor of Pointe*Orlando and enjoy budget-friendly Cajun dishes like jambalaya and crawfish étouffée.... *Tel 407/354-1122. www.lulusbaitshack.com. Pointe*Orlando, 9101 International Dr. AE, MC, V. $–$$*

See Map 9 on p. 93.

Mama Della's Ristorante (p. 84) UNIVERSAL ORLANDO *ITALIAN* Mama Della welcomes you to her "home," pushing pasta on you with a "Mangia! Mangia!" Sounds hokey, but who cares when the food's so good?... *Tel 407/224-9255. Portofino Bay Hotel, 5601 Universal Blvd. AE, MC, V. $$–$$$*

See Map 9 on p. 93.

Mama Melrose's Ristorante Italiano (p. 84) WDW *ITALIAN* A casual trattoria with great pizza—and shorter lines than at other Disney–MGM Studios eateries.... *Tel 407/WDW-DINE. Disney-MGM Studios. AE, DC, DISC, MC, V. $–$$$*

See Map 7 on p. 90.

Manuel's on the 28th (p. 72) DOWNTOWN ORLANDO *CONTINENTAL* Splurge-worthy dining atop the Bank of America Building in downtown Orlando. The food is actually more amazing than the views at this award-winning restaurant.... *Tel 407/246-6580. www.manuelsonthe28th.com. 390 N. Orange Ave, 28th floor. Jackets preferred. Reservations recommended. AE, DC, DISC, MC, V. $$$$*

See Map 6 on p. 89.

Matsunoma Lounge (p. 77) WDW *JAPANESE* One of Epcot's best-kept secrets (till now). Sneak away to the second floor of the Mitsukoshi Department Store at World Showcase Japan, nibble sushi, and sample a sake martini.... *Tel 407/WDW-DINE. Epcot. AE, DC, DISC, MC, V. $–$$$*

See Map 8 on p. 92.

Mel's Drive-In (p. 77) UNIVERSAL ORLANDO *AMERICAN* A 1950s-themed classic diner a la *Happy Days*. Great atmosphere; so-so food.... *Tel 407/363-8000. Universal Studios Florida. AE, DISC, MC, V. $-$$*

See Map 9 on p. 93.

Morton's of Chicago (p. 82) INTERNATIONAL DRIVE *STEAKS* This steakhouse serves up expensive steaks and cigars. A manly man's type of joint.... *Tel 407/248-3485. www.mortons.com. The Marketplace at Dr. Phillips, 7600 Dr. Phillips Blvd. AE, DISC, MC, V. $$-$$$$*

See Map 9 on p. 93.

NASCAR Cafe Orlando (p. 71) UNIVERSAL ORLANDO *AMERICAN* Raise the checkered flag—uh, tablecloth—and dig into "down-home American" cuisine amid grease-monkey decor (no dieting here!). If the thought of this makes your heart race, have at it. Otherwise skip it.... *Tel 407/224-3663. www.nascarcafe.com. CityWalk. AE, DISC, MC, V. $-$$$$*

See Map 9 on p. 93.

NBA City (p. 71) UNIVERSAL ORLANDO *AMERICAN* Average food at chain-restaurant prices; indifferent service. Only worth your time if you're a huge basketball fan.... *Tel 407/363-5919. www.nbacity.com. CityWalk. AE, DISC, MC, V. $-$$$*

See Map 9 on p. 93.

1900 Park Fare (p. 80) WDW *AMERICAN/CHARACTER MEAL* This buffet-style restaurant, dominated by Big Bertha, a century-old Parisian band organ, offers breakfast with Mary Poppins and prime-rib dinner with Cinderella.... *Tel 407/WDW-DINE. Grand Floridian Resort & Spa, 4401 Floridian Way. Advance Reservation recommended. AE, DC, DISC, MC, V. $$-$$$$*

See Map 7 on p. 90.

'Ohana (p. 80) WDW *PACIFIC RIM/CHARACTER MEAL* Offers character breakfasts in the morning and a Polynesian-themed dinner at night.... *Tel 407/WDW-DINE. Disney's Polynesian Resort, 1600 Seven Seas Dr. Advance Reservation recommended. AE, DC, DISC, MC, V. $$-$$$$*

See Map 7 on p. 90.

The Palm (p. 83) UNIVERSAL ORLANDO *STEAKS* Known nationwide for their great steaks and seafood. Pricey but worth it.... *Tel 407/503-2467. www.thepalm.com. Hard Rock Hotel, 5000 Universal Blvd. Reservations recommended. AE, DISC, MC, V. $$$-$$$$*

See Map 9 on p. 93.

Pat O'Brien's Orlando (p. 78) UNIVERSAL ORLANDO *CAJUN/CREOLE* An authentic reproduction of the original in New Orleans. On offer are the usual Creole faves (catfish, jambalaya), plus the famous Hurricanes and dueling pianos. "Two for Tuesday" drink specials and the cheapest cheeseburger at CityWalk help the budget-minded.... *Tel 407/224-2690. www.patobriens.com. CityWalk. AE, DISC, MC, V. $-$$$*

See Map 9 on p. 93.

Pebbles (p. 72) LAKE BUENA VISTA *WEST COAST* An antidote to theme overload—not a kooky costume or wild animal to be found, just pale wood and plants and really tasty food.... *Tel 407/827-1111. www.pebblesworldwide.com. Crossroads Shopping Plaza, 12551 Apopka-Vineland Rd. (S.R. 535). AE, DC, DISC, MC, V. $$-$$$$*

See Map 7 on p. 90.

Pecos Bill Café (p. 86) WDW *AMERICAN* This counter-service restaurant allows you to substitute carrots for fries and offers an enhanced fixin's bar complete with mushrooms and onions.... *Tel 407/WDW-DINE. Magic Kingdom. AE, DC, DISC, MC, V. $-$$*

See Map 7 on p. 90.

Portobello Yacht Club (p. 85) WDW *ITALIAN* Styled in New England nautical, this Pleasure Island restaurant can be bustling and noisy, but the northern-Italian cuisine compensates. Save room for the traditional Sicilian cannoli.... *Tel 407/934-8888. www.portobellorestaurant.com. Pleasure Island, 1650 Buena Vista Dr. Advance Reservation recommended. AE, DC, DISC, MC, V. $-$$$$*

See Map 7 on p. 90.

Race Rock (p. 71) INTERNATIONAL DRIVE *AMERICAN* A shrine to motor sports, decked out with race cars, race boats, and Bigfoot, the world's largest monster truck. Fare runs to sandwiches, salads, pasta, pizza, and prime rib.... *Tel 407/248-9876. www.racerock.com. 8986 International Dr. AE, DC, DISC, MC, V. $-$$$*

See Map 9 on p. 93.

Restaurant Akershus (p. 77) WDW *SCANDINAVIAN/CHARACTER BREAKFAST* An all-you-can-eat Norwegian *koldtbord* (buffet, to you and me), in a large, medieval-fortress-style dining room. The princess character breakfast is extremely popular with the very young ladies.... *Tel 407/WDW-DINE. Epcot. Advance Reservation recommended. $$-$$$$*

See Map 8 on p. 92.

Restaurant Marrakesh (p. 75) WDW *MOROCCAN* Adventurous eaters will be rewarded with delicious kabobs and other Moroccan delicacies served in a palatial dining room. Strolling belly dancers contribute to the exotic atmosphere. One of the best dining values at Epcot.... *Tel 407/WDW-DINE. Epcot. Advance Reservation recommended. AE, DC, DISC, MC, V. $-$$$$*

See Map 8 on p. 92.

Restaurantosaurus (p. 80) WDW *AMERICAN/CHARACTER MEAL* The Big Cheese, Goofy, Donald, and Pluto (usually in Safari-wear) entertain at this bountiful breakfast buffet. It's fast food the rest of the day.... *Tel 407/WDW-DINE. Disney's Animal Kingdom. AE, DC, DISC, MC, V. $–$$$*

See Map 7 on p. 90.

Rose & Crown Pub and Dining Room (p. 76) WDW *BRITISH* British pub grub served in huge portions that attracts even Her Majesty's visiting flock. Belly up to the pub's bar and toss back a pint. The outdoor seating offers good views of IllumiNations. A jolly good show.... *Tel 407/WDW-DINE. Epcot. Advance Reservation recommended. AE, DC, DISC, MC, V. $–$$$*

See Map 8 on p. 92.

Roy's (p. 73) INTERNATIONAL DRIVE *PACIFIC RIM* Award-winning chef Roy Yamaguchi offers Euro-Asian cuisine amid an inviting Oriental decor of bamboo and mahogany.... *Tel 407/226-3900. www.roysrestaurant.com. 7760 Sand Lake Rd. AE, DC, DISC, MC, V. $$$$*

See Map 9 on p. 93.

Ruth's Chris Steak House (p. 83) INTERNATIONAL DRIVE *STEAKS* Big, buttery, fork-tender slabs of beef, broiled at scorching temps—what's not to like? Carnivores will love it here, though the price tag will set you back a bit.... *Tel 407/226-3900. www.ruthschris.com. 7501 Sand Lake Rd. Reservations recommended. AE, DC, DISC, MC, V. $$$$*

See Map 9 on p. 93.

Samba Room (p. 74) INTERNATIONAL DRIVE *LATIN* Serves a delicious Latin-fusion menu in fun surroundings reminiscent of 1960s Rio. Cigar lounge for those who partake; live bands on the weekend.... *Tel 407/226-0550. www.e-brands.net. 7468 Sand Lake Rd. AE, DC, DISC, MC, V. $$–$$$$*

See Map 9 on p. 93.

San Angel Inn (p. 73) WDW *MEXICAN* This enchanting Mexican restaurant serves up a romantic atmosphere and specialties like **mole poblano** (chicken with mole sauce). Killer margaritas, too.... *Tel 407/WDW-DINE. Epcot. Advance Reservation recommended. AE, DC, DISC, MC, V. $–$$$*

See Map 8 on p. 92.

Sci-Fi Dine-In Theater Restaurant (p. 86) WDW *AMERICAN* Cool—this place really does feel like a 1950s drive-in, as you slip into a convertible and watch sci-fi and B-movie trailers playing on a giant screen. Decent burgers, sandwiches, and milkshakes. Just don't get caught up in the moment and start making out in the back seat—the rest of us are trying to eat, okay?... *Tel 407/WDW-DINE. Disney–MGM Studios. Advance Reservation recommended. AE, DC, DISC, MC, V. $–$$$*

See Map 7 on p. 90.

Seafire Inn (p. 80) SEAWORLD *AMERICAN* In the morning you can have breakfast with Shamu. The rest of the day enjoy huge steak burgers (big enough for two), stir-fry entrees, and more.... *Tel 407/351-3600 (toll-free 800/423-8368). www.seaworld.com. SeaWorld. AE, DISC, MC, V. $$*

See Map 9 on p. 93.

Shamu Stadium (p. 80) SEAWORLD *AMERICAN* Home to "Dine with Shamu," a nightly dinner with a private killer-whale performance. Pricey but very worth it. One of the best dinner shows in Orlando.... *Tel 407/351-3600 (toll-free 800/423-8368). www.seaworld.com. SeaWorld. Reservations essential. AE, DISC, MC, V. $$–$$$$*

See Map 9 on p. 93.

Sharks Underwater Grill (p. 84) SEAWORLD *AMERICAN* Dine with sharks instead of swimming with them. The Floribbean food's worth sinking your teeth into.... *Tel 407/351-3600 (toll-free 800/423-8368). www.seaworld.com. SeaWorld. Reservations essential. AE, DISC, MC, V. $–$$$*

See Map 9 on p. 93.

Shula's Steak House (p. 83) WDW *STEAK* This is about as good as it gets: great cuts of meat, expertly prepared and served to perfection in a manly, clubby atmosphere. Priced high but worth every penny.... *Tel 407/934-1362. www.donshula.com. Walt Disney World Dolphin, 1500 Epcot Resorts Blvd., off Buena Vista Dr. Advance Reservation recommended. AE, DISC, MC, V. $$$$*

See Map 7 on p. 90.

Siam Orchid (p. 78) INTERNATIONAL DRIVE *THAI* Huge menu of Thai classics best enjoyed family style for maximum pig-out. Coconut ice cream is not to be missed.... *Tel 407/351-0821. 7575 Universal Boulevard. AE, MC, V. $$–$$$*

See Map 9 on p. 93.

Spoodles (p. 81) WDW *TAPAS* Dig into a platter of tapas and sip some sweet sangria and you'll swear you're in Costa del Sol, not Costa del Disney. The all-you-can-eat breakfast platter is a good value, by Disney standards anyway.... *Tel 407/939-3463. Disney's BoardWalk, 2101 N. Epcot Resorts Blvd., off Buena Vista Dr. Advance Reservation recommended. AE, DC, DISC, MC, V. $–$$$$*

See Map 7 on p. 90.

Sunset Sam's Fish Camp (p. 84) LAKE BUENA VISTA *SEAFOOD* A Key West–inspired menu of seafood served on a boat inside a hotel's man-made lagoon. They've even got a steel-drum band playing while you eat.... *Tel 407/586-0000. www.gaylordpalms.com. Gaylord Palms Hotel, 6000 Osceola Pkwy. AE, DC, DISC, MC, V. $$–$$$$*

See Map 7 on p. 90.

Tijuana Flats Burrito Company (p. 71) CITYWIDE *MEXICAN* A 5-minute drive north of Universal will land you two-handed burritos and other traditional Tex-Mex items. The real treat is the rotating 12-slot, serve-yourself hot-sauce bar featuring such titles as "Endorphin Rush" and "Smack My Ass and Call Me Sally."... *Kirkman Road: Tel 407/822-4257. www.tijuanaflats.com. 2320 S. Kirkman Rd. AE, DC, DISC, MC, V. Call for other locations. $$–$$$*

See Map 6 on p. 89.

Todd English's bluezoo (p. 73) WDW *SEAFOOD* Celebrity chef English serves innovative seafood in an unusually vibrant setting. Raw-bar items will put the smallest dent in your wallet.... *Tel 407/934-1111. www.thebluezoo.com. Walt Disney World Dolphin, 1500 Epcot Resorts Blvd., off Buena Vista Dr. Advance Reservation recommended. AE, DC, DISC, MC, V. $$–$$$$*

See Map 7 on p. 90.

Tune-In Lounge (p. 87) WDW *BAR FOOD* Just off the main lobby of the 50's Prime Time Cafe, this little nook offers an escape from the hectic pace of the park. Enjoy a cold one at the bar.... *Tel 407/WDW-DINE. Disney–MGM Studios. AE, DC, DISC, MC, V. $–$$*

See Map 7 on p. 90.

Victoria & Albert's (p. 72) WDW *INTERNATIONAL* Disney's best restaurant features top-of-the-line cuisine that will easily set you back $100 or more per person (before the wine). Romantic elegance is laid on with a trowel by way of floating violinists, fresh flowers, gleaming china, and low lighting.... *Tel 407/WDW-DINE. Disney's Grand Floridian Resort & Spa, 4401 Floridian Way. Advance Reservation required (up to 180 days in advance). AE, DC, DISC, MC, V. $$$$*

See Map 7 on p. 90.

Whispering Canyon Cafe (p. 81) WDW *AMERICAN* A rustic setting and wood-smoked meats and chicken make this family-friendly restaurant the best bet at the Wilderness Lodge. Food is all-you-can-eat, served family-style.... *Tel 407/WDW-DINE. Wilderness Lodge, 901 W. Timberline Dr. Advance Reservation recommended. AE, DC, DISC, MC, V. $–$$$*

See Map 7 on p. 90.

White Wolf Cafe (p. 75) DOWNTOWN ORLANDO *CONTINENTAL* A real gem just north of downtown Orlando, with inspired flavorful choices for vegetarians and meat eaters alike. Open for lunch and dinner. Try the vegetarian plate with black-bean hummus and mango-nut tabbouleh. Closed Sunday.... *Tel 407/895-9911. www.whitewolfcafe.com. 1829 N. Orange Ave. AE, MC, V. $–$$*

See Map 6 on p. 89.

Wolfgang Puck Cafe (p. 73) WDW *WEST COAST* Super Chef Puck's wood-fired pizzas and pastas, and an extensive sushi bar. Grab 'n go on the main floor or spend bigger bucks in the upstairs dining room. *Tel 407/938-9653. www.wolfgtangpuck.com. Downtown Disney West Side. AE, DC, DISC, MC, V. $–$$$*

See Map 7 on p. 90.

Yachtsman's Steakhouse (p. 83) WDW *STEAKS* Yacht club burgees (flags) and a glassed-in butcher shop alone can't make this into a tempting option. You're better off walking over to Le Cellier in Epcot if you want a good steak.... *Tel 407/WDW-DINE. Disney's Yacht Club Resort, 1700 Epcot Resorts Blvd., off Buena Vista Dr. Advance Reservation recommended. AE, DC, DISC, MC, V. $–$$$$*

See Map 7 on p. 90.

DIVER

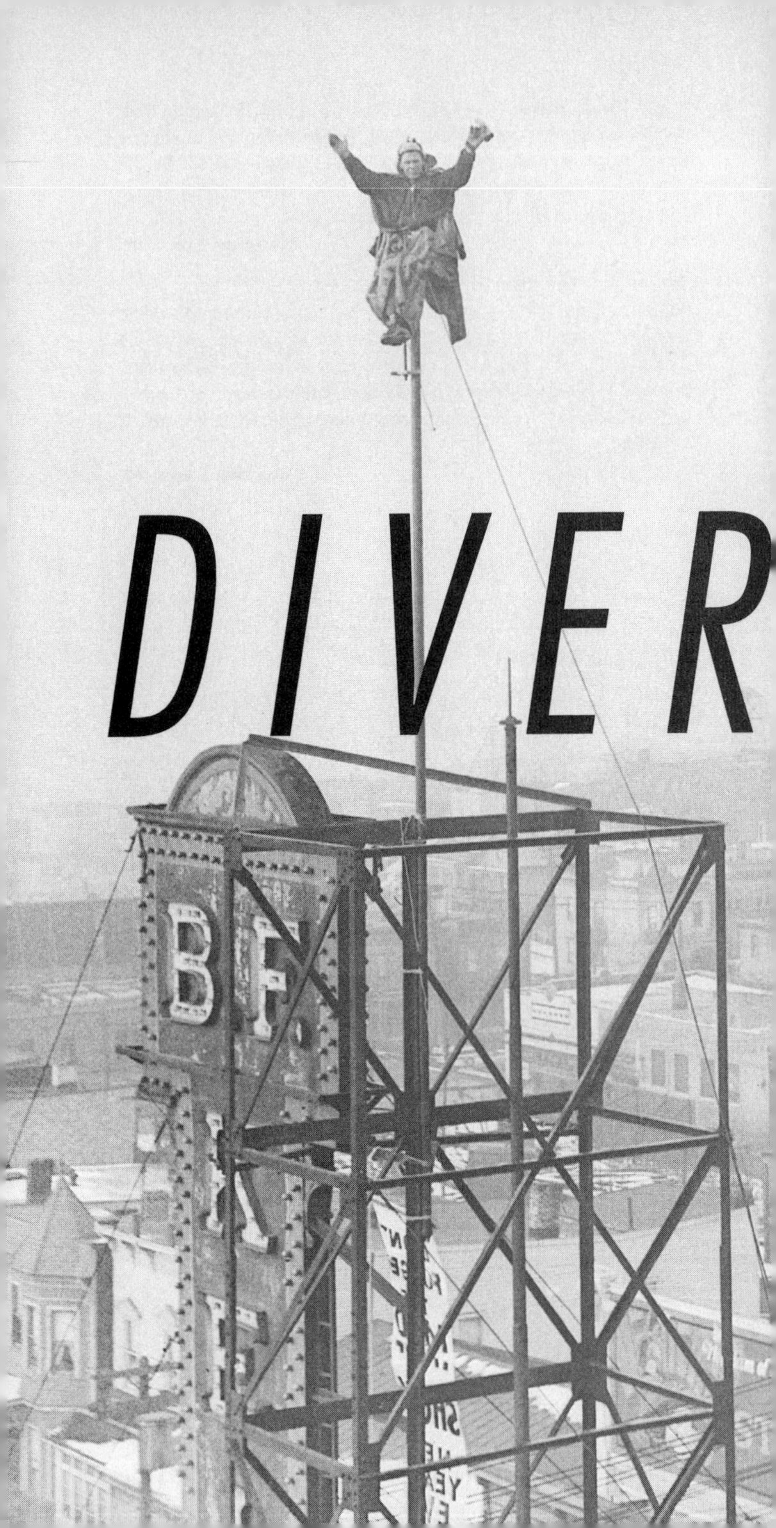

SIONS

3

Basic Stuff

If you can't find anything to do in Orlando, then you simply aren't trying. For better or worse, Orlando is the ultimate playground, where no matter what your age, you'll find some excuse to revert back to your childhood. Not that that's all bad. But when you're paying up to $67 a ticket for 1 day's entertainment, jumping in without some kind of plan can just suck you dry.

Of course, you need to do the Big Three: Disney, Universal, and SeaWorld. Each has its own charm and must-do's. From there, if you still have time (and money), there's everything from Gatorland to Ripley's Believe It or Not. From dinner shows to indoor skydiving, just about every interest is represented in glorious form, just waiting for you to partake in its charm.

However you feel about the Disney empire, a visit to its theme parks will show you what this company does best: create an environment where no detail is overlooked, where every scrap of litter is whisked away the moment it's dropped. No other theme park welcomes so many international visitors, yet homogenizes every "cast member" (don't ever call them employees) into a perennially Prozac-perky welcome wagon that won't offend anyone. Seriously—every cast member attends "Disney University," where they are trained, down to hand gestures, how not to accidentally offend any park guest, regardless of nationality.

Eventually, Disney's 27,000-acre spread will offer every form of entertainment known to man, neatly packaged and perfected. Even now, it could take you a week just to skim Disney's highlights, what with all the golf courses, horseback rides, watersports, and myriad other offerings that most day guests are too overwhelmed to scope out.

If you're a tourist, the insidious ease and self-containment of Walt Disney World, along with its reliability—always clean, always friendly, always scrupulously maintained—can suck you in like quicksand. If you're a traveler, though, you might be tempted to break out beyond the gates of Walt Disney World. Not that there's anything particularly rustic or authentic out there. Orlando's theme parks and attractions number almost 100, but if you make enough passes along I-4, you'll swear there are more, what with all the high-tech billboards grabbing your attention.

At the other end of what's known as the tourist corridor of I-4, there's turbo-charged Universal Orlando, which is the most visited attraction in the country after the Disney theme parks.

Once upon a time there was one park, Universal Studios Florida. Today Universal Orlando has mushroomed into a complete destination resort, including two major amusement parks, Universal Studios Florida, and Islands of Adventure; the CityWalk entertainment complex, featuring a mix of restaurants and cafes, live music, nightclubs, theaters, and specialty shops; and a cluster of themed hotels and resorts. Somewhere in between Disney and Universal, you'll find SeaWorld and its sister attraction, Discovery Cove, both treading the line between theme park and conservation aquarium.

There are a few attractions off the beaten path. Travel into Kissimmee and you'll find Gatorland, where one of the featured shows presents live alligators jumping up to snatch dead chickens.

Getting Your Bearings

Here's the drill: **I-4** (also known as, Interstate 4, the main tourist thoroughfare) officially runs east and west, no matter what it looks like on the map (where it always mysteriously appears to go north-south), and the exit numbers go higher as you head east.

The southern edge of WDW's borders rides along **U.S. 192** (also known as the Irlo Bronson Memorial Hwy.), which is the main east-west road through Kissimmee. Locals know it as "Hotel Row," as most of the budget properties in town are located here. Head south out of the Magic Kingdom and you'll eventually run into U.S. 192. **Florida Highway 535,** known also as Apopka-Vineland Road, runs northwest diagonally from U.S. 192, past I-4 and Disney, and up to Sand Lake Road and beyond. Epcot Center Drive (which originates...oh, go ahead and guess) becomes **Florida Highway 536** once you pass I-4, and goes on to Highway 535 and I-Drive before turning into **Florida Highway 417** (a toll road also known as the Central Florida Greenway). If you follow the **Osceola Parkway** (also known as Florida Hwy. 424, because every major road in Orlando appears to have multiple-personality disorder) out of the Animal Kingdom, it eventually runs through the northern edge of Kissimmee, right near Gatorland, before intersecting the **Florida Turnpike** (no nickname—it should protest!). U.S. 192 also intersects the Florida Turnpike about 30 minutes east of Disney.

If you're headed over to SeaWorld, the main road to remember is International Drive (known better as **I-Drive**), which runs north-south until it gets up to Wet 'n' Wild and borders SeaWorld on the east. The Central Florida Parkway borders SeaWorld on the south, I-4 on the west, and **Highway 528** (better known as the **Bee Line Expressway**) on the north. The Bee Line also runs out to Orlando International Airport.

Up by Universal, you'll first encounter **Sand Lake Road** (also known as Hwy. 482), which intersects with I-Drive near that street's northern end. **Kirkman Road** (Hwy. 435) runs from Sand Lake Road, north past Universal and beyond. The Florida Turnpike runs from eastern Kissimmee and intersects I-4 just east of Universal. See how easy all of this is to understand (okay, my editor didn't think so either, so she ordered me to tell you to get yourself a really good map before you set out—and that there are a lot of gas stations around if you get lost).

Finding your way around Walt Disney World itself is actually more complicated, though the signs have gotten better over the last few years. Most newcomers stagger around at first, awestruck by the sheer size and scope of Disney World—which encompasses nearly 50 square miles' worth of theme parks, resort hotels, golf courses, and water parks. For starters, there are the Big Four—the Magic Kingdom, Epcot, Disney–MGM Studios, and Animal Kingdom—as well as Downtown Disney (see the Dining and Nightlife & Entertainment chapters), and Blizzard Beach and Typhoon Lagoon (see the Getting Outside chapter). Each park is miles from the others, carved into a landscape that once consisted of mangrove swamps and orange groves; guests navigate the property by bus, car, monorail, and ferryboat. To survive, you've got to get map-happy: Stop at Disney's Transportation and Ticket Center (or the guest-services desk at a Disney resort), where, along with plunking down loads of money for those essential park passes, you can pick up a good map of the entire property along with route information for Disney's monorail, buses, and boats. Grab another map every time you enter a theme park, and you won't be forced to drop a breadcrumb trail.

Jump the Lines

Even though Disney practically invented the art of line distraction—designing diversions to preoccupy you while you wait hours in line, they perfected a method—originally introduced at Universal Studios Hollywood—for jumping the line (without risking the wrath of the universe) at the busiest attractions. The idea behind the miraculous FASTPASS is that instead of

Learn the Disney Lingo

Attraction: *Ride or theater show*

Attraction host: *Ride operator*

Backstage: *Behind the scenes, out of view of customers*

Bull pen: *Queuing area*

Cast member: *Disney employee*

Character: *Disney cartoon character impersonated by an employee*

Costume: *Work attire or uniform*

Dark ride: *Indoor Ride*

Face character: *A character who doesn't wear a head-covering costume (Snow White, Cinderella, Jasmine)*

In rehearsal: *Operating though not officially open, or in preview*

Lead: *Foreman or manager; the person in charge of an attraction*

On stage: *In full view of customers*

Preshow: *Entertainment at an attraction prior to the feature presentation*

Role: *An employee's job*

Security host: *Security guard*

Soft opening: *A park or attraction becoming operational before its stated opening date*

Transitional experience: *An element of the queuing area and/or preshow that provides a story line or information essential to understanding the attraction*

waiting hours on end in line, you put your ticket in a machine that spits back out your ticket (don't forget it!) and a reservation slip with a time window imprinted on it (usually an hour, but sometimes less). So while everyone else is sweltering in line, you're now free to go to a different attraction. When your assigned time arrives (and for the primo rides, it may be a while), you get into a relatively short line, give the cast member your slip, and climb aboard. Note that you can only get up to two FASTPASS slips at a time. Until you use one, you won't be able to get another. Not 100% perfect, but a solution that works wonders in soothing the savage tourist. All the major attractions at the Disney theme parks are now outfitted with the FASTPASS.

Universal has gone one step better, offering a few different options for those not wanting to languish in horrendous lines. UNIVERSAL EXPRESS is similar to the FASTPASS in principle: You get a ticket that allows you to come back at a later time to get in the shorter line. However, guests staying at any of

Universal's three resorts (the Portofino Bay, Hard Rock Hotel, and Royal Pacific) can use their room key to instantly jump into the EXPRESS line—no waiting for a ticket time. The room keys also work for line-jumping at most restaurants in the parks and at CityWalk, and all line-jumping privileges are good from the day you check in to the day you check out (not just through checkout time, but the whole day!).

Theme-Park Strategy

You've gotta have a game plan at the World, or the overwhelming sprawl will leave you dazed and confused, wondering, "Did I leave the kids at Splash Mountain, or was it Big Thunder Mountain? Did I park at the 'Chip' lot, or was it 'Dale'?" A few tips:

- If your time is limited, consider staying at a Disney hotel; you'll spend less time commuting in most cases, and thus more time at the parks, and you may also be able to benefit from the special early-admission mornings.
- If you plan to visit either of the Universal parks, consider staying a night at their resorts for the room-key privileges described above. During high season especially, this can be a lifesaver, as Universal's attractions often have longer and slower-moving lines than Disney's.
- If you can come during the off season, that's all the better for avoiding lines. Basically that's anytime except major U.S. school holidays, mid-March to mid-April, Christmas, and summer.
- Unless you're a huge Disney-character fan, skip the midafternoon parades and head for the most popular rides while the parades are going on, when lots of park visitors have been siphoned off to stand on the sidewalks craning their necks at floats and costumed characters. If a parade's being staged (such as when the Magic Kingdom is open late for peak periods) twice, skip the earlier one—the later one will be less crowded.
- If you start to burn out midday, take a break (for a late lunch, a swim, or a nap) and return to the park around 5 or 6pm, refreshed and raring to go—when everyone else is heading home. Reentering the park is allowed, even if you're not a Disney guest, as long as you keep your ticket and get your hand stamped on your way out.

- Don't waste your time at the parks' full-service restaurants, except at Epcot, where the restaurants are as much fun as the attractions. Instead, stuff your backpack full of goodies (although this is technically against the rules), and just grab snacks, fruit, and fast food on your theme-park days.

Price Tag for the Kingdom & Beyond

Note: All prices in this section include tax and were rounded up to the nearest dollar unless indicated otherwise.

When it comes to Disney admission prices, things have gotten much simpler than the days of overlapping vacation packages and seemingly random price hierarchies. Everything is now a la carte. First you select how many theme-park tickets you want, for how many days, and the ages of the ticket holders. With this basic setup, you can visit one particular theme park per day only. Next, you choose if you want to add the **Park Hopper** option, which allows you to "hop" from park to park at will on the same day—choose among the Magic Kingdom, Epcot, Disney-MGM Studios, and Animal Kingdom. The next upsell is the **Water Park Fun & More** option, which lets you access Blizzard Beach, Typhoon Lagoon, DisneyQuest, and Wide World of Sports. Lastly, you can spend a little more on the **No Expiration** option, which means that unused days on your tickets are good forever (until you choose to use them, of course).

What does this all cost? Disney wants you to buy more days and more options, so the more you buy, the more your cost-per-day goes down. Let's start with the basics, adding tax to all prices: a **1-day, 1-park ticket** costs $67 adults, $56 children (ages 3–9). You could add options and make this 1-day ticket absurdly expensive (up to $163), but no one would buy options on a 1-day ticket—they'd never hit all the parks in so short a time.

Let's try a more sensible comparison. A **3-day ticket** costs $192 for adults, $160 for children. A **3-day Park Hopper** ticket goes for $237 adults, $205 children. The **3-day Park Hopper, Water Park Fun & More** option is $287 adults, $255 children. And if you add the **No Expiration** option, you're looking at $302 adults, $270 children. And so it goes. You can play with all the price points on Disney's website, www.waltdisneyworld.com.

On the non-Disney front, **1-day/1-park admission** to Universal Studios Florida or Islands of Adventure (including tax and rounded up) is $68 for adults and around $56 for children 3 to 9. If you plan to visit Universal Orlando parks more than 2 or

3 days, consider getting an **annual pass** (currently around $180, plus tax), which not only allows unlimited park admission, but offers discounts on dining and shopping, as well as free parking. Note that Universal almost always offers some kind of ticket or pass deal on its website at www.universalorlando.com.

SeaWorld's **single-day admission** is $68 (adults) or $55 (children 3–9), though you can save 10% if you purchase 7 or more days in advance online (www.seaworld.com) and print out your ticket. A good value for those wanting to spend more than 1 day at the park is the **Fun Card,** which is usually on sale from January to April. For the same price as a 1-day ticket, you get unlimited admission through December 31 of the year you purchase the pass. Save even more with a range of **annual Passports,** many of which not only include other Anheuser-Busch parks nationwide, but can be purchased using the company's EZPay plan (no-interest monthly payments and no credit check, though you must have a credit card to purchase them).

Discovery Cove, SeaWorld's sister park, offers daily packages with and without a personal dolphin swim. With the dolphin swim, the price is between $249 and $279 per day (without the dolphin swim, $149–$179). These prices may seem steep, but they include lunch, snorkel, use of goggles and wet suit, and a 7-day admission pass to SeaWorld or Busch Gardens.

For those interested in park hopping between several non-Disney parks, the **Orlando FlexTicket** offers unlimited admission to Universal Studios, Islands of Adventure, SeaWorld, and Wet 'n' Wild Orlando for 14 consecutive days from the first day the pass is used. A four-park ticket is $197 for adults and $161 for children ages 3 to 9. A five-park ticket, which adds Busch Gardens in Tampa (and includes free shuttle service to the park), is $240 for adults and $203 for children 3 to 9. There is also a shuttle bus from many I-Drive locations to Busch Gardens that runs about $10 round-trip per person.

The Lowdown

Best use of technology... Nods to Universal for three of its over-the-top attractions, which their spin masters call the "most thrilling and technologically advanced rides and attractions ever made...." Who's to argue after taking a ride (let's call it a trip) on the **Amazing Adventures of Spider-Man**? This ride combines the sensory tricks of the famed Back to the Future...The Ride attraction and the 3-D accomplishments of Terminator 2. Spider-Man is with you all the way, seemingly within your grasp, as your car hurtles through New York street scenes, past spewing water pipes and raging fires, smashing into vehicles as you go. The ride culminates when Doc Ock takes aim at you with his anti-gravity gun, sending you into a 400-foot sensory plunge. It's not to be missed, though you'll have to be prepared to stand in line for the thrill; waits of 60 to 90 minutes are not uncommon. Next door, at the Studios, you'll find **Revenge of the Mummy,** which combines a coaster run with magnetism and the best cinematic special-effects technology (flame ceilings, scarabs pouring out of the walls) for a ride that will touch on your worst phobias. Universal also offers **Terminator 2 3-D,** a live-action and special-effects spectacular that is one outrageous outing. Even diehard fans of the movie will be impressed. Not to be outdone, Disney's infamous **Tower of Terror** at Disney–MGM Studios features randomized drop sequences...not even the cast members herding you into the elevator know which one you'll get. And over at Epcot is **Mission: Space,** where NASA technology helps create an astronaut simulator so effective they've had to install "lunch bags" for all the motion sickness it causes. Animal Kingdom's new **Expedition Everest** not only sports the highest mountain in Florida (artificial or otherwise), it also features a menacing climax in the form of an 18-foot-tall Abominable Snowman, said to be the most complex and realistic Audio Animatronic robot ever produced by Disney's Imagineers.

Where the wild things are... Is it a theme park? A zoo? A nature preserve? Disney's **Animal Kingdom** tries to be all of these things. Animals and more sedate experiences are the main focus to be sure, but the addition of Expedition Everest considerably upped AK's thrill quotient. But if it's daylong thrills you seek, you're better off sticking to the tried-and-true theme parks. If you're not a big animal fan, this park probably won't even take you half a day to navigate. However, if you do like the idea of spending the day with assorted beasts and creatures, you'll really enjoy this park. **Kilimanjaro Safaris** is one of the more popular attractions, usually accumulating long lines early in the day. Riding in special safari trucks, you head out into the African wilderness (well, one manufactured by Disney to replicate their version of the Dark Continent). There's a hokey story line about saving elephants from poachers, and a rickety bridge that threatens to fall apart (this is Disney—you miraculously escape), but if you can ignore all that, you'll enjoy seeing giraffes and zebras wandering by. Just be sure you come early or later in the day—most animals (unlike many of the humans here) know better than to go traipsing around during the heat of the day, so they snooze during the afternoons. Three other walking tours of exotic-animal habitats not to miss are **Pangani Forest Exploration Trail** (gorillas, meerkats, and so on), **Maharajah Jungle Trek** (tigers, rare birds), and the **Discovery Island Trails** around the Tree of Life (birds, tortoises, lemurs).

If your animal tastes run to the aquatic, **SeaWorld** is a wonderful place to spend a day or two. Where else can you get up close with sea lions, manatees, dolphins, stingrays, and killer whales? SeaWorld's sister park, **Discovery Cove,** offers the ultimate in aquatic thrills. Play tag with stingrays in a small lagoon or swim side-by-side with schools of fish; you can even frolic with playful dolphins. You don't just observe at this park, you're part of the action.

It's a scream.... When it comes to haunted houses, it doesn't get much worse (or better, depending on your point of view) than **Skull Kingdom,** an independent attraction located outside Orlando's major theme parks. Skull Kingdom is very, very scary. You'll be sent off into pitch-dark corridors, feeling your way around as sinister and spooky characters—sometimes live and sometimes animated robots—jump out at you at every corner. Special effects like blasted air, falling spider webs, opening doors, and loud noises will keep you jumping each step of the way. Nicely done. Universal's **Revenge of the Mummy** can induce outright fear in the extremely phobic. Fear of coasters? Check. Fear of the dark? Check. Fear of bugs? Check. Fear of flames? Check. The ride itself isn't that scary. It's the phobias it taps into that do the real damage. **Dinosaur** at Animal Kingdom takes riders back 65 million years in order to rescue the planet's last dinosaur before a meteor slams into Earth. You'll encounter the requisite robotic dinos along the way, experience the herky-jerky when you encounter meteor showers, and spend a good amount of time in the dark. But it's the last few dinosaurs that have most people screaming on this ride.

It should come as no surprise that any ride based on Rod Serling's famous take on people's fears and phobias leaves its riders screaming. And you'll hear plenty of shrieking at **The Twilight Zone Tower of Terror** in Disney–MGM Studios. Admittedly, some of the screams are because of the random precipitous drops in the dark (not to mention the incredibly eerie atmosphere), but those drops are downright scary. So frightening, in fact, that a Disney Imagineer who helped design the ride has never ridden it and turns white at the very thought of boarding.

Best places to lose your lunch... Despite its undisputed position as Theme Park Central, Orlando's great parks were once devoid of top-notch roller-coaster thrills. Not anymore. **Islands of Adventure,** promoted as the world's "most technologically advanced theme park," offers some of the best stomach-lurching thrills in existence. The **Dueling Dragons** ride, a mass of intertwining metal, hurls dragon-shaped racing cars at each other for a high-speed, near-miss nightmare. The cars travel up to 60 mph and come within (what seems like) less than 12 inches of each other. The **Incredible Hulk Coaster** shoots riders up 10 stories with the same G-force power as a fighter jet, then turns them upside down and sends them into a maze of tracks, plunging them under a bridge, and into underground trenches. (And, in concert with some of its riders, it actually glows green at night—how's that for realism!) You can't miss the 200-foot steel tower that houses **Doctor Doom's Fearfall.** Another variation on the classic tower plunge, the Fearfall benefits from the high views granted by its outdoor location, but it's really not worth the massive lines that frequently accumulate in its bull pens. Disney has countered Universal's entries with Disney–MGM Studios' **Rock 'n' Roller Coaster starring Aerosmith,** its first high-speed launch (0–60 mph in 2.8 seconds), upside-down roller coaster ride. On this ride, you'll be fastened into a mock "stretch limo" and thrown into a mangled maze of twists and turns, including three upside-down segments. Along the way, there are familiar Tinseltown scenes (though who's paying attention?) and a loud (there are 120 onboard speakers in each coaster train) Aerosmith soundtrack synchronized to every twist and turn (but, again, who has time to notice?). During the coaster's grand opening, the ride even made Aerosmith's Steven Tyler a bit weak in the knees. Let's not forget **Kraken** over at SeaWorld. It may not be as smooth as its Universal or Disney counterparts, but it makes up for that with height, speed, and some tantalizing near-smashups with the ground. As for **Mission: Space,** don't even try this one if you're prone to motion sickness. Not sure? Pick up some Dramamine before you hit Epcot—due to the laws of supply and demand, motion-sickness medication costs significantly more at Mouse Gears, the closest store to this ride.

Best thrill rides for weenies... It happens to the best of us. You don't want to be relegated to the kid rides, but the sight of two inverted corkscrews makes you practically pass out. Try **Big Thunder Mountain** at the Magic Kingdom—it's basically a rickety ride on a runaway mine train, with cool props such as skeletons that you may not notice as you're whipping around. A few sudden plummets and high-speed curves will give young ones and ride weenies some mild thrills as they travel through old-mining-town scenery of faux rocks, fake chickens, and rushing waterfalls. Other than the speed factor, it's probably the tamest of all the adult coasters. ***Note:*** This one's better at night when you can't see where you're going. Epcot's **Test Track** also relies on speed, among other things, for its thrills. Where else can you slam your car into a wall (well, almost) and walk away with nary a scratch? Also at Epcot, try **The Maelstrom** in Norway. It's a pretty tame water ride with only a couple of small drops; you won't even have a lap bar. And, of course, there's the perennial favorite, **Space Mountain,** which is tame enough for most chickens, yet thrilling enough for regular coaster crazies. The main fright factor on this coaster is the darkness...it is literally pitch black in the dome that houses this indoor ride. ***Tip:*** A good way to judge the fear factor of any coaster is to look at the safety rig on each seat. If there's just a lap bar, the ride is mostly speed with a few drops. Anything that requires a shoulder harness is usually going to flip you upside down at least once.

Stimulating simulators... Each of the Big Three offers up a simulator-type ride. Generally, these involve getting into a "car" of some sort that moves side to side, up and down, in time with the movie being projected on the screen in front of you. At Universal Studios Florida, **Back to the Future...The Ride** does a convincing job of hurtling you, herky-jerky, through space (and nearly down a dinosaur's throat) in a souped-up DeLorean (far more successful in this fantasy than it ever was in reality). SeaWorld has **Wild Arctic,** a lurching helicopter "flight" through the heart of a glacier. The long-running **Star Tours** is a *Star Wars*–inspired adventure (the Force is definitely with this one) at the Disney–MGM Studios with a sense of humor (and the absolute coolest queue area). Sit in the last row to get the most oomph from the action. Disneyland's Soarin' Over California simulator has been imported to Epcot simply as **Soarin',** and the mild but exhilarating sense of actually flying over an IMAX-movie landscape is not to be missed.

Wipe out... Water rides: Either you love 'em or hate 'em. If you're in the former group, you won't find a better drive-and-drench ride than the **Jurassic Park River Adventure** at Islands of Adventure. Riders travel through a prehistoric land inhabited by fierce, unbelievably real-looking dinosaurs. Creatures five stories tall growl and bare their teeth, some within inches of your face. The ride speeds up as you try to escape from a Tyrannosaurus rex, ending in a stomach-flopping, 85-foot plunge into water. (Steven Spielberg, who helped design it, could stomach the dinosaurs, but not the drop—he reportedly asked to be let off before the big nose dive when he rode it at Islands' grand opening). A bit tamer, but just as wet, is **Dudley Do-Right's Ripsaw Falls.** This water flume ride sends riders plummeting 75 feet at 50 mph until you actually head beneath the surface of the water (the H_2O is contained by glass, but, fear not, you'll still get soaked). **Splash Mountain** at Magic Kingdom is a 12-minute log flume ride featuring the characters and music from *Song of the South.* Riders travel through Brer Rabbit's land of gardens, swamps, and caves, before a thrilling 87-foot, 40-mph drop at the end that will leave you completely drenched if you're seated in the first log. This is the best part of the ride, and it's the section that people see when they pass by or stand waiting in line. (Typically shrewd placement on Disney's part.) At Disney's Animal Kingdom, you can cool down on the popular **Kali River Rapids.** The faux setting is the turbulent Chakrandi River, and along the way you'll be bumped, dipped, rolled, and properly drenched. Similar in tone (but actually bouncier and faster) are Islands of Adventure's **Popeye & Bluto's Bilge-Rat Barges.** If you can avoid getting waterlogged on the simulated white-water rapids (you can't), the kids too short to ride this one man high-powered water canons along the route and are only too happy to take out their frustrations on you. *Bon Voyage!* It's only fitting that SeaWorld should have its own water-coaster thrill ride. On **Journey to Atlantis,** riders are plunged eight at a time into a battle for the lost city of Atlantis (which has mysteriously risen to the surface of a Greek harbor, and is naturally the subject of a media frenzy) via a swirling vortex, with blasting fountains and sprays of water along the way. You know the first plunge is coming (you can see this one from the queue), but just when you think it's over, you'll get your second dip-and-drench. Special effects include evil sirens, morphing sets (a golden sea-horse turns into Hermes, who doubles as guide and fighter for the forces of good), and maelstroms that threaten to swamp the boats. As with the Popeye boats at Islands of Adventure, Journey to Atlantis makes it even more sadistic by allowing passersby to man water cannons that are aimed right at your boat following the first drop.

For Mario Andretti wannabes... Think you can handle a few laps of white-knuckled, heart-pounding speed? Then don a crash helmet and your rookie stripes, and hop into the shotgun seat of a stock car at the **Richard Petty Driving Experience** (Tel 800/BE-PETTY). This fantasy experience costs $99 for a three-lap simulated Winston Cup qualifying run. The car, driven by one of Richard Petty's professional instructors, travels up to 145 mph. If you'd like to get your own hands on the wheel and your foot on the gas, sign up for the 3-hour Rookie Experience ($399). The racetrack is in the Magic Kingdom parking lot; drive to the entrance of Magic Kingdom and you'll hear the engines roar. ***Tip:*** Tell the attendants you're going to Richard Petty, and you won't have to pay for parking. Epcot's **Test Track** sends riders screeching through hairpin turns and spins at speeds of up to 65 mph. It's the longest (distance-wise anyway), fastest ride in Disney history. So what if you're not actually doing the driving?

The Kingdom for kids and the young at heart... Now some of you may be toting kids to these parks. Tiny tots are the Magic Kingdom's biggest fans—and Disney's bread and butter—so it comes as no surprise that they've added more to please them in recent years. At **Mickey's Toontown Fair,** little ones get to visit Mickey's and Minnie's houses, cool off in a mini–water park, and ride **Goofy's Barnstormer,** a tame, just-for-kids roller coaster. The biggest draw is meeting Mickey and his friends. Stand in line and you'll get a one-on-one meeting with the Big Cheese himself. **The Many Adventures of Winnie the Pooh** in Fantasyland takes you through the Hundred Acre Wood on a very "blustery day." A bit of bounce and twirl adds to the whimsical journey. Expect long waits, however, for a ride that ends way too soon. The heaviest nostalgia trip for adults can be found at Fantasyland, where preschoolers gape in wide-eyed wonder at **Cinderella's Golden Carousel.** Perhaps the most imaginative ride in Fantasyland is **Peter Pan's Flight,** a 4-minute excursion in which you journey to Neverland and pass over an especially enchanting view of nighttime London. It's unusual in that your "ships" are suspended from a rail above instead of on the usual track. The downside: The lines are almost always excruciating, so unless you FASTPASS it, you'll age several years before you get aboard.

Snow White's Adventures used to give every 6-year-old nightmares; that nasty old witch seemed to pop out at every turn. The ride was refocused on lovely Snow White, rather than the poison-apple-bearing witch, but it's still dark and menacing enough to frighten the very young. The international animatronic community of **It's a Small World** continues to pump out its excruciatingly catchy tune after all these years—now with better sound and updated sets. I like to torture people by taking them on this one; it's a hazing ritual that challenges one's sanity, and everyone should go through it at least once. After winding through the displays of 289 dolls with the song playing continuously, they all but run me over trying to get off the ride (though it's a great place to cool off in summer). Many will also find the **Country Bear Jamboree** a tortuous rite of passage, but kids love this animatronic musical show.

The ever-popular **Pirates of the Caribbean** reopened in July 2006 after undergoing renovations to make it more thematically similar to the hit moves it inspired. Expect at least an Audio Animatronic version of Johnny Depp's Captain Jack Sparrow lurking somewhere. In Liberty Square the best thing going is the **Haunted Mansion,** a G-rated fun house with friendly ghosts and lots of special effects. It's a cult favorite that attracts many a return visitor. This one's fine for the apprehensive—nothing reaches out and grabs you. This is Disney, after all. Check out the cute (if corny) tombstones as you leave. And a special note for those who think all Disney cast members are programmed with smiles plastered on their faces: You won't find a grin here, except on the ghosts. It's hauntingly refreshing.

Working on the notion that if you like one ride...you'll like it again somewhere else, Disney sometimes recycles ideas. Take the basic premise of a bunch of cars spinning slowly around a center with each car able to raise and lower by a lever controlled by the rider. Now name the ride. You'd be correct if you said **Dumbo the Flying Elephant** (Fantasyland), **Magic Carpets of Aladdin** (Adventureland), **Astro Orbiter** (Tomorrowland), or **TriceraTop Spin** (DinoLand U.S.A./Animal Kingdom). And if the whole family seems on the verge of collapse, take a rest on the **Walt Disney World Railroad** that leaves from Main Street and circles the entire Magic Kingdom with stops in Adventureland and Mickey's Toontown. (***Hint:*** This is a great way to get from one side of the park to another on crowded days.)

Best place to find Mickey in person... Three little words, spoken in a whisper, have enough power to ripple through a crowd and clear the lines at Space Mountain: "Look, there's Mickey." (Tempting, huh?) If you think the line was long at the teacups, wait till you wait for the Big Cheese's paw print. Our first suggestion: Sign up for at least one character meal. Some folks we know make reservations for two or three "meet-and-eat" sessions (featuring different characters at each meal) during their stay. This guarantees that their kids will get to hug their favorite friends and fill their autograph books (these are sold for about $6 at nearly every Disney shop). You'll avoid disappointment and save more time for the park's rides and attractions, instead of spending your precious hours hunting down Winnie and friends. That said, Disney has improved matters for young paparazzi. At Magic Kingdom, head for **Mickey's**

Toontown Fair: You'll find two separate lines, one waiting to greet Mickey, the other featuring Mickey's pals (Minnie, Pluto, and others). You'll wait in line, but the payoff is a sure shot at a one-on-one encounter with the world's most famous mouse. You'll also find Ariel sitting in her Grotto over in Fantasyland. At Disney–MGM Studios, characters like Goofy and Donald hang out in front of the **Sorcerer's Hat** every day around 4pm. Several characters can also be found along Mickey and Tigger avenues. At Animal Kingdom, you'll want to make a beeline for **Camp Minnie-Mickey.** The character-greeting trails feature top stars such as Mickey, Minnie, Pluto, Goofy, Winnie, Tigger, and more. Rafiki (of *The Lion King* fame) and Pocahontas hang at **Conservation Station.** Chip 'n' Dale are often found greeting tykes along the boulevard leading to Africa. Character greetings at Epcot tend to be more serendipitous. Some characters can be spotted in the country from which their story originated: Aladdin in Morocco, Snow White in Germany, and so on...but don't count on it. Either look for the double-decker character bus that shows up in the afternoon or head over to the **International Gateway** (between Britain and France) where several characters are usually perched. Be sure to check with Disney when visiting as to who's appearing where, as the character lineups are always in flux.

By the way, Disney doesn't have the lock on character friends. At Islands of Adventure you can hardly get away from the cartoon and movie characters wandering about. You're likely to encounter Spider-Man, Captain America, and Wolverine at **Marvel Super Hero Island,** or bump into **Thing 1** (or was it 2?) and the **Cat in the Hat** at Seuss Island, or Olive Oyl at **Toon Lagoon.** And on the Studios side of Universal, expect to run into Shrek and Fiona, along with miscellaneous characters from classic movies still in the Universal repertoire.

The Magic Kingdom for big kids...err...adults... Some attractions are perfect for all ages. The best in this category is **Buzz Lightyear's Space Ranger Spin,** a ride that pits two players against each other in a ride through a shooting gallery to save Earth from the evil emperor Zurg. Want to score higher points? Never take your finger off the trigger. Pumping the trigger like a normal gun only causes breaks in the laser targeting system, which can make you score lower. For a low-tech blast to your childhood: Just try to make it across the barrel bridge on **Tom Sawyer Island** without giggling. **Mickey's PhilharMagic** is a fun 3-D romp through various Disney movies as Donald chases Mickey's sorcerer's hat. This 3-D show also adds a fourth "dimension": smell-o-vision. You may walk out craving an apple pie.

Only if the lines in the Magic Kingdom are non-existent... The **Tomorrowland Speedway,** featuring motorized, slow-moving go-carts that are confined to a narrow track, is definitely a bore unless you're 5 years old and really think you're driving. Zzzz. Nobody seems too enchanted by the **Swiss Family Robinson Treehouse** (in nearby Adventureland) either—it always seems to have a long, noisy line, and it doesn't seem worth the agony just to see a man-made tree (covered with vinyl leaves) housing a giant treehouse. If the kids really need to stretch their legs and you need to sit for a spell, take the raft trip to **Tom Sawyer Island** (in Frontierland), where kids can explore a cave, a fort, and a secret passageway. Can you tolerate cute, cuddly, and corny? Take in the **Country Bear Jamboree,** where audio-animated bears sing, dance, and tell silly jokes. The **Enchanted Tiki Room,** complete with characters from *Aladdin,* falls into the same category, with more than 200 birds, plants, and statues chirping and chatting in a tropical serenade. It seems to strike a chord with toddlers and nostalgia buffs—this was Disney's first audio-animated attraction—but considering Orlando's other offerings in the special-effects department these days, why bother?

Epcot's greatest hits... After the Magic Kingdom, **Epcot** is a letdown for the 6-and-under set, which makes it perfect for adults who can swallow its earnest sugarcoated educational stuff. The first thing you'll see at Epcot is the massive silver geosphere called **Spaceship Earth** (you know, the giant golf ball). Most guests stop right here and take the ride through the history of communication, but you should bypass it until the end of the day, when the slow pace and air-conditioning will make it worthwhile. Instead, head to **The Land** pavilion (behind Innoventions West, adjacent to The Living Seas) to take in the new **Soarin'**

free-flight simulator, as it's become the most popular attraction in the park. Then mosey next door to the **Imagination** pavilion and the wild-'n'-crazy **Honey, I Shrunk the Audience**—definitely a wake-up call if you've arrived at Epcot bleary-eyed. This is the wackiest attraction at Epcot, a 3-D film featuring Rick Moranis from *Honey, I Shrunk the Kids,* and the special effects are terrific for adults as well as kids. You'll jump out of your seat—literally. I wouldn't hang around this pavilion afterward though; instead, cut through **Innoventions Plaza** and go directly to the side-by-side **Test Track** and **Mission: Space** rides. **Universe of Energy** has employed Ellen DeGeneres and Bill Nye the Science Guy to tell the tale of fossil fuels and alternative energy sources in the very entertaining **Ellen's Energy Adventure.** Just watch out for those spitting dinosaurs.

If you've already done Splash Mountain, you'll probably want to skip Norway's **The Maelstrom,** where you board a Viking ship and navigate a North Sea storm, with trolls peering at you from behind the rocks. If you do ride, look behind you after the first drop for a quick thrill. The biggest lines are found at **The American Adventure,** an unabashedly patriotic show featuring Audio Animatronic characters in a journey through American history. It's a feel-good history lesson that can induce tears in some viewers and snores in others. Perhaps one of its best features is its length: 30 minutes, long enough for you to sneak in a nap.

What not to miss at USF... So you did pretty well in your last 10K road race? It'll serve you well at **Universal Studios Florida.** It's nearly impossible to cram all the rides here into 1 day, but it can be done. Just get plenty of sleep the night before, wear comfortable shoes, and be ready to hustle, big time. Pick up a map and daily entertainment schedule, and circle the rides and shows on your "must-see" list. Then as soon as you're through the gate, run like hell to **Revenge of the Mummy,** which always has long lines. Stop en route to pick up a quick EXPRESS pass for **Shrek 4-D** (if you don't have a Universal resort-room key). This attraction uses 3-D movie effects married with seats that move and bounce to continue the story of Shrek and Fiona. It's fun for all ages and *very* popular! ***Tip:*** Those with bad backs or those who are pregnant should request seats in the front row as they are stationary. **Terminator 2 3-D** features the creepy-steely T-1,000,000, and live-action doubles of Arnold Schwarzenegger and Edward Furlong, who roar onto the stage on Harleys and then into a giant movie screen, a very cool trick. To tell you more would spoil the fun—see this one for yourself. Your adrenaline pumping? Excellent time to hit **Men in Black Alien Attack,** where you can zap icky aliens as you ride through the streets of New York. You zig, you zag, you hurtle through the city at breakneck speed—a lot like a *real* Big Apple cab ride. Shoot the alien with the newspaper—it's Steven Spielberg. For maximum points, watch for the red button to light up and hit it for a quick 100,000 points...otherwise, you may end up as Bug Bait. Next, in order of importance, are **Back to the Future...The Ride**—a fast-paced simulator ride through space and time in a mock DeLorean; **Earthquake: The Big One** (a cable-car ride through the great San Francisco earthquake); a cruise in the **Jaws** boat, where everybody can be shark bait for a day (I can tell when the shark is coming, but it always scares most people); and the **E.T. Adventure,** a swooping bike ride through the sky that ends with a personal thank-you from E.T. himself. The only show that has ever disappointed me at this park is **Twister.** Based on the movie (as are all things in USF), I expected to be thrust into a mock tornado. What I got was a lot of wind serving up a small tornado in the distance as I stood on a "patio" with the rest of my group. Then a bucket of water was flung at my face. Woo hoo.

If (and only if) you've got younger kids, you can try to get them slimed on-air at **Nickelodeon Studios,** an homage to the all-kids network (best time is midafternoon). They'll also love the **Jimmy Neutron's Nicktoon Blast** simulator ride—just beware the Chicken Dance. Regardless of age, don't miss the very cute **Animal Planet Live!** show, which demonstrates why actors are almost always upstaged by animals.

Best and worst of Islands of Adventure... The endless lines say it all: At the Islands, thrill rides are the thing. Like carnival rides on steroids, the **Incredible Hulk** and **Dueling Dragons** roller coasters are truly gut-twisting, while **The Amazing Adventures of Spider-Man** is the ultimate high-tech adventure (it's only slightly less intense if you whip off the 3-D glasses). **Doctor Doom's Fearfall** is a dumbed-down version of Disney's **Tower of Terror,** and it's rarely worth the long lines. Meanwhile, at the replicant version of Jurassic Park (Steven Spielberg was a creative consultant on this attraction, which first debuted in Universal Studios Hollywood), you'll be scared witless as velociraptors stalk you inside the diabolical **Jurassic Park River Adventure.** Then board the charming **Pteranodon Flyers,** but only if you've got a small child in tow, or at least a very short adult—somebody in your pair has to be *56 inches tall or less* to "glide" in the two-person gondolas, which hang suspended from a curving track. (And note that the line for this one can reach back all the way to the Jurassic period.) Nostalgic fun for all ages is **The Cat in the Hat** ride at Seuss Landing, where you'll spin (and spin some more) through the book's familiar story line.

Star productions at Disney–MGM Studios... If you found the Magic Kingdom so sweet it made your teeth ache, and Epcot a bit too heavy in the dining-and-shopping category, here's your reward. **Disney–MGM Studios** has action aplenty. Impromptu fires, rainstorms, explosions, and gunplay are among the predominant themes at this amusement-park-cum-movie-and-TV-studio. Only a couple of attractions here are geared solely toward little kids: **Honey, I Shrunk the Kids Movie Set Adventure** (not to be confused with Honey, I Shrunk the Audience at Epcot), and **Playhouse Disney: Live on Stage!** Most everything else can be equally enjoyed by adults, school-age kids, and hard-to-please teens. Thrill seekers will want to bolt to the **Rock 'n' Roller Coaster.** An original Aerosmith soundtrack, created exclusively for the ride, blasts into your "limo" as it travels at breakneck speed through Tinseltown. Try to hit this ride before lunch. There are lots of twists and turns, and three upside-down inversions. The **Twilight Zone Tower of Terror** is the—ahem—towering achievement of Walt Disney Imagineering. You'll see it as you drive into the park; the structure looms as a delightfully Gothic presence at the end of Sunset Boulevard, all cracked pink stucco with a sparking electric sign and gaping hole in the wall. This one's got all the goodies that have made TZ a cult favorite for decades: levitating eyeball, "doo-doo-doo-doo" theme, Rod Serling, even holographic ghosts. Then there's the moment you enter the you-know-what and free-fall 13 stories in the out-of-control service elevator, only to do the whole thing all over again. At the end, you may want to spring for the souvenir photo of yourself, mouth agape, taken as the plunge begins. For a study in contrasts, make your next stop the ***Beauty and the Beast*** **stage show.** It's your typical beast-meets-girl love story, performed by live actors, and the music is terrific. How romantic is it? Notice how many couples are holding hands as they leave the theater. Or maybe they just don't want to get separated as they make a mad dash for **Star Tours,** a vastly popular motion-simulation ride—get there early or late to avoid long lines. Even if the *Star Wars* plotlines have faded somewhat from your memory, the Force will still be with you; on this ride, the story's beside the point. The real thrill is lurching through time and space (while dodging in-your-face asteroids) in a runaway "Starspeeder" (read: mechanized simulator).

Everybody knows the real stars in action flicks are the stunt doubles. See them in action—minus the boring retakes and makeup sessions—at the **Indiana Jones Epic Stunt Spectacular.** Special effects, razzle-dazzle stunts, and pyrotechnics make this show worth the (incredibly long) wait. Wear a bright-colored shirt, wave your arms spastically, and you might be called up on stage as an extra. (***Warning:*** If you sit in the front row, you'll be so close to the action your eyeballs will sizzle.) For even more stupendous stunts, check out the new **Lights! Motors! Action! Extreme Stunt Show,** an import from Disneyland Paris. It's pretty much what you'd expect: cars and motorcycles zoom, boom, and carom off each other. Had enough mechanized action? Tops in the gee-whiz techno category is, believe it or not, **Voyage of the Little Mermaid.** People without kids in tow might bypass this "sleeper" attraction—but if they do, well, it's their loss. This stage show combines animation, puppetry, lasers, and live performers in a mini-version of the Disney movie. No, you're not just getting misty at this story of boy meets fish, you're actually getting misted. And if the names Kermit, Miss Piggy, and Gonzo mean anything to you (and even if they don't—for shame!), don't miss the wonderfully wacky **Jim Henson's Muppet*Vision 3-D.** Housed in a perfect re-creation of the Muppets' theater (complete with the blessedly crotchety

Statler and Waldorf critiquing the action from the balcony), it's a zany mix of 3-D film, animatronics, live-action, and special effects.

By now, your hair's soaked and your clothes reek of propane, signs you're having a swell time at Disney–MGM. Time to go win some prizes at **Who Wants to Be a Millionaire—Play It!** Based on the popular game show (before Disney overran it on ABC and killed it), everyone in the audience gets to participate in the lightning quiz round. Advance to the hot seat and you can work your way up to the grand prize (usually a Disney cruise). And shame on you if you don't make it to **The Great Movie Ride,** Disney–MGM's homage to the magic of the movies. After watching a delightful montage of movie clips in a prestaging area (housed in a replica of Grauman's Chinese Theatre), you'll take a tram ride through re-created movie sets enhanced by Audio Animatronics (the *Wizard of Oz* set will make you wonder why Dorothy ever wanted to go back to Kansas). And just when you think you know what this ride is about, the tour guide announces—you've got it—"Something's wrong, folks!"

If you have the time and inclination, check out **Journey into Narnia: Creating the Lion, the Witch, and the Wardrobe** for a low-impact walkthrough of how the fantasy movie was made, including close-up looks at various props and creatures.

Best in show... And the prize goes to...Indiana Jones and his stuntmen and -women, stars of the **Indiana Jones Epic Stunt Spectacular** at Disney–MGM Studios. It's a not-to-be-missed live-action show full of out-of-control vehicles, real explosions, falling rocks, flying spears, crumbling buildings, and amazing movie stunts. You'll recognize some of the settings from the movies, and you'll get a peek at the secrets behind the scenes. Similar vehicular violence can be observed at the **Lights! Motors! Action! Extreme Stunt Show,** though you may be ready for something a bit more low-key after sitting through all that mayhem. The **Festival of the Lion King** at Animal Kingdom offers up a Broadwayesque version of the famous Circle of Life. It's one of the best shows in town—don't miss it.

Also compelling is SeaWorld's 30-minute **Odyssea.** Similar to Cirque du Soleil, it combines acrobatics, music, comedy, and special effects in a set that transports guests into a faux underwater world. Very well done and a great way to escape the Florida heat. **Pets Ahoy!** is SeaWorld's entry into the animal-show arena, featuring silly skits (the emcee seems totally embarrassed to be there) with a menagerie of dogs, cats, birds, rats, even potbelly pigs. The warm, fuzzy side of this is that most of these animals were rescued from shelters.

To sea or not to see... Anheuser-Busch, the owner of **SeaWorld Orlando,** has pumped a ton of money into this park to make it a player. There's a lot more to this place than Shamu these days, including thrill rides, new shows, and a stomach-lurching roller coaster. Still, Shamu rules, charming even the most jaded of us, especially kids (who insist upon sitting close to the action—the first few rows are usually the splash zone—so that everybody in their party gets drenched). Even if you've seen the **Shamu Adventure** show before—and they change it regularly to keep things interesting—you'll still "ooh" and "ahh" as the sleek, black-and-white killer whale shoots out of the water, straddled by a trainer. Beyond Shamu and the resident dolphins, sea lions, and otters, this park packs some exciting surprises, including some thrill rides that can compete with the best of the bunch over at Universal and Disney. (***Hint:*** Pay attention to the motion-sickness warnings.) The **Kraken** roller coaster is a must-do for coaster crazies. SeaWorld calls it the longest, tallest (15 stories, to be exact), fastest in Orlando.... You'll hurl; you'll twirl; your stomach will lunge and your heart will plunge.... Are we having fun yet? It features a floorless design—that is, your feet will dangle—and you also have nothing in front of you to wrap those white-knuckled fingers around.... The coaster exceeds 65 mph with seven inversions, including a cobra roll, zero-gravity roll, and vertical loops and spins. The **Wild Arctic** is a simulated helicopter ride (you can also do this without the jostling motion) through a glacier. Strapped in your seat, you dodge icebergs and zigzag through a frozen landscape, then walk through re-created arctic settings to view real polar bears and walruses. (***Hint:*** Don't do this immediately after the Shamu show, when you're soaking wet, because the thermostat is set to chilly and pneumonia just isn't cool.) Then there's **Journey to Atlantis,** SeaWorld's ambitious water-coaster thrill attraction, which combines cool special effects (they call them "aqualusions") with a hair-raising boat ride.

Rides aside, the action at SeaWorld centers around its shows; you plan your itinerary around them, and spend the rest of your time touring walk-through exhibits. At any of the aquatic shows, the first few rows are the splash zones—you will get wet sitting there, so place your butt accordingly. My favorite show is **"Clyde & Seamore Take Pirate Island,"** a sea-lion-and-otter show. Get up close and personal with two sea lions and an otter as they enact a pirate skit with their trainers. Another of SeaWorld's virtues is its **Shark Encounter** aquarium, a walk-through tunnel populated with the scarier denizens of the deep, such as moray eels, barracudas, rays, scorpion fish, and (of course) sharks. It's way cooler than the Living Seas at Epcot. I'd also make it a point to take a peek at the sea lions at **Pacific Point Preserve** and the so-ugly-they're-cute manatees at **Manatee Rescue.** These walruslike creatures, sometimes called sea cows, are a Florida treasure, currently threatened by red tide and motorboat propellers. Over 21? Make sure to visit the **Hospitality Center** at the far back corner of the park for your free samples of various Anheuser-Busch liquid refreshments. You can even take a short beer class here; upon completion, you'll receive an Honorary Brewmaster certificate. Now that's entertainment!

Another roadside attraction... So, you've done Disney, and the adventurers in your group are moaning the B-word...what next? **DisneyQuest,** five stories of virtual reality, will keep them busy for hours. Its various zones offer tons of options, including the opportunity to design a roller coaster and then ride it (not so adventurous now, are we), take a mini-course in animation, play vintage video games (Centipede anyone?), and battle 3-D pirates for hidden treasure. The cost seems steep at first ($38 adults; $31 for kids 3–9), but imagine how many quarters you've dropped in an hour at the local arcade. If you want to see wild animals (in non-Disney habitats), head out to **Gatorland.** That this 50-year-old park still competes against entertainment giants such as Disney and Universal is endearing, and one can only hope that the old-fashioned, Florida-flavored attraction will survive. You enter Gatorland through a giant, tooth-filled 'gator's jaw, and plan your day (3 hours should do it) around shows including **Gator Wrestlin'** (self-explanatory), **Upclose Encounters** (ditto), and **Gator Jumparoo** (wherein gators leap high out of the water to be hand-fed a snack of dead chickens—it's actually quite the crowd pleaser). Gatorland is a commercial alligator farm covering some 110 acres, whose gators have been featured in myriad TV commercials and movies, including *Indiana Jones and the Temple of Doom.* Try not to think about the fact that their cousins end up as belts in the boutique and as gator chowder in Pearl's Smoke House restaurant. Nice features of the park include its natural Florida setting, a cypress swamp, and its role as a wading-bird sanctuary and rookery. From February through summer, snowy egrets, American egrets, herons, and other shorebirds build hundreds of nests and care for their young amid the alligators' 10-acre breeding marsh. The gator wranglers and snake handlers also share a lot of information about their charges in a down-home, folksy manner, along the lines of "Never insult an alligator until you've crossed the river," and this bit of advice on how to recognize a deadly coral snake: "If the nose is black, that's bad for Jack." You'll leave the park with a healthy respect for these toothy reptiles, especially as they emerge from the gator-wrestling nonsense with their dignity intact.

Meanwhile, *Titanic* fever lives on at **Titanic: The Experience,** at the Mercado shopping center on I-Drive. This permanent exhibition combines the historic (*Titanic* dinnerware and other artifacts), the dramatic (actors pretending to be ship's passengers and survivors), and the weird (a chess table made from wood floating around the *Titanic* wreck site). Ultimately, it's both sad and chilling. Of course, you're snapped back to reality when you see Leo's costume from the James Cameron *Titanic* flick, and copies of the famous necklace in the gift shop. **Ripley's Believe It or Not!** doesn't even pretend to take itself seriously. Even the building is a joke: It's set into the ground at an angle, enough so that the exit is dizzying, as though the whole thing were being sucked into a giant sinkhole. Among the bizarre exhibits on display are replicas of the world's tallest man and the world's fattest man (so far, it sounds like typical talk-show fare), the man with two pupils in each eye, an actual shrunken head, and a 1907 Rolls Royce crafted from matchsticks. If you're drawn to carnival freak shows and

Diane Arbus photographs, you'll love the place. Just don't touch the fertility statues—several years ago when the attraction first received them, several women on staff became pregnant. Coincidence? Do you really want to find out?

Finally, if you'd like to add a little educational value to your entertainment, check out the wacky **WonderWorks** at Pointe*Orlando on International Drive. This interactive entertainment center, housed in a zany, upside-down building, features a variety of unusual activities. Sit in an electric chair, experience the sensation of an earthquake or hurricane, play computer-simulated basketball, make giant bubbles, see what you'll look like 25 years from now (yeah, you really want to do that)...and more. Basically a science exhibit gone mad.

For something a little less interactive, how about the **Monument of the States** in Kissimmee? Following the attack on Pearl Harbor in December 1941, a local doc got the idea to erect this tall mass of rocks (it looks kind of like a Jenga game with an Eagle on top) as a symbol of America's unity. So he wrote the governors of each state (and FDR, for good measure) asking them to send him a bit of local rock to contribute to the monument. Miraculously, they did! And (shades of "if you build it, they will come") so did many others. The monument includes donations from 22 countries for a total of 1,500 stones (and some odd additions, including a petrified apple, a cannonball, and...a map of Holland?).

One of the most controversial attractions in town is **The Holy Land Experience,** an attraction that claims to tell the life of Jesus through "dramatic musical productions" and "biblical presentations" on grounds designed to look like Jerusalem at the time of Christ. Most Orlando rabbis protest that it's nothing but a giant conversion ploy. The facilities are all on par with the Big Three parks in terms of special effects and set design, and the artifact museum is actually quite impressive. But be aware that this is at root an evangelistic enterprise—if you go to the Holy Land Experience, you will be preached at. Of course, they do sell tasty Goliath Burgers, so there's that.

Join the parade... *Not.* Unless you have a child who absolutely insists on attending Disney's overcrowded street displays, or you're a huge fan of Disney characters, your best bet is to avoid them like the plague. Instead, take advantage of the chance to hit the more popular rides while the lines are shorter. Check the schedule for parade times, or just watch as folks begin to claim their space on the streets, sometimes an hour before the show begins. At the Magic Kingdom, the **Share a Dream Come True** parade is held at 3pm daily, and at that time the route along Main Street is packed with elbow-to-elbow, stroller-to-stroller crowds waiting to watch the extravaganza of floats, giant inflated Disney characters, live dancers, clowns, and more. The same holds true for Magic Kingdom's nighttime **SpectroMagic.** The 20-minute spectacle walks the 3.4-mile Main Street parade route, and includes a host of giant Disney characters outlined in glittery lights. It really is beautiful to watch, even if you're not a Disney devotee. Problem is, folks start lining up for the event a full 1 to 2 hours beforehand! Ditto for **Mickey's Jammin' Jungle Parade** at Disney's Animal Kingdom, where the scene is always depressingly the same: sweat-drenched, irritable crowds waiting for the floats, costumed performers, and music to arrive. Better to attend your hometown parade and spend your time here at the park's rides and attractions. The **Fantasmic!** show at Disney–MGM Studios is a nightly spectacular of lights, lasers, and water, and it's a must for Disney fans. The extravaganza, which features music and characters from Disney classics

Post-Theme-Park Pampering

After hours spent trekking through theme parks, what could be finer than a few hours at a luscious spa? Disney has three full-service spas (at ***Disney's Grand Floridian, Disney's Saratoga Springs Resort & Spa,*** *and* ***Walt Disney World Dolphin****) that offer a number of soothing treatments, including an herbal eye-lift number that eliminates (at least temporarily) those tiny furrows that develop from waking up at 4am to beat the crowds at the Magic Kingdom. Nearby, the staff at the* ***Buena Vista Palace*** *perform a special theme-park foot massage that leaves weary feet feeling refreshed and baby's-bottom soft. My first choice at Universal Orlando: the European, full-service* ***Mandara Spa*** *at the Portofino Bay Hotel. Try a soothing herbal body wrap, or maybe one of their mud therapies, followed by a shiatsu massage. (See the Accommodations chapter for info on all of the above resorts.) But if you're at USF and have at least a quarter, head over to the restrooms in front of* ***Animal Planet Live!*** *or at Richter's Burgers and you'll find a small coin-operated foot massager. Plunk in a little silver and get enough instant relief to carry you through the rest of the day.*

(what else?) lasts about 25 minutes, but (and this is a big but), you'll usually need to get in line at least an hour ahead of time to snag a seat (it's inside an amphitheater, so, alas, you can't see it from outside), unless you pay for a Fantasmic! Dinner Package (see the Dining chapter), which gives you a jump-the-line pass and offers seating in a special section at the show.

Got game?... Disney does, at its gigantic (220 acres!) **Wide World of Sports** complex. You can fulfill your sports fantasies by throwing pitches, shooting hoops, and so on, at the Multi-Sports Experience. If you'd rather watch someone else sweat, more than 30 different sporting events, including football, tennis, track, soccer, baseball, and more are featured, and all levels—amateur, youth, and professional—are represented. The Atlanta Braves and Tampa Bay Buccaneers conduct spring training at this facility. If you want to catch a game, pick up a schedule—something is going on here every day of the year. You can also see top-notch Orlando Magic basketball action at the downtown **T.D. Waterhouse Center,** but tickets may be tough to come by. Sometimes fans can pick them up outside the arena the night of the game (scalping is illegal, but cops generally look the other way). In early spring, the Houston Astros baseball team holds spring training at the **Osceola County Stadium and Sports Complex** in Kissimmee. Minor-league baseball action goes on most of the year at this complex, as well. Also check the schedule for the **Florida Citrus Bowl,** where a number of professional sports events are hosted, including an occasional NFL game (usually an exhibition), NCAA Division I college football contests, and soccer matches. The Citrus Bowl is held here annually, and both World Cup and Olympic soccer action have taken place here.

For a look at Orlando before Mickey arrived... Long before there were theme parks, there was Central Florida, a hot, isolated wilderness that was home to cattle ranchers, orange growers, and those looking for a tropical paradise far from civilization. Take a look at Orlando's pioneer past at the **Orange County Regional History Center,** a quiet oasis on Central Boulevard. While much of this small museum consists of archival materials, there's an old

(1926—that's old for Florida) fire station and a re-created pioneer kitchen, newspaper press room, and Victorian parlor. Located in the Loch Haven Park complex is the **Orlando Museum of Art,** one of the best museums in the South. Its permanent collections feature 19th- and 20th-century American, pre-Columbian, and African art; artists represented include Childe Hassam and Judy Pfaff. Finally, if you've got young kids hanging with you, inside the same complex, there's the **Orlando Science Center,** a hands-on science museum geared toward children that is a great favorite with local grade-school groups (and thus an avoid-at-all costs spot if you want to avoid kids).

Behind the scenes... Did you realize that more than 10,000 rosebushes decorate the World Showcase grounds? Or that the **Morocco** pavilion was a gift from the Kingdom of Morocco and is made up of more than 9 tons of handcrafted tile? Bet you didn't know that the **Swiss Family Treehouse** has 600 branches and 800,000 vinyl leaves. If you have a passion for detail (or maybe you're boning up to compete on *Jeopardy!*), check into one of the many backstage tours offered at the theme parks. The **Hidden Treasures of the World Showcase** ($59, plus admission) is a 3½-hour walking tour that concentrates on the architecture and construction techniques of Epcot's individual country pavilions. Don't want to walk? No problem. How about **Around the World at Epcot,** which lets you tour the park on a futuristic Segway riding machine for 2 hours. You must be 16 or older and 250 pounds or less to participate...oh, and willing to part with $80, *plus* park admission. At SeaWorld, frolic with beluga whales in the **Beluga Interaction Program** ($179, plus park admission), or get up close and personal with Jaws and 50 of his closest friends at the **Sharks Deep Dive** ($150, plus park admission). True water-critter fanatics can embark on the **Marine Mammal Keeper Experience** ($399; includes 7-day pass to SeaWorld) and you'll do everything from helping with food preparation and area clean-up to learning training techniques and interacting with the killer whales, sea lions, otters, walruses, and bottlenose dolphins. Make sure to book at least a month in advance, especially during summer. The park also offers some less-pricey Behind-the-Scenes tours, each lasting about an hour ($16 adults, $12 children

3–9) and including some very limited animal interaction; "touch a penguin," for example. The cheapie tours often don't fill up even on busy days (few people are aware they exist), but reserve in advance if you feel the need.

You have to have an extraordinary interest in Disney to endure, much less enjoy, the **World's Backstage Magic** tour ($199 per person), which takes guests behind the scenes to see how Disney does it. You'll explore the "utilidor" system beneath the Magic Kingdom and travel backstage at three of the Disney theme parks. The good news is that you'll skip the lines, you don't have to pay park admission, and lunch is included; the bad news is that the tour lasts 7 hours and sometimes feels like a day at school. The 4½-hour **Keys to the Kingdom** tour ($58) is similar to Backstage Magic—you'll see the utilidors and production center—but you'll have to wait in line at the attractions and pay park admission. This one is open to guests 16 years old or older. The 3+-hour **Backstage Safari** tour ($65) is a look at how Disney created the Animal Kingdom and cares for its animals. For availability and reservations for all these tours, call Tel 407/WDW-TOUR. If none of these sound like your kind of pleasure, and you have 10 or more in your group, you can always sign up for a **Disney VIP** tour (cost: $125 an hour, with a 5-hour minimum), a custom-designed program tailored to your individual interests; it might include a shopper's tour of the Kingdom, a behind-the-scenes look at one or all of the theme parks, or whatever else you might have in mind. (How about a no-waiting-in-lines tour? Nope. Even VIPs don't get to jump the lines at Disney.) To book, call Tel 407/560-4033 up to 48 hours in advance (not available Dec 25–31).

There are also 5-hour **VIP tours** at either Universal Studios Florida or Islands of Adventure, which include a guided tour and line-cutting privileges at a number of high-profile attractions, for $100 to $120 per person. A 7-hour, two-park VIP tour covers both parks and costs $125 to $150 per person. Prices for both tours *do not include admission to the parks!* For more information on the VIP tour, call Tel 407/363-8295.

Bright lights and Disney nights... Forget about spotting the Big Dipper in this town: Nightly fireworks finales pepper the skies over Disney World. The impressive **Electrical**

Water Pageant is the kind of presentation Disney does best: A come-to-life cartoon character travels the Seven Seas to the strains of music and light. Watch as King Neptune slithers through the water, leading an array of animated sea life (okay, it's actually a 1,000-ft. barge, transporting an imaginative maze of lights and music, weaving through the Seven Seas Lagoon and Bay Lake). Combine this with dining at a Disney resort—you can see the show from the Polynesian (where it begins at about 9pm), and the Grand Floridian, Wilderness Lodge, Fort Wilderness, and Contemporary resorts. **Wishes!,** the nightly closing show at the Magic Kingdom, is rather impressive. But you don't really get the scope of how large the fireworks display is until you watch it from one of the area resorts. And I can't imagine how much they have to pay "Tinkerbell" to slide down the wire from the castle to Tomorrowland. Yikes! The **IllumiNations** show at Epcot is hugely popular—people start lining up along the lagoon hours before showtime. Fireworks and laser lights are set off over the World Showcase Lagoon, to classic musical scores, as each "country" lights up. It's stirring but not necessarily worth a special trip (though if you happen to be in town, stick around). If you want to see this, be prepared to stake out your viewing spot up to 2 hours before showtime. Finally, it's **New Year's Eve** every night at **Pleasure Island,** as a laser-and-light show, fireworks, and professional dancers help ring in a hectic, ever-recurring new year (go ahead, make that pledge and you may actually be able to keep it until the next celebration). The Pleasure Island cast tries hard to make you have fun, and the party-hearty tourists lining the streets don't seem to have too many problems getting into the mood while throwing confetti—and knocking back cocktails.

One size does not fit all.... It'd be nice if we were all one size...the seats at theme-park attractions could accommodate everyone without difficulty. But for those not born with a Madison Avenue build, here's a basic primer so you don't have to worry about getting squished, bumped, or bruised. At Disney, the only rides where a bigger booty or chest could be a real problem are: **Dinosaur** (Animal

Kingdom)—the seats are narrow, lack legroom, and may leave bruises from all the jerking around; **Rock 'n' Roller Coaster** (Disney–MGM Studios) has a shoulder harness that may not fit larger chests (leave that WonderBra at home); **Space Mountain** (Magic Kingdom) has a T-bar lap harness that may not come down securely on those proportioned with large thighs or long legs; **Test Track** (Epcot) doesn't offer much arm space between seats so ask the cast member to leave the middle seat empty for more upper body room. SeaWorld bats 50/50; **Journey to Atlantis** has plenty of seat room. **Kraken,** on the other hand, has a shoulder harness that may not fit larger chests. There's a sample seat at the front of the attraction line—if you can't fit that, you won't be able to ride. **Islands of Adventure coasters** also sport harness issues; try the seats hanging at the entrances to each ride to see if you'll fit (look for the double-strap examples as they have more room than single-strap seats). **Dudley Do-Right's Ripsaw Falls** is seriously height-challenged—the long-legged will have lots of kinks to massage out upon exiting the flume.

The future is getting clearer.... Universal Orlando has considerable open real estate that may shape up into new attractions someday (mainly the recently closed Nickelodeon Studios area). For now, the only Universal news is a reworking of the malfunction-plagued **Sylvester McMonkey McBean's Very Unusual Driving Machines** at Islands of Adventure's Seuss Landing. One assumes it will still be a driving/riding thing, but nobody knows for sure, despite a projected summer 2006 startup. For its part, SeaWorld is opening a few new shows and constructing a large children's area, complete with kiddie coaster, all of which are supposed to come online at various times throughout 2006. With major openings like Mission: Space, Soarin', and Expedition Everest finally in the rearview mirror, the only newbies on the Disney side are the more movie-friendly **Pirates of the Caribbean** in the Magic Kingdom (scheduled for June 2006), and **The Seas with Nemo and Friends** (scheduled for fall 2006), a simulator at Epcot's The Living Seas based on the movie *Finding Nemo.*

Map 10: Orlando Attractions

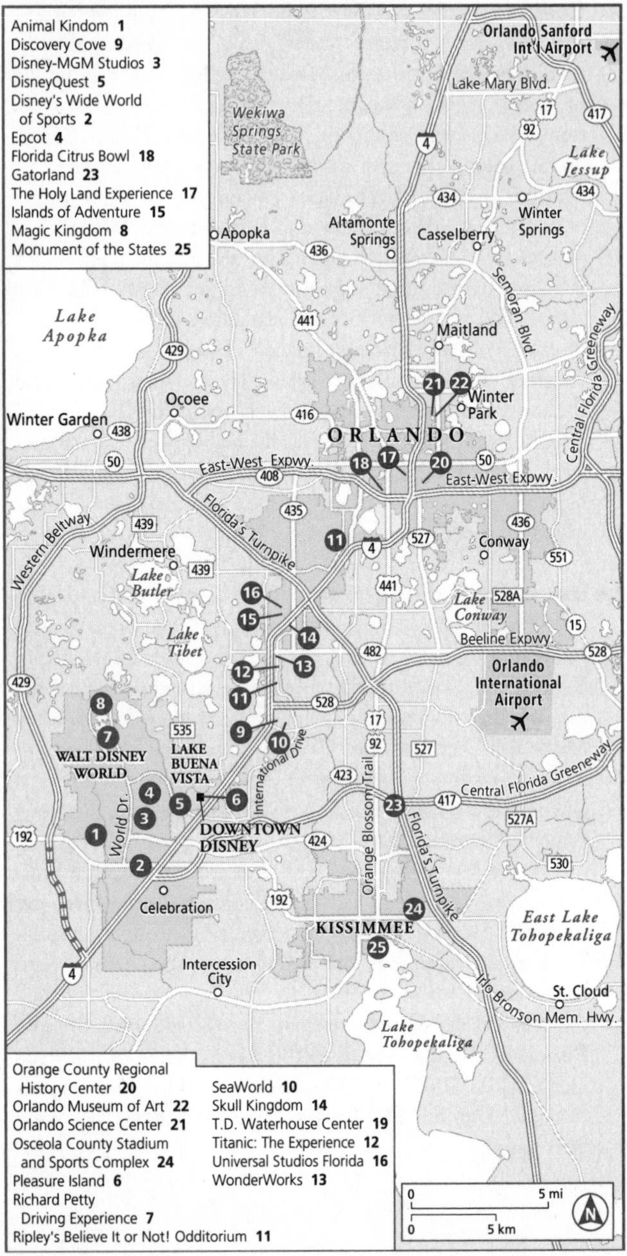

The Index

Animal Kingdom (p. 119) WDW Jam-packed trails littered with natural barrier cages serve as the homes for everything from moles to gorillas.... *Tel 407/824-4321. www.disneyworld.com. Walt Disney World. Daily; hours vary seasonally though the park closes at dusk. Single-day admission $68 adults, $56 children 3–9. Discount multiday-pass options available.*

See Map 10 on p. 144.

Discovery Cove (p. 120) INTERNATIONAL DRIVE SeaWorld's sister park offers daily all-inclusive packages with and without a personal dolphin swim.... *Tel 407/370-1280 (toll-free 877/434-7268). www.discoverycove.com. 6000 Discovery Cove Way. Hours vary seasonally. Admission with dolphin swim $249–$279 ages 6 and up; without dolphin swim $149–$179 ages 6 and up. Tickets must be reserved in advance.*

See Map 10 on p. 144.

Disney–MGM Studios (p. 131) WDW One hundred thirty-five acres of TV and movie magic.... *Tel 407/824-4321. www.disneyworld.com. Walt Disney World. Daily; hours vary seasonally. Single-day admission $68 adults, $56 children 3–9. Discount multiday-pass options available.*

See Map 10 on p. 144.

DisneyQuest (p. 135) WDW A giant modern-day arcade with five floors of virtual-reality fun. Design a roller coaster, battle evil aliens, or find lost treasure.... *Tel 407/828-4600. www.disneyquest.com. 1486 E. Buena Vista Dr., in Downtown Disney West Side. Sun–Thurs 11:30am–11pm; Fri–Sat 11:30am–midnight. Admission $39 adults, $32 children 3–9.*

See Map 10 on p. 144.

Disney's Wide World of Sports (p. 139) WDW You name it, it's played here. Sports nuts play out their fantasies at the Multi-Sports Experience.... *Tel 407/939-1500. www.disneysports.com. 6910 S. Victory Way, near Magic Kingdom. Daily 10am–5pm. Admission $11 adults, $8 children 3–9.*

See Map 10 on p. 144.

Epcot (p. 128) WDW Walt Disney's visionary community comes across as an educational-toy-store-cum-faux-United-Nations. It's the best of the Disney parks for the adult set.... *Tel 407/824-4321. www.disneyworld.com. Walt Disney World. Daily; hours vary seasonally. Single-day admission $68 adults, $56 children 3–9. Discount multiday-pass options available.*

See Map 10 on p. 144.

Florida Citrus Bowl (p. 139) DOWNTOWN ORLANDO Home to a number of sports events, including Division I college football and soccer matches.... *Tel 407/423-2476. 1 Citrus Bowl Place. Hours and ticket prices vary according to event.*

See Map 10 on p. 144.

Gatorland (p. 135) ORLANDO Florida's largest alligator farm, housing 5,000 gators and crocs.... *Tel 407/855-5496 (toll-free 800/393-5297). www.gatorland.com. 14501 S. Orange Blossom Trail (U.S. 441), between Osceola Pkwy. and Hunter's Creek Blvd. Daily 9am–5pm, though closing times vary seasonally. Admission $22 adults, $14 children 3–12 including tax.*

See Map 10 on p. 144.

The Holy Land Experience (p. 137) ORLANDO Jesus Christ goes head-to-head with Mickey. For this religious theme park, you gotta be a believer.... *Tel 407/367-2065 (toll-free 866/872-4659). www.holylandexperience.com. 4655 Vineland Rd. Daily 9am–4pm. Admission $30 adults, $20 children 4–12.*

See Map 10 on p. 144.

Islands of Adventure (p. 121) UNIVERSAL ORLANDO Tops in town for thrills and chills, the park features state-of-the-art coasters, 3-D film, live-action and simulator rides, and water flumes.... *Tel 407/363-8000 (toll-free 800/711-0080). www.universalorlando.com. 1000 Universal Studios Plaza. Daily; hours vary seasonally. Single-day admission $68 adults, $56 children 3–9. Discount multiday-pass options available.*

See Map 10 on p. 144.

Magic Kingdom (p. 125) WDW The 100-acre Magic Kingdom is the sugarcoated heart of Walt Disney World.... *Tel 407/824-4321. www.disneyworld.com. Walt Disney World. Daily; hours vary seasonally. Single-day admission $68 adults; $56 children 3–9. Discount multiday-pass options available.*

See Map 10 on p. 144.

Monument of the States (p. 137) KISSIMMEE A statue erected after Pearl Harbor as a symbol of America's unity.... *No telephone. Lakefront Park, 300 E. Monument Ave. Daily 24 hr. Free admission.*

See Map 10 on p. 144.

Orange County Regional History Center (p. 139) DOWNTOWN ORLANDO Explore Orlando's pioneer past through old photographs, and re-created settings.... *Tel 407/836-8500 (toll-free 800/965-2030). www.thehistorycenter.org. 65 E. Central Blvd. Mon–Sat 10am–5pm; Sun noon–5pm. Closed Thanksgiving, Christmas, and New Year's. Admission $7 adults, $3.50 children 3–12.*

See Map 10 on p. 144.

Orlando Museum of Art (p. 140) ORLANDO Hosts special exhibitions throughout the year, and the permanent collections feature 19th- and 20th-century American art, pre-Columbian art, and African art.... *Tel 407/896-4231. www.omart.org. 2416 N. Mills Ave., in Loch Haven Park. Tues–Fri 10am–4pm; Sat–Sun noon–5pm; closed Mon and major holidays. Admission $15 adults, $5 children 6–18.*

See Map 10 on p. 144.

Orlando Science Center (p. 140) ORLANDO Small and child-friendly, this museum features interactive science exhibits and a planetarium.... *Tel 407/897-6350. www.osc.org. 777 E. Princeton St., between Orange and Mills aves., in Loch Haven Park. Mon–Thurs 9am–5pm; Fri–Sat 9am–9pm; Sun noon–5pm. Admission (includes exhibits, Cinedome film, and planetarium) $15 adults, $10 children 3–11.*

See Map 10 on p. 144.

Osceola County Stadium and Sports Complex (p. 139) KISSIMMEE Home of the Houston Astros baseball team's spring training.... *Tel 407/839-3900. www.osceola.org. 631 Heritage Park Way, off Bill Beck Blvd. at Hwy. 192. Ticket prices and hours vary.*

See Map 10 on p. 144.

Pleasure Island (p. 142) WDW Every night is New Year's Eve at Disney's biggest club-and-bar district.... *Tel 407/934-7781. www.disneyworld.com. 1590 Buena Vista Dr., in Downtown Disney. Daily 7pm–2am. Admission $22.*

See Map 10 on p. 144.

Richard Petty Driving Experience (p. 124) WDW Race a 600-horsepower Winston Cup car at breakneck speeds.... *Tel 407/939-0130 (toll-free 800/237-3889). www.1800bepetty.com. 3450 N. World Dr., off Magic Kingdom parking lot. Daily 9am–5pm. Admission $105–$1,330 depending on package option selected (prices include sales tax).*

See Map 10 on p. 144.

Ripley's Believe It or Not! Odditorium (p. 136) INTERNATIONAL DRIVE The oddities and exhibits displayed at this museum are mighty strange indeed.... *Tel 407/345-8510. www.ripleysorlando.com. 8201 International Dr. Daily 9am–1am. Admission $19 adults, $13 children 4–12.*

See Map 10 on p. 144.

SeaWorld (p. 134) INTERNATIONAL DRIVE Pay your respects to Shamu and take a side trip to Key West at the world's most popular marine-life park.... *Tel 407/351-3600 (toll-free 800/327-2424). www.seaworld.com. 7007 SeaWorld Dr. Daily; hours vary seasonally. Single-day admission $68 adults, $55 children 3–9. Discount multiday-pass options available.*

See Map 10 on p. 144.

Skull Kingdom (p. 120) INTERNATIONAL DRIVE Spooky attraction, full of dark corners, special effects, and live characters.... *Tel 407/354-1564. www.skullkingdom.com. 5933 American Way, just off the intersection of International Dr. and Universal Blvd. Mon–Fri 10am–5pm; Sat–Sun 6pm–midnight. Admission: day show $10, night show $15 per person.*

See Map 10 on p. 144.

T.D. Waterhouse Center (p. 139) DOWNTOWN ORLANDO Home to the Orlando Magic basketball team.... *Tel 407/849-2001 for information; 407/839-3900 for tickets through Ticketmaster. www.orlandocentroplex.com. 600 W. Amelia St., between I-4 and Parramore Ave. Ticket prices and hours vary.*

See Map 10 on p. 144.

Titanic: The Experience (p. 136) INTERNATIONAL DRIVE This permanent exhibit combines authentic artifacts, movie memorabilia, and costumed actors. Only for true *Titanic* buffs.... *Tel 407/248-1166. www.titanicshipofdreams.com. The Mercado, 8445 International Dr., 3 blocks south of Sand Lake Rd. Daily 10am–8pm. Admission $21 adults, $15 children 6–11.*

See Map 10 on p. 144.

Universal Studios Florida (p. 129) UNIVERSAL ORLANDO An excellent mix of top-shelf thrill rides and movie-themed shows and simulators.... *Tel 407/363-8000. www.universalorlando.com. 1000 Universal Studios Plaza. Daily; hours vary seasonally. Single-day admission $68 adults, $64 children 3–9. Multiday discount-pass options available.*

See Map 10 on p. 144.

WonderWorks (p. 137) INTERNATIONAL DRIVE Amusing interactive exhibits like the bubble machine and virtual-reality sports.... *Tel 407/351-8800. www.wonderworksonline.com. Pointe*Orlando, 9067 International Dr. Daily 9am–midnight. Admission $22 adults, $15 children 4–12.*

See Map 10 on p. 144.

GETTING

OUTSIDE

4

Basic Stuff

Ask Orlandoans what they like best about living in Orlando and most will tell you "the weather." They'll boast about an average annual temperature of a very pleasant 72°F (22°C), with plenty of sunshine and soft breezes. But, we ask, what about the hot and humid summer months, when all of Central Florida turns into one giant buggy sweatbox? No matter. Frequent afternoon thunderstorms sweep through to cool things down; there's always air-conditioning; plus you get used to it. What humidity? The weather, it seems, is what keeps Orlandoans in Orlando and gets them outdoors to play.

Of course, the area's appeal is more suited to some activities than it is to others. Suffice it to say that this ex-swamp-turned-tourist-mecca will never pass muster with the rugged, gorp-chomping crowd. Try as they might, even Disney's wild Imagineers and gigantic budgets can't turn Orlando into a scenic paradise. Face it: Thunder Mountain is not the Tetons. The Wilderness Lodge hot springs do not compare to Old Faithful. And no matter how many sangrias you drink, the grounds surrounding the Coronado Springs Resort will never look like the Mojave Desert. Not surprisingly, recreation in Central Florida centers on water, courts, and courses. There are more than 300 lakes in the greater Orlando area, and hundreds of elaborate hotel pools. Golfers will think they've died and gone to heaven, with more than 150 courses located within a 45-minute drive of downtown Orlando. Sure, it gets hot out on the course during the summer, but the plummet in greens fees (sometimes as low as half price, starting in May) makes up for the rise in temperature.

Golf, tennis, boating, fishing, and water-skiing are all offered at Disney, mostly in pristine, man-made environments, *sans* mosquitoes and flies. (We don't even want to know how they get rid of the buggers.) Outside the parks, you'll find even more activities to choose from. You could spend a day at Discovery Cove, swimming with bottlenose dolphins and snorkeling in a coral-reef lagoon. Grab a rubber mat and zip down a wet slide or tube the white-water rapids at one of five water parks in the area. Canoe the scenic Wekiva River, take a guided horseback tour through the woods, float in a hot-air balloon above Cinderella Castle, or hop in an airboat to go gator hunting. All that and more is here to be tried—without ever stepping into an amusement park. Just be sure to bring your sunscreen.

Resources for Golfers

Duffers, pay attention: The Orlando CVB operates a **GolfOrlando** (Tel 866/246-1449; www.golforlandoinfo.com) program in conjunction with **Golfpac** (Tel 407/260-2288 or 888/848-8941; www.golfpacinc.com), an organization that packages golf vacations with accommodations and other features and prearranges tee times at more than 45 Orlando-area courses. Request the program's brochure or head online to check out all their offerings. **Tee Times USA** (Tel 888/465-3356; www.teetimesusa.com) and **Teebone Golf** (Tel 866/833-2663; www.floridagolfing.com) are two other reservations services that offer packages and course information for public, semiprivate, and private courses across the state, as well as advice on where to play. You can usually reserve tee times up to 3 months in advance, or just give them a call when you wake up to a gorgeous-day-for-golf morning. All golf courses offer high- and low-season rates. Most courses give big price breaks in the early morning and midafternoon, and it's usually cheaper to golf midweek than on the weekends. Disney resort guests get a discount at WDW courses. But check with your hotel, too; many offer coupon discounts to a number of local courses. ***Note:*** All greens fees listed in this book are for nonguests in high season.

The Lowdown

Thrills and chills... It's 90°F (32°C) and about 100% humidity—where do you want to be? It's no surprise that water parks are big attractions here. Walt Disney World alone has two—Blizzard Beach and Typhoon Lagoon. The independent player is Wet 'n' Wild. Which is the best? Your choice will depend on your favorite method for getting wet. No matter which option you choose, you'll be handing over a chunk of change (about $35 for adults, $18 seniors, $29 kids 3–9, free for kids under 3) for the privilege of getting soaked.

If you like stomach-lurching plunges—the steeper the better—try **Wet 'n' Wild,** 6200 International Dr. (Tel 407/351-1800), the water park that claims to be the world's first and the nation's best-attended. Those who are experts on these places—teens—label this one "awesome." The park's **Hydra Fighter** is a hit, combining favorite kid-pleasing ingredients for summer fun—swings, water, and squirt guns. How can it miss? You'll grab a seat in one of the back-to-back high-powered swings equipped with its own personal water cannon. Want to go higher? Faster? Keep firing that cannon to keep the water pressure rising. Wet 'n' Wild's biggest entry into the thrill-slide wars is **Der Stuka,** a six-story speed chute that plunges you 250 feet, then coasts you to a (hopefully) gentle stop along 115 more feet of level, watery "runway." The **Black Hole** is a wet version of Disney's Space Mountain; you ride a two-person raft through a pitch-black corkscrew, propelled by a 1,000-gallon-a-minute blast of water. Other rides include the **Surge,** a five-person tube ride that careens along twisted, banked curves, and the **Bubba Tub,** a triple-humped flume that you ride in family-size tubes. And, of course, there's the ever-popular vertical free-fall slide, **Bomb Bay,** which hurtles you through the air in a capsule before splashdown. Perhaps one of the strangest attractions ever conceived (for a water park or otherwise) is **Disco H_2O,** where you ride a raft into a waterlogged 1970s disco (after passing a bouncer, even). You float around to the music and dance floor FX before getting flushed out the door at the other end. Other good features about Wet 'n' Wild: It's open late on summer weekends, making it a great place to hang on sultry Orlando nights; live music is offered at night; and if you arrive after 5pm, prices are slashed 50%. By day, prices are comparable to Disney's, but unlike the Disney parks, Wet 'n' Wild runs discount coupons in several visitor magazines.

If the idea of bodysurfing in a wave pool attracts you, hotfoot it over to Disney's **Typhoon Lagoon** (Tel 407/824-4321). The scene is pure Disney: It's the aftermath of a typhoon. A shipwrecked boat teeters on a mountaintop, and, just below, a surf machine generates knock-your-suit-off tidal waves about every 90 seconds in the world's largest wave pool. You hear the roar of the wave approaching; everyone squeals; then, a 6-foot wall of water, shaped like a perfectly crested wave, sends you flying forward or diving for cover. This is rip-roaring good fun, if you can avoid landing in a pileup of bathers. At **Shark Reef,** you can suit up frogman-style and snorkel across a pool with tropical fish, stingrays, and (somehow non-life-threatening) hammerhead sharks. This can be adventurous but a bit rush-rush; avoid it if it's super-crowded or you'll spend forever waiting in line, compared to a very short time actually in the

Super Soakers: Wet 'n' Wild vs. Disney

*Which is the best water park—**Wet 'n' Wild,** or Disney's twins, **Blizzard Beach** and **Typhoon Lagoon?** Admission prices are similar at all three parks. If you're a water-slide purist, though, there's really no contest. The slides at Wet 'n' Wild are wilder, higher, weirder, and more numerous. Just the drop through the enclosed corkscrew plumbing inside the **Black Hole** slide is worth the price of admission. On the other hand, Wet 'n' Wild has zero theme; beyond the fun of the sun and the water, the park is a completely charmless expanse of concrete and palm saplings. What the Disney parks may lack in pizzazz, they make up for in looks. Typhoon Lagoon is a jumbled tropical cove, while Blizzard Beach is a Floridian paradise that fictitiously (and unsuccessfully) attempted to become a ski resort by way of improbable winter weather. The Disney parks also have more shade as part of their overall more salubrious designs, and this can be critical in summer. However, Wet 'n' Wild has one ace up its sleeve: It stays open until 11pm in high season, while the Disney parks close around 5pm. For that reason alone, Typhoon Lagoon and Blizzard Beach are best enjoyed as a half day in the morning or afternoon, before or after a similar half day in the theme parks (or maybe before or after a half-day nap). If you do go the Disney water-park way, be advised that Blizzard Beach caters more to thrill slides and flash, while Typhoon Lagoon is a bit more sedate and laid-back.*

water. Then there's **Castaway Creek,** one of those meandering tube rides. The Disneyized version of this takes you through a grotto and a rainforest. This can be heaven on a hot day, but it, too, is nightmarish when crowded, unless you like the idea of being jammed against concrete riverbanks. The ride can also be ruined by aggressive types who mistake it for a bumper-boat attraction. **Humonga Kowabunga**'s three 214-foot water slides provide 30-mph fun, but the real thrills come when women opt for fashion over sense and two-piece bathing suits become one on the way down (there are even bleachers for those looking for the occasional peep show, though Disney claims they're there for parents to watch their kids). The new **Crush 'N' Gusher** calls itself a "water roller coaster," using water jets to blast one or two people in long tubes through a wrecked fruit-processing plant. You can choose which slide you'll attempt, with variations in twists, drops, curves, and plunges.

Disney's **Blizzard Beach** (Tel 407/824-4321) wins points for creativity. As the story goes, a freak snowstorm dumped powdery white stuff on Disney World (and the park's mascot, Ice Gator). Ski-resort operators quickly moved in to create Florida's first ski resort on the mountain of snow. But, alas, temperatures quickly climbed to normal levels, leaving behind slush, bobsled rides, and slalom courses—and the makings of a wild and woolly water park. A landscape of dripping icicles and patches of snow (you'll touch them to make sure they're not real), melting ice caves (complete with freezing water), a ski lodge, even a working chair lift, carry the theme to its limits. Tops with teens and daring adults is the **Summit Plummet** slide, the world's fastest and a serious test of your bravado. You take the chairlift to the "ski jump" on top of Mount Gushmore, then free-fall 120 feet (at 65 mph) into a pool at the bottom. Then you wait in line another hour or so and do it again. One adrenaline junkie describes the experience as "15 seconds of paralyzing fear." The usual water-park mix of inner-tube rides, rafts, and wave pools is also offered. This place gets crowded and often closes due to capacity limits shortly after the doors open. Get here early.

Birdies and bogeys... There are as many golf packages as there are ways to get a hamburger in this town; golf-and-room packages abound, and many resorts offer free transportation and preferred access to otherwise private courses.

While the rest of your group is meeting the Terminator, you can try to straighten out that slice at the **Arnold Palmer Golf Academy,** 9000 Bay Hill Blvd. (Tel 407/876-5362 or 800/523-5999). Golfers from all over the country come to the academy, located at the Arnold Palmer's Bay Hill Club and Lodge (see the Accommodations chapter). Check into one of the lodge rooms or suites (about $224–$324 a night) and you'll have a 27-hole championship course right outside your door.

A number of top area courses welcome nonmembers, which is good news for all Orlando-bound golfers. The top-notch **Mission Inn Golf and Tennis Resort,** 10400 County Rd. 48, Howey-in-the-Hills (Tel 800/874-9053; www.missioninnresort.com), about 35 minutes northwest of Orlando, offers two championship courses and attracts a loyal following of return players. El Campeón (The Champion), designed in 1926 by C. E. Clarke of Troon, Scotland, is consistently voted one of Florida's top 25 courses by *Golfweek* magazine. Rolling hills, towering pines, and tee boxes that put you up to 85 feet in elevation will make you think you've been transported to Scotland. Rates include a cart and run about $90 to $150; the public is welcome. Some duffers fork out the big bucks for a room at the **Hyatt Regency Grand Cypress,** 1 Grand Cypress Blvd. (Tel 407/239-1234; see the Accommodations chapter), just to get onto its golf course. What's not to like? Here you'll find 45 holes of Jack Nicklaus–designed golf, a 9-hole pitch-and-putt course, and a staff willing to please. Greens fees run about $180. Six lakes weave through wide fairways lined by ancient oaks and cypress trees at the **Grande Pines Golf Club,** 6351 International Dr. (Tel 407/239-6909; www.grandpinesgolfclub.com). Friendly greens with state-of-the-art yardage systems and soft bunkers keep frustration levels here to a minimum. Nonmember tee-time policy varies; call ahead for details. Greens fees run about $64 to $134. It's the greens themselves that'll keep bringing you back to the **Eastwood Golf Club,** 13950 Golf Blvd. (Tel 407/281-4653; www.eastwoodgolf.com), an 18-hole championship layout by Lloyd Clifton that's widely known in the area as having the best Bermuda greens in Central Florida. Tee times are available 7 days in advance. Greens fees are $44 to $99.

A number of top courses are located in Kissimmee. The course at **Kissimmee Bay Country Club,** 2801 Kissimmee Bay Blvd. (Tel 407/348-4653; www.kissimmeebaycc.com), designed by architect Lloyd Clifton around century-old oak trees and lush foliage, has been nominated by *Golf Digest* as one of America's best new courses. Tee times for nonmembers must be reserved 7 days in advance; greens fees are $50 to $79. **Orange Lake Country Club Resort,** 8505 Irlo Bronson Hwy. (Tel 407/239-1050; www.golforangelake.com), boasts an 18-hole Arnold Palmer–designed course divided into The Links (the Scottish-style front 9) and The Pines (the picturesque back 9). Tee-time reservations can be made 24 or 48 hours in advance; the general public pays $25 to $139 in season, but resort guests get a price break. Ask about their afternoon specials; they run around $25 to $45, including cart and greens fees. **Kissimmee Oaks Golf Club,** 1500 Oaks Blvd. (Tel 407/933-4055; www.kissimmeeoaksgolf.com), remains a standout for beauty and challenge. They don't call it "The Oaks" for nothing: You'll walk through great stands of the mighty trees, trying to stay on course. Greens fees are around $50 to $79.

Disney for duffers... If you're not incredibly sick of cartoon cuteness by the time you hit the golf course, you surely will be when you round the sixth hole at the **Magnolia Golf Course** and find a sand trap shaped like Mickey. (I suggest investing in an overpriced set of balls with the big mouse's face printed on them, then whacking the crap out of them. It's a great stress reliever.) Given the long yardages on this championship course, you might be feeling pretty stressed pretty soon. Disney has five PGA courses in all, plus a 9-hole practice course. These courses are popular with both resort guests and day visitors. Greens fees run from about $120 to $145 for resort guests (nonguests pay about $10 more), but you'll get a big break—more than a 50% discount—if you play late in the afternoon, generally after 3pm. Disney resort guests get preferred tee times and, often, free transportation from the resort to the course. Tee times at all of Disney's golf courses can be booked by calling Tel 407/WDW-GOLF (939-4653).

The **Osprey Ridge** course, located at the Bonnet Creek Golf Club, is the toughest and most interesting corner of Disney linkdom. Lots of work and dollars went into turning swampland into this very manicured rolling terrain, now dotted with lakes and streams. Disney guilt (after its major alteration of the natural order of things) must have prompted the placement of nesting platforms for local ospreys throughout the course, hence the name. Greens fees run $145. The **Eagle Pines** course, also at Bonnet Creek, is lined with pine needles and sand, giving it a beachlike look. It offers less of a challenge than most other Disney courses (greens fees run around $150).

The **Palm** (greens fees $119) and **Magnolia** (greens fees $129) golf courses, both at the Shades of Green resort, are great examples of what can be done with landscaping when money is no object. They're best for duffers who prefer long, narrow, and tight challenges. The 9-hole **Oak Trail** course, located across from the Polynesian Resort, features a combination of par-5s, par-3s, and par-4s. It's an inexpensive (about $20–$38 per round) walking course, mainly used by duffers to brush up on their games. I'd stay away from the **Lake Buena Vista Golf Course.** This short, uninteresting course near Downtown Disney attracts tons of tourists and weekend hackers, but it's barely worth the moderate-to-high price tag of $99. Finally, what town would be perfect without its own golf course? Celebration, Disney's eerie attempt at the perfect planned community, boasts the **Celebration Golf Club,** 701 Golf Park Dr. (Tel 888/275-2918; www.celebrationgolf.com), an 18-hole course designed by Robert Trent Jones, Sr. Greens fees cost $95.

Cruisin' Disney... Fun, fun, fun; will it ever end? Stop by **Sammy Duvall's Water Sports Centre** (Tel 407/939-0754), located at **Disney's Contemporary Resort Marina,** to select your on-the-water pleasure...wake boarding, parasailing, skiing, knee boarding, inner-tubing, and more. As the name implies, this is watersports central. Several Disney resorts also rent watercraft, including Fort Wilderness, Polynesian, Grand Floridian, Wilderness Lodge, Yacht and Beach Club, and the Swan and Dolphin hotels; the marinas at Port Orleans, Old Key West, and Disney Village Marketplace offer them as well. Rentals are available to nonresort guests, too. Unfortunately, you'll share the waters with zillions of others, including jet-skiers and Disney shuttle launches. Not a real nature lover's getaway. Rentals out of the Fort Wilderness Campground ($6.50 an hour for a paddleboat or canoe) offer the best opportunity for solitude and peace. Of course, never underestimate the power of the fountains located at the Downtown Disney Marketplace. I'm sure parents are thrilled to spend all of their money to bring the family to Walt Disney World only to have the kids spend hours running through these fountains for free.

Away from it all... Slow the internal clock down with an excursion to nearby Winter Park, about 5 miles north of Orlando. This affluent and historic area in Central Florida is laced with lakes and waterways, ancient trees, and elegant homes and gardens. The best way to see the scenery is to take a **Winter Park Boat Tour,** 312 E. Morse Blvd., Winter Park (Tel 407/644-4056; www.scenicboattours.com), a relaxing pontoon-boat ride that's been a tradition in Winter Park for more than 50 years. The 1-hour narrated cruise ($10 adults, $5 kids 2–11) takes you through a chain of lakes and canals lined with giant cypress trees and ancient oaks dripping with Spanish moss. The narrated tour passes Rollins College, Kraft Azalea Gardens, and historic mansions. Or venture out to Clermont, a mere half-hour north of Disney, to the **Lakeridge Winery,** 19239 U.S. 27 North (Tel 800/768-WINE; www.lakeridge winery.com). Take a free tour of the vineyards, and then sample several of the wines made by the winery. Visit in August for the annual grape-stomping festival.

Hook, line, and sinker... Some of the best fishing in the state can be had in the lakes and streams surrounding the greater Orlando area. Bass fishing is big here, and you'll find lots of guide services to show you where to cast your line—for about $200 to $300 a day (usually for a party of two). **Pro Bass Guide Service,** 398 Grove Court, Winter Garden (Tel 407/877-9676 or 800/771-9676) is so sure of their angling expertise that they have a "no bass, no pay" policy on their all-day trips, guaranteeing you'll hook 'em. Capt. Paul Solomon operates out of nearby Winter Garden and runs a big, nasty bass boat on the Butler Chain of Lakes.

If these catch-'em-and-eat-'em outfits offend your sensibilities, check out the more politically correct **Bass Challenger Guide Service,** P.O. Box 679155 (Tel 407/273-8045 or 800/241-5314; www.basschallenger.com) in Orlando. "Catch a Memory" is its very sweet slogan; they practice CPR—catch, photograph, and release. Veteran guide Eddie Bussard caters to everyone from first-timers to experienced casters to those with disabilities. Excursions supply drinks, ice, and the ultimate in Florida necessities: polarized sunglasses and sunscreen!

For a real backwoods excursion, try **Backcountry Charter Service,** 31 Cunningham Rd., DeBary (Tel 407/668-5516 or 800/932-7335; www.floridabackcountry.com). You'll travel about 1½ hours to the world-famous (at least among anglers) Indian River Lagoon, near the Kennedy Space Center, where you'll go after inshore saltwater game fish. Watch as manatees, dolphins, and stingrays circle the boat. If you prefer big-game fishing, connect with **Atlantic White Water Sport Fishing,** P.O. Box 2145, Melbourne (Tel 321/783-0268; www.whitewater2.com). Capt. Mike Kane will take you out for some serious deep-sea sport fishing off the shores near the Kennedy Space Center.

Disney dunks... The heaviest largemouth bass caught and recorded at WDW was 14 pounds, 6 ounces. Don't count on landing one that size, but the odds of snagging one weighing, say, 6 or 7 pounds are pretty good. Seems that back in the '60s, the Disney folks stocked **Bay Lake** with 70,000 bass. Bay Lake, by the way, is the largest lake in the World (Disney World, that is). This is where you're likely to head if you sign up for one of Disney's 2-hour guided excursions. No fishing license is needed to fish Disney waters, by the way. The bass excursions cost between $200 and $230 for a party of up to five people, and the price includes refreshments, gear, guide, and tax. Note that the program is strictly catch-and-release. To make the mandatory reservations for these excursions or for more information, call Tel 407/939-7529 up to 2 weeks in advance. For a less rigid (and expensive) jaunt, most of Disney's resorts (notably Fort Wilderness and Port Orleans) offer catch-and-release pole fishing in their "rivers" and "lakes." Pole rentals will run you about $4 per half-hour, or $14 a day.

Flying on water... If you've just gotta get out on the water and feel the wind in your hair, then hop on an airboat. Zipping through swamps at roller-coaster speeds is a uniquely Floridian experience. You'll get the speed you crave and a nice look at Florida's natural side at **Boggy Creek Airboat Rides,** 3702 Big Bass Rd. (Tel 407/344-9550; www.bcairboats.com), in Kissimmee. Their 30-minute tours offer a scenic view of East Lake Toho as you travel to five different wetland areas. The leisurely idle down a natural creek ends in a high-speed (50 mph) race across the swampy lake ($20 adults, $16 for kids 3–12; 1-hr. night tours run $25–$30).

Tennis, anyone?... Orlando has more than 800 tennis courts for visitors. You'll find courts in most of the larger hotels and resorts; many of them will rent equipment, arrange lessons, or even set up matches for you. If you're looking to improve your game, courts are available to visitors at the pretty **Mission Inn Golf and Tennis Resort** (see "Birdies and bogeys," earlier in this chapter), about 35 minutes northwest of Orlando. Play a few games, and then drink in the views of rolling countryside and lush grounds. The **Grand Cypress Racquet Club** at the Hyatt Regency Grand Cypress (see the Accommodations chapter) in Orlando is a full-service facility that draws some names to its courts. You'll get state-of-the-art lessons, video analysis, hard-court play, and lots of court-time instruction.

Disney courts... Disney answers with 26 courts in its World, including a 10-court tennis center at the **Disney Wide World of Sports** complex. Day visitors are welcome at the **Racquet Club at the Contemporary** resort (six clay courts lit for night play), and **Fort Wilderness Campground** (no reservations are taken, but the court time is free). Court time at the Contemporary costs about $18 an hour (for both day visitors and Disney resort guests). Private lessons are offered for $75 an hour at the Contemporary. At Disney's **Old Key West, Yacht Club, BoardWalk Inn,** and **Grand Floridian** resorts, complimentary courts are available only to resort guests. For more information or to reserve a court (reservations cost $10), call Tel 407/939-7529.

Skimming the surface... Feel like a little water-skiing? **Sammy Duvall Watersports Centre** at Disney's Contemporary Resort (Tel 407/939-0754; www.sammyduvall.com) arranges water-skiing trips on Bay Lake for $140 per hour (including boats, drivers, equipment, and instruction). Make the mandatory reservations up to 14 days in advance (the sooner the better). (For those bucks, you better be a fast learner. Or take some friends—the fee covers up to five people per boat.)

Mini-golf... Take a quick drive down International Drive in Orlando or U.S. 192 in Kissimmee and you'd swear that putt-putt golf is the official sport of Orlando. There are adventure/mini-golf courses around every corner, and all of them seem to be full of rambunctious kids swinging for the hole-in-one prizes. If this is your kind of fun, you'll be delirious with pleasure. Take your pick. Naturally, Disney jumped on this bandwagon in a large way, with two centers: **Fantasia Gardens Miniature Golf** (Tel 407/560-4870), located off Buena Vista Drive across from Disney–MGM Studios, offers two 18-hole miniature courses drawing inspiration from the Walt Disney classic cartoon of the same name. You'll find hippos, ostriches, and alligators on the **Fantasia Gardens** course, where the Sorcerer's Apprentice presides over the final hole. It's a good bet for beginners. Seasoned mini-golfers probably will prefer **Fantasia**

Fairways, which is a scaled-down golf course complete with sand traps, water hazards, tricky putting greens, and holes ranging from 40 to 75 feet. Disney's **Winter Summerland** (Tel 407/560-3000) mini-golf complex has two themed courses—one is fun in the sun, the other a winter wonderland. Santa and his elves play at both. Of course, Disney does mini-golf bigger and better than local entrepreneurs, but it'll mean waiting in line and paying more, too. Putting in Mickeyville costs $11, while Orlando/Kissimmee mini-golf usually runs about $8. Because you'll likely get plenty tired of cartoon characters seen in every imaginable shape, form, and texture, why pay more? You'll have just as much fun at **Pirate's Cove Adventure Golf,** with locations at 8601 International Dr. (Tel 407/352-7378; www.piratescove.net) and in the Crossroads Shopping Center just outside of Disney (Tel 407/827-1242). Both feature all the windmills, waterfalls, mazes, and traps that make mini-golf a hoot. Toss in soft-serve cones and rock 'n' roll, and you've got a sure winner for a mere $8.50 a round ($13 if you play two).

Who wants to be an animal trainer?... If your final answer is "me," sign up for one of **SeaWorld's animal interaction programs.** If you're ready to get up close and personal with the animals and don't mind devoting a day to it (and a hefty amount of cash), consider the **Marine Mammal Keeper Experience.** Included in the $399 fee is a 7-day admission pass to SeaWorld, lunch, souvenir book, and T-shirt. Because the program is an up-close, intimate experience, only three people at a time can play trainer each day. Participants must be in good physical condition, at least 13, and a minimum of 52 inches tall. Call Tel 800/327-2424 for information and reservations, or check out the details on www.seaworld.com.

Always feel like you're swimming with the sharks? Well, now you can do it for real. One of SeaWorld's other cool hands-on programs, **Sharks Deep Dive,** lets you swim with the toothy denizens of the deep. Sort of. Two at a time, guests don wet suits for a 30-minute encounter inside a cage that rides a 125-foot track. Part of the cage is above water, but participants can dive up to 8 feet underwater for a close-up look at the denizens. Okay. So you're in a cage because the residents may think you're lunch, but it's the thought that counts. Right? The cost is $150 per person (minimum age 10). The price includes a souvenir booklet, T-shirt, and photo, but does not include the required park admission fee (you didn't expect a measly $150 would get you in, did you?).

Wet, wild, and wonderful... You've already had breakfast with Mickey and lunch with Pooh—so how about a day swimming with Flipper? Okay, the critter isn't really Flipper (who lives in Miami), but it *is* the real thing. At **Discovery Cove** (Tel 877/434-7268; www.discoverycove.com), located adjacent to SeaWorld, you'll spend the day swimming with dolphins, snorkeling with manta rays, and floating among tropical fish and sea animals. This beachy oasis features acres of sugar-white sand, thatched-roof huts, cabanas, robin's-egg-blue lagoons, and winding rivers. Coached by professional animal trainers, guests can swim and play with dolphins in three lagoons. How about a high-speed dorsal-fin ride? Adventurous snorkelers can also swim among rays, some up to 4 feet in diameter (take care to avoid those tails!), and go nose-to-nose with sharks and barracudas (safely separated by clear underwater partitions). There are coral reefs and underwater ruins to explore, or you can swim under a waterfall into a tropical aviary. Admission to Discovery Cove is limited (they let in only 1,000 guests per day—peanuts compared to the other parks), so you won't be fighting crowds or spending much time waiting for the fun to begin. The cost is $249 to $279 plus tax for the day, and includes all gear, a personal guide, the dolphin swim encounter, a 14-day pass to SeaWorld, and lunch. Subtract $100 to go without the dolphin swim. Reservations are mandatory and should be made as far in advance as humanly possible. The high price tag hasn't deterred the masses from swimming with the fishes here. Call Tel 877/434-7268 for information and reservations.

Under the seas... Granted, Central Florida is not a diving mecca, but if you want to get under the water and swim with the fish, you can do it here. It's no surprise that the most talked-about dive is one manufactured by Disney. Daily scuba dives are available in the 6-million-gallon aquarium at **The Living Seas Pavilion** at Epcot. Each day at 4:30 and 5:30pm, all certified divers (with proof) can take the Disney plunge. The program includes an orientation to The Living

Seas, a 40-minute dive, and (what else?) a T-shirt. All this for about $140. Reservations are required; call Tel 407/939-8687. I say, save the cash and do Discovery Cove (see "Wet, wild, and wonderful," above) instead if you want to dive.

Back in the saddle again... No one would ever mistake Florida for the Wild West, no matter how often residents here remind you that this was once cowboy country. That was a long time ago; today, the grasslands are gone and the cows are on the dinner plates, but horseback riding is still here. At the world-class **Grand Cypress Equestrian Center,** 1 Equestrian Dr. (Tel 407/239-1938 or 800/835-7377; www.grandcypress.com) in Orlando, three different guided riding tours are offered, depending on your abilities. Beginners can hop in the saddle for a walking tour; intermediates can walk and trot; and experienced English saddle riders can canter on the trails surrounding the Grand Cypress Golf Course. Trips run about $45 to $85 and last 45 minutes; maximum weight is 220 pounds. The **Fort Wilderness Resort & Campground** (Tel 407/939-7529) offers beginner trail riding. You can take a 45-minute guided tour (a slow-paced, often hot and buggy, walk) through woods and along waterways. Maximum rider weight is 250 pounds; rides cost about $32. At **Horse World Riding Stables,** 3705 S. Poinciana Blvd. (Tel 407/847-4343; www.horseworldstables.com) in Kissimmee, you can ride on 750 acres of wooded trails. Guided nature and private trail rides are available. It costs about $39 to $69 per person, depending on the trail option you choose.

In the air... I understand the appeal of hovering aloft over Vermont's fall foliage, or the Grand Canyon, but over Race Rock restaurant and Wet 'n' Wild ? Somehow, Orlando's pancake-flat topography doesn't seem dramatic enough to warrant a flyover. If you want to see Orlando's attractions from on high, you could simply go up to the 27th-floor bar at the Buena Vista Palace hotel and have a drink. Or ask for a window seat on the plane flight home. But then again, a hot-air-balloon flight over the distinctly Orlando skyscape (read: neon globes, futuristic balls, towers of terror, and castles...) may be an experience you won't soon forget. If so, you can sign up for one with **Orange Blossom Balloons** in

Lake Buena Vista (Tel 407/239-7677; www.orangeblossomballoons.com) and go soaring through the air for $175 per person. Want a little more thrill to your air ride? Take the controls of a World War II Warbird airplane at **Warbird Adventures, Inc.** They give you a short instruction, take you up with a pilot, and then let you control the plane for a few minutes (Tel 407/870-7366 or 800/386-1593; www.warbirdadventures.com). The adventures last 15 to 60 minutes and range in price from $130 to $580.

A walk in the park... You've had it, right? Too much noise, too much concrete, too much whizbang. What you need is a nice, quiet stroll. The Orlando area has a number of pockets of green peace where you can slow down and smell the flowers. Venture downtown to pretty **Lake Eola Park,** a tiny oasis in the center of Orlando, and walk around the flower-lined brick paths that circle the lake. If you're feeling romantic, rent one of the whimsical swan boats and paddle around the lake. Or try **Big Tree Park** (Tel 407/788-0405) in Altamonte Springs, home to one of the oldest and largest trees in America. The 3,500-year-old, 138-foot bald cypress tree is named "The Senator" after Senator H. G. Overstreet, who donated the tree and land to Seminole County. Who says there's no history in Orlando? **Blue Springs State Park,** located in Orange City (Tel 386/775-3663), has a warm-water spring where you can see wintering manatees.

Turkey Lake Park (Tel 407/299-5594), off I Drive in Orlando, is a popular daytime picnic area. You'll find biking and hiking trails, a swimming pool, a wooden fishing pier, canoe rentals, and a petting zoo on its 300 acres. Not exactly wilderness, but a nice getaway. Another good spot to go on a very hot day is **Wekiwa Springs State Park** (Tel 407/884-2009). The river spouts a cool spring, the closest thing Central Florida has to a Vermont swimming hole. There are lots of recreational activities, including canoeing, boating, camping, fishing, hiking, and tubing.

Walks around the World... As if you'll need to do any more walking than the gazillion miles you'll put in at the theme parks.... But say you've opted to stay out of the parks for the day and need a little exercise, you could always stroll the 1.5-mile walk around the lake at **Disney's Caribbean**

Beach Resort. Disney's Port Orleans Resort also has a number of walkways and promenades spread throughout the resort. Disney's **Fort Wilderness Resort & Campground** offers a relatively peaceful oasis in the World; more than 700 acres of cypress and pine woods surround the resort, with lots of biking and walking paths. There's no charge for day guests. Bike rentals are available as well, or take out a canoe and explore the maze of waterways. There's also a 2.25-mile fitness course with exercise stations. For information on all of these resorts, see the Accommodations chapter.

Garden strolls... Sunshine every day and subtropical weather make this region prime growing territory for lush gardens and magnificent flowers. It's hard to top the flower displays at **Epcot.** If you're a garden lover, you can spend days roaming the grounds, strolling the paths, and, well, smelling the flowers—some three million plants and annuals, and 10,000 roses. Green-thumbers might consider the special behind-the-scenes **Gardens of the World** tour (sign up at The Land pavilion at Epcot; see the Diversions chapter). This 3-hour walking tour focuses on the special effects and design concepts of several World Showcase gardens. You've got to really be into plants to enjoy this tour, though; most people will consider it a big yawn. If you time your visit for the month of May, you can catch **Epcot's International Flower & Garden Festival,** a celebration of horticulture featuring millions of blossoms, topiary designs, demonstrations, workshops, guest speakers, guided tours, how-to sessions, and world-class horticulture displays.

In Orlando, the **Harry P. Leu Gardens,** 1920 N. Forest Ave. (Tel 407/246-2620; www.leugardens.org) boasts the largest camellia collection and formal rose garden in the South. Guided tours of the 50-acre property and restored-house museum are offered, and admission's just $5. It's a beauty, but most visitors have enough trouble finding time to see the major theme-park attractions, so only truly devoted flower people should pencil it in on their schedules.

SHOP

PING

5

Basic Stuff

Star-struck? Mouse-obsessed? Bargain-mad? Orlando is the place to buy things like the Rasta cap with attached dreadlocks and the original framed Disney animation cels. Orlando may not be a shopping mecca on the scale of, say, Milan or Paris, but when it comes to kitsch, it has no peers.

Need it be said that this isn't the place to stock up on Harris tweeds and snappy skirted suits? While you can certainly purchase designer names at Orlando's outlet malls, and even at Disney character stores (Nicole Miller lends her cachet to Mickey tote bags, for example), the real finds are those things you'd never buy at home: the *Pulp Fiction* poster signed by John Travolta, Quentin Tarantino, and Samuel L. Jackson ($695 at Sid Cahuenga's One-of-a-Kind); a baseball bat autographed by 19 members of the 1927 Yankees (a mere $65,000 at Starabilias); the floor lamp shaded with a froth of lime-green hair ($140 at Hoypoloi); or the handblown-glass replica of Cinderella Castle (yours for the princely sum of $25,000 at the Magic Kingdom's Crystal Arts shop). The area can lay claim to eight shopping malls, six outlet centers, two giant flea markets, and a shop at the end of each ride (sung to the tune of "The Twelve Days of Christmas"). With a lineup like this, is it any wonder that Orlando reigns as the fastest-growing retail market in the country? Now is the time to snag those delicious little glow-in-the-dark bikini panties ($9 at Spencer's) and that cunning aviator cap ($26 at the Rocky & Bullwinkle Shop, Islands of Adventure). On a budget? You can have a grand time sleuthing out tacky-terrific trinkets, whether you go uptown (the Disney shops) or downtown (Flea World, billed as "America's largest flea market under one roof").

As if all this wasn't enough, three shopping centers bulk up the mix even more. Right across from Belz (a complex of outlet stores) is **Festival Bay,** a 1.1-million-square-foot shopping/dining/entertainment complex. Also new on the block is **Orlando Premium Outlets,** off exit 27 near SeaWorld, which promises savings of 25% to 65% on such high-profile names as Louis Feráud, Kenneth Cole, Oilily, Tod's, and Versace. Catering to the high end is the **Mall at Millenia,** on I-4 at Conroy Road, featuring Tiffany, Gucci, and Bloomies, among 200 or so upscale stores and restaurants. Vacationers, pray for a rainy day.

And you thought you'd be stuck with another "Honk if you love Florida" T-shirt.

What to Buy

Well, that should be obvious: souvenirs, and plenty of 'em. Orlando is more than happy to oblige. Within Walt Disney World itself, you'll find more souvenir shops than I can name (though I've made a valiant effort in the Index). While the lowly T-shirt is by far the biggest seller of all Disney-character merchandise, you could, in fact, create a whole wardrobe around Mickey, starting with Mickey-face silk briefs or cotton bikinis and the ever-wholesome Mickey bra; and topped with a Mickey sundress, shorts, sweater, shirt, vest, tie, blazer, socks, a cap, and fanny pack or tote bag. But why stop there? Why, you could outfit your entire home in Mickey lamps, wallpaper borders, glassware, sculpture, and designer leather furniture. If Martha Stewart can do it, why not Mickey? And for that Mickey Mouse operation you call a business, how about a Mickey mousepad, desk blotter, and datebook? You could get this carried away; I wouldn't. But if you want a little something Disney as a memento of your trip—something a bit more sentimental than a Visa bill—you won't have a lick of trouble finding it at any of the Disney theme parks, not to mention every hotel gift shop, convenience store, and gas station.

For those with a taste for tack, Orlando is Shangri-la reincarnated. The stores lining U.S. 192 on the way into town feature some of the cheesiest mementos ever made: iridescent sand-sculpture alligators, varnished cedar clocks, souvenirs made from shells, Florida snow globes (useful, as it never snows here). Best of all, every store carries pretty much the same tacky

Rumor Mill: Pin Trading

Not since Disney offered guests the privilege of paying $35 for a 1-inch-square photo tile on Epcot's "Leave a Legacy" sculpture has the House of Mouse come up with as profitable a boondoggle as this. Pin trading is just what it sounds like—you typically pay $15 for an official Disney metal pin, featuring some Disney character, scene, event, symbol, or whatever. (You can pay up to $100 for special pin sets, if you really must.) Then you waltz around the theme parks trading pins with Disney cast members or other pin fanatics. Be advised that there's an official etiquette regarding how such pin trades are conducted—check www.officialdisneypintrading.com for details. We're not sure what happens to etiquette violators, but we're guessing such incidents come with one of those "I'm not angry, just disappointed" lectures. At the end of the day, Disney has everyone's money, which you'll forgive us for describing as "pinevitable" anyway.

merchandise, so there's no need to shop around. If you're looking to outfit a shrine to bad taste, go for it.

Target Zones

Personally, I wouldn't waste my time ducking into the shops at the theme parks when there's so much else to do (and I've paid so dearly to do it). But some of the shops are so cute it's tough to resist them. Hard-core shoppers may want to troll Main Street at the **Magic Kingdom,** a villagey strip where you can buy all things Disney. Elsewhere in the Magic Kingdom, shops tie in with their surrounding areas: nautical and pirate gear at Adventureland, Americana at Liberty Square, country-and-western crafts at Frontierland, and so on. **Epcot** has nearly 70 shops; the most interesting are among the re-created foreign villages at World Showcase, where you can find unusual souvenirs and playthings such as sheepskin drums from Morocco, wild-animal masks fashioned from wood, and pots of assorted silver beads, waiting to be selected and strung for a one-of-a-kind keepsake. (Other than the huge **Mouse Gears,** skip the shops at Future World.) **Disney's Animal Kingdom** is the place to outfit your kids in a safari motif. Dress 'em up as the hunter (safari vests and pith helmets) or the hunted (leopard-print shirts and shorts sets) at **Wonders of the Wild,** in Safari Village. Check out **Mombasa Marketplace/Ziwani Traders** for authentic African gifts. This shop stocks cool drums, wooden animal sets, Nigerian straw baskets (great for carrying your other souvenirs), and my most fabulous find: carved wooden salad tongs with a zebra motif ($8). The shops scattered around at **Disney–MGM Studios** carry the typical character merchandise, but also some fun stuff for movie buffs. Check out **Sid Cahuenga's One-of-a-Kind** for vintage movie posters, celebrity-autographed black-and-white publicity stills, and movie props. At **Universal Studios Florida** and **Islands of Adventure,** the shops fit so seamlessly into the motifs that you might miss them. Be assured, though, there's themed shopping available outside every attraction. Look for that "Pet Tornado" kit at **Aftermath** (the Twister store) and those *Terminator 2*–style wraparound shades at **Cyber Image** (the shop outside T2 3-D), and so on.

Downtown Disney is a restaurant-and-retail complex apart from the theme parks, near the main entrance to Walt Disney World. Connected via footbridge, Downtown Disney West Side, Downtown Disney Marketplace, and Pleasure Island are home to several shops, including the Largest Disney

Shop on Earth!—**World of Disney.** It's a bit like Bloomies, but if you look closely, you'll realize that everything is Mickeyfied, from evening bags to undies. Sounds positively Goofy, but some of this stuff is awesome, if you can get past the fact that it celebrates a rodent. Would you believe a bejeweled evening bag featuring Mickey's likeness in Austrian crystals? It's fabulous! Baby boomers who refuse to grow up will adore **Once Upon a Time,** a 16,000-square-foot extravaganza of interactive toys and games. Fun stuff includes new playthings developed by Disney and Hasbro that you won't find anywhere else—like retro favorites, Lincoln Logs, and Tinkertoys—yup, they've even given Mr. Potato Head some Mickey Mouse ears. Two other standout shops here are the **LEGO Imagination Center** and **Starabilias.** You can have a grand time at the LEGO store without actually setting foot inside the place; outside are 75 incredible LEGO creations and LEGO play stations for small fry. (Nobody frisks the little tykes when they leave, but it's considered good form to leave the LEGO pieces behind when you depart.) Check out the LEGO sea monster in Lake Buena Vista (the birds in the water are LEGO-ed, not feathered, as well), the snoring grand pop, and best of all, the tourists who peer back at you with little LEGO eyes. Starabilias is the place to go for Coca-Cola collectibles (the big seller here; we don't get it, either), vintage license plates, and an autographed photo of Nirvana, signed by the late Kurt Cobain. Hours are generally 9:30am to 11pm. A short stroll away is **Pleasure Island,** the nightclub/entertainment complex that is Disney's foray into cooldom. Pleasure Island aims for "hip" with a few shops that try to be trendy but don't quite make it. You can't shop Pleasure Island's stores until 7pm, and because that's when the clubs open, you pay a cover charge. **Crossroads at Lake Buena Vista** benefits from a great location—this strip shopping center is just a hop and a skip from the entrance to Walt Disney World Village and all the hotels at the junction of I-4 and State Road 535. Disney-maintained, this center offers one-stop shopping for vacationers, including a 24-hour supermarket with a pharmacy and 1-hour photo lab on premises. There's also a Disney character shop, in case you missed the other million opportunities. (Is there some sort of Orlando ordinance requiring a character shop every 200 ft.?) Crossroads also has a good selection of restaurants, operating at a much more relaxed pace than their theme-park counterparts.

Right across from the convention center is a glorified shopping mall called **Pointe*Orlando.** It's just a quick hop (or trolley ride) from the hotels on International Drive. Shop options here include **Spencer's,** where you can buy that must-have giggling Mona Lisa pillow; and **Florida Wild,** which features stuff made in the Sunshine State, like those dreadful glittery T-shirts, and a Florida version of that old standby, Monopoly. Then there are the usual suspects: **A/X Armani Exchange, Chico's,** and **Victoria's Secret.** You might as well tie in a visit to Muvico Cinema's IMAX 3-D theater while you're here, or pop across the street to **WonderWorks** (see the Diversions chapter), since you're already paying for parking.

The **Mercado** has a built-in clientele; it's within walking distance of the numerous hotels on International Drive. The intent here was to create a Mediterranean village atmosphere, with shops in little alleyways centered on an open-air courtyard. Despite the fact that some of the merchandise is fairly high-end (and some is very cheesy), the Mercado has kind of a low-rent feel. Maybe it's because displays tend to tumble out into the walkways, and the small shops are crammed with merchandise.

Then there are the traditional retail malls. The Orlando area has—count 'em—eight. Together, they offer—would you believe it—1,200 stores. Scary. Mall-wise, the **Florida Mall** seems like the place to go these days, thanks to A-list tenants such as Saks Fifth Avenue, Burdine's, J. Crew, Pottery Barn, Restoration Hardware, and even an Abercrombie & Fitch for kids, offering mini-versions of their must-have sportswear for label-conscious tykes. And in the "Recession? What recession?" category, there's a high-end contender, the **Mall at Millenia,** where Tiffany's and Gucci join anchor stores Bloomingdale's, Macy's, and Neiman-Marcus. (Hey, who on vacation doesn't need a $9,000 evening gown?)

Bargain Hunting

You can't consider yourself a bona fide shopaholic unless you include an outlet mall on your vacation itinerary. Orlando makes it easy; there are two outlet pods on the north end of International Drive: **Belz Factory Outlet World** and **Belz Designer Outlet Centre.** Together, the two enclosed malls and four strip centers (or annexes, as they call them) house more than 170 stores. Naturally, the good stuff is spread around: Head to Mall 1 for shoes (Bally, Bruno Magli, Stride-Rite), Mall 2 for upscale kiddie duds (Baby Guess, OshKosh B'gosh,

Umbro)—oops! I also found Birkenstock lurking there—and the various annexes for brands like Tommy Hilfiger, Timberland, Calvin Klein, and Reebok. Because you buy directly from the manufacturers, Belz lets you save up to 75% on first-quality goods—overstocks, as well as the occasional irregular pieces and odd sizes, and last year's fashions. Belz Designer Outlet Centre is skewed toward the high end, with 45 outlets offering discounts of 30% to 60% off full retail. The prices aren't rock bottom, but if you have an educated eye and can discern what this stuff is really worth (perhaps that DKNY tunic really is a steal at $149), you're likely to come away with some great deals. Names include Ann Taylor, Coach Leather Goods, Kenneth Cole, Donna Karan, Cole Haan, and Fossil. Some of the same names crop up at **Orlando Premium Outlets,** plus the added cachet of Versace, Armani, and Burberry. Look for savings of 25% to 65% off full retail. If you're big into Disney-character duds, check out **Character Warehouse**—you might find that $30 Animal Kingdom sweatshirt you've been looking for marked down to $9.99. **Lake Buena Vista Factory Stores** offer direct-from-the-manufacturer savings of up to 75% on over-run products and last season's merchandise.

But you haven't really shopped Orlando-style until you've had the Flea Market Experience. If you've cut your teeth on yard sales, tag sales, rummage sales, church bazaars, even Greek agoras and Moroccan souks, you may be ready for the ultimate shopper's challenge: finding the gems among the junk at **Flea World,** the largest open-air flea market in the country. More than 1,700 dealers sell their wares here. We've all read the stories: "Art Dealer Finds Priceless Painting"; "Housewife Pays $15 for Fabergé Egg." Of course, what you'll probably go home with is a 12-pack of tube socks or a potbellied pig, so you'd better enjoy the entertainment value of the hunt and the haggling over prices. Where else can you get tattooed and body-pierced, buy an adult video, adopt a cockatiel, and hire a lawyer, all in the same afternoon? Come to think of it, if you buy all that stuff, you'll probably need a divorce attorney.

Every other store along U.S. 192 sports big signs shrieking "Bargain!" and "Five T-shirts, $10!!" Many of the stores have the word "bargain"—or some variation thereof—right in their names. ***Beware:*** Just because a store looks like a discounter doesn't mean it has discount prices. These places carry a lot of Disney and Universal Studio apparel and souvenirs, some licensed and some not, as well as anything and everything with the word "Florida" imprinted on it. I compared prices of identical items at two of the biggie discount stores, **Bargain World** and **Smart Department Store,** and found them to be about the same. These stores also carry discounted brand-name items from Nike, Reebok, and L.A. Gear, as well as licensed sports apparel.

Hours of Business

Most stores open at 10am and close at 9 or 10pm. Some stay open longer, including Pointe*Orlando (10am–11pm), the Mercado (10am–11pm), Disney Downtown Marketplace (9:30am–11pm), and Pleasure Island (7pm–1am, but you'll pay a cover charge). Factory-outlet malls and traditional retail malls are usually open from 11am to 6pm on Sunday. Hours may be extended in high season. With stand-alone stores, it's always wise to check first, especially if you're making a bit of a trip (and with Orlando traffic, it's *always* a bit of a trip). Most are open 7 days a week.

Sales Tax

Tax rates are determined by county. Orange County has a 6.5% tax rate; Seminole County has a 7% tax rate. All prepared food is taxable.

The Lowdown

For the hard-core Disney fan... If your love of Mickey knows no bounds (including good taste) and price is no object, head to **Art of Disney** at Downtown Disney Marketplace. This is also the place to find limited-edition Disney figurines, original animation cels of Disney cartoons, and production cels of Disney cartoons and movies. The more absurdly expensive tchotchkes of past emporiums ($8,000 Mickey figurine, anyone?) have been replaced by a raft of specialists. **World of Disney** added a cluster of interactive shopping "experiences," allowing you to get pampered like a princess, search for pirate booty, and so on, as long as you're willing to fork over the cash to cap off the "experience." The **Team Mickey Athletic Club** offers jerseys, hats, and sweats with Disney characters splattered in strategically sporty locales. You might think **Mickey's Mart** represents Disney finally caving to clearinghouse fever, since everything's priced at $10 or less. But it's actually just a clever grouping of cheap souvenirs and trinkets one can find elsewhere in Disney World for the same prices. That doesn't seem to bother the crowds of bulk-purchasing customers, though. If you don't want to go to those extremes but want just a touch of Disneyana in your decor, I suggest **Disney's Days of Christmas** in the Downtown Disney Marketplace. There you can find baubles, balls for your tree celebrating such hallowed figures as Goofy and Donald Duck, and collectible Seven Dwarfs ornaments made by Christopher Radko. Then there's the all-important Santa Hat with Mouse Ears...c'mon, you know you want one.

Funky finds... If all that MM gear sends you reaching for the MMaalox, seek out a store with less mouse and more attitude. At the New Age **Hoypoloi** in Downtown Disney West Side, you'll discover floor lamps shaded with Day-Glo green or pink wigs ($140), desk lamps shaped like martinis, and a great alternative to the hotel wake-up call, the Zen Alarm Clock, which rouses you with gradually increasing chimes ($140). Cheaper, tackier, and even more fun are the goods at **Dapy,** CityWalk, where accent pieces include a giggling Mona Lisa pillow (press her belly and she titters) for $25, a life-size cardboard cutout of Austin Powers' Dr. Evil, black-light art and lava lamps, and everything Elvis. And at Pointe*Orlando, you'll find **Spencer's,** a store dedicated to all things black-light friendly and great for a dorm room.

For the Minnie wannabe... Alas, she can't actually grow up to be Minnie or Mickey ("After all, there's only one Mickey and Minnie," a WDW public relations type told me, with a perfectly straight face), but she can look the part. **World of Disney,** at Downtown Disney Marketplace, has an assortment of totally cute costumes, including Snow White, Cinderella (post-makeover), Ariel the Mermaid, Tinkerbell, Jasmine, and, of course, Minnie; each will hit you for a $59 price tag. Do the smart thing: Head over to the **Character Warehouse** at the Belz Outlet Mall (Mall 2) and you'll find many of the same Princess dresses for around $20.

You have a little Pooh on your shirt.... If you're one of the millions that would rather be sportin' some serious bear, Disney has two shops that will accommodate you. At the end of the Many Adventures of Winnie the Pooh ride in the Magic Kingdom, you'll find Pooh's Thotful Shop, a small merchandise area with T-shirts and baby items. You can also pick up plush toys and sleepwear featuring the Hundred-Acre gang at **World of Disney Kids** at Downtown Disney Marketplace.

His 'n' hers... What's with all the boudoir gear in the theme-park shops? Someone in Marketing obviously caught on to the fact that not all of us are into wispy black lace and peek-a-boo panels. Get a load of the cute-and-comfy Grumpywear pj's at **World of Disney.** And I'm a sucker for the his-and-hers matching Mickey silk underwear—for her, a silk chemise; for him, sexy boxers. If your significant other spends a bit too much time hunched over the newspaper, grab his or her attention in your snappy little Sunday Funnies printed silk pajamas ($55 on sale) or boxers ($20) at **Toon Extra,** in Islands of Adventure. S/he'll have to get *real* close to read that last panel of Hagar the Horrible.

We can't imagine what kind of twisted soul would want a *Titanic*-logoed bathrobe, but somebody must: They're available at the gift shop at **Titanic: The Experience.** Far more tasteful, I think, is Rose's heart-shaped sapphire necklace, as seen on Kate Winslet's neck in the James Cameron movie. The loveliest—and alas, priciest—version of this little trinket sells for $750 at the Titanic shop.

For the Jimmy Buffett wannabe... Maybe it's the heat, but there's something about O-Town that can turn even Brooks Brothers types into Bubbas and Bubbettes. One minute you're checking your e-mail, the next you're buying a T-shirt that reads "Life is short—drink faster!" Might as well look the part: Pick up a baseball cap that sports its own curly gray ponytail from **Dapy** at CityWalk. Cover those not-ready-for-prime-time gams—please—with a pair of longish surfer shorts from **Boardwalk Surf and Sport** (Pointe*Orlando). Never mind that the nearest ocean is hours away—we be jammin'.

Incredible edibles... Not even the scary witch dunking apples (poisoned?) into caramel will keep the kids (and kids at heart) away from **Disney's Candy Cauldron** (Downtown Disney West Side). Buy 'em a bag of gummi gators, then treat yourself to the *good stuff* at **Ghirardelli Soda Fountain & Chocolate Shop.** ("Like sex, kids are too young to appreciate good chocolate," whispered the gal at the counter. Who's gonna argue?) For a serious sugar rush (or potent PMS antidote), try the World's Largest Chocolate Bar, a 5-pound, foil-wrapped hunk of heaven. They also serve outrageously expensive—and delicious—ice cream concoctions. Figure it this way: Even at 5 bucks a scoop, it's cheaper than Prozac. Nobody beats the French when it comes to luscious pastry, so indulge in sublime tartlets, brioches, and éclairs at **Boulangerie Patisserie** in the France pavilion at Epcot. I can't guarantee the bakers were all born in France, but their recipes and methods are all properly Gallic. And don't say I didn't warn you about Mickey Roni & Cheese, available all over WDW. Talk about your shameless hucksterism! Once you've scarfed down these cunning little cheese-covered Mickeys at $2.95 a box, you'll never again be happy with Kraft's 80¢ version of same.

To bring out the Nicklaus in you... You may have discovered Orlando's world-class golf courses and the fact that golf legends Arnold Palmer and Gary Player own developments here. If all this only intimidates you because your game is strictly bush league, maybe your equipment's to blame. **Special Tee Golf and Tennis** carries links equipment and apparel by more than 100 manufacturers. Then again, maybe the problem is your swing. Each Special Tee shop (there are two on I-Dr.) offers a fitting range so you can analyze your swing and try out a variety of clubs.

To bring out the Nicholson in you... Ya gotta have shades. Even if you're not interested in creating an aura of mystery and raw sexual power, sunglasses are *de rigueur* in Orlando, where eyes need protection from the searing tropical sun. You can find cheapo models at every convenience store and supermarket, but you'll find the best selection of stylin' shades at **Sunglass Hut Outlet** in Lake Buena Vista Factory Stores, where they carry lines such as Revo, Oakley, and polarized Maui Gem at 20% to 30% off.

Fun finds for small fries... Gotta bring home a present for your nieces and nephews (or have them along for the ride)? First, a word of warning: Even if you're not a shopper, you'll end up in more gift shops than you thought possible during your Orlando stay. Theme-park engineers are now craftily designing rides that disgorge passengers directly into gift shops. You could blindfold the kids at this juncture, or hustle them right on through the place before their little eyes have time to focus on, say, that giant stuffed Shamu. I say: Good luck. You might as well bite the bullet and steer them toward the really fun (read: less pricey) finds. At SeaWorld's **Wild Arctic Gift Shop,** there are piles and piles of adoptable plush, including some unusual creatures such as stuffed manatees and narwhals, in a range of prices. Meanwhile, at **Shamu's Emporium** (the SeaWorld shop with the widest selection of merchandise), you'll find irresistible shark-shaped squirt guns and inflatable, ride-on Shamu water toys. You can't go wrong with the squeaky Shamu puppet, a natural for back-seat puppet shows. At Universal Studios Florida, check out the **Universal Studios Store** for cool stuff aimed at the preteen set, like the Pet Tornado ($25) and other *Twister*-themed gear, as well as the classic, 24-inch E.T. figure, and the DeLorean car (of *Back to the Future* fame) that drives in circles. ***Tip:*** Don't waste your time in the post-ride shops at Islands of Adventure. They've put all the goods from every Island under the same roof at **Islands of Adventure Trading Co.** (near the park entrance/exit). Look for huggable plush like E.T., the Cat in the Hat, and the Grinch, as well as cool Spider-Man backpacks. Also worth a stop: **Dr. Seuss' All the Books You Can Read,** chock-full of Seuss classics such as *One Fish, Two Fish...*, videos, and software. After all this, if you've somehow avoided picking up any souvenirs or Mickey ears, **Once Upon a Toy** at Downtown Disney presents an irresistibly huge assortment of toys and games ranging from classics to the latest high-tech amusements.

The most interesting shops are at Epcot's World Showcase, where stock includes animal masks and sets of tiny wooden animals from Kenya, Pocky candy from Japan, and fragrant soaps from China. The shops at Magic Kingdom are heavy on character merchandise, but you can find some cute items in Frontierland at **Frontier Trading Post,** including Daniel Boone–style coonskin caps and woven leather bracelets. At Disney–MGM, the **"Indy Truck"** pushcart has giant rubber snakes, humongous fake cockroaches (or Palmetto bugs, as they're genteelly known in Florida)—perfect for sending Grandma into cardiac arrest when you scatter them around her kitchen—as well as politically incorrect cap guns. Got a *Star Wars* fan on your shopping list? **Tattooine Traders,** also at Disney–MGM Studios, carries exclusive merchandise, as well as the usual light-saber toys. **World of Disney** certainly has its share of trinkets, such as plush character key chains, wraparound Winnie-the-Pooh sunglasses, and the irresistible Mickey Mouse propeller beanie.

Best Cheapie Souvenir

It costs 50¢ to press a penny (okay, make that 51¢) at Disney. Short of a sale...oops... special-value item being greatly reduced, you probably won't find a less expensive memento of your vacation (though the mark-up is beyond obscene). Each machine has three or more patterns, including various Disney characters, and machines are scattered throughout the parks. Use pennies made before 1982; pennies made after have less copper and can turn green during the pressing process.

Character duds at a discount... For cut-rate Disney clothing (remainders, close-outs, and past-season stock, but who cares?), try the **Character Warehouse** at Belz Factory Outlet World, Mall 2. The stock changes from day to day, but I found "Twilight Zone Tower of Terror" T-shirts for a realistic $5, and silk-screened Mickey sweatshirts for $10 (similar shirts inside the park sell for around $30). Adorable little infant "onesies" printed with Disney pals were priced at $5 and up. Generally, stuff crops up here a few months after it debuts in the Disney stores. Items include toys and garments tied in with Walt Disney Co. animated films, as well as Mickey-and-friends merchandise. Next door in Mall 1, you'll find another Disney discount store, **Character Premier.** Surprisingly, each store does get different merchandise shipments, so it's worth your time to check both. Another Character Premier can be found at the Orlando Premium Outlets, and **Character Corner** is over on Orange Blossom Trail. All of these Disney discount retailers sell over-runs and past-season character clothing, toys, and accessories at savings of up to 75%. You won't find the range of merchandise you'll find at the shops in Disney, but at these prices, so what? **Mickey's Mart** in the Downtown Disney Marketplace doesn't actually sell anything at a discount, but they do carry a huge variety of souvenirs, toys, and the occasional baby tee, with everything priced at $10 or less. Even at the theme parks, it's possible to find the bargains. Universal and SeaWorld don't mind putting up the "sale" signs, offering great savings on logo merchandise. In fact, both Universal Studios Florida and Islands of Adventure have sale stores located just to the right of each park's exit. But at Disney, you have to know the code phrase..."special value." "Sale" makes it look tacky, they say. As long as I'm saving money, I don't care what they call it.

Fashion, Florida-style... Everybody's done it: bought something that looked great on vacation, brought it home and unpacked it, then shrieked, "What was I thinking?!" and exiled it to the back of the closet where it won't offend anybody. **Pointe*Orlando,** on the other hand, offers relatively risk-free shopping with the likes of A/X Armani Exchange, Abercrombie & Fitch, Banana Republic, and Chico's. And, of course, several other well-known names are represented at all of Orlando's outlet malls, where you may strike it lucky (or you may be faced with a lot of stuff that didn't sell at full retail for good reason).

Glass act... What little girl wouldn't be dazzled by her very own Cinderella-style glass slipper (to be displayed on a bureau top, not worn)? **EUROSPAIN by the Arribas Brothers** at the Downtown Disney Marketplace features the requisite crystal characters along with lots of twinkling glass creations—vases, bowls, goblets, lamps, jewelry—from all over the world. Glassblowers work on the premises to create tiny, multicolored glass figurines of animals, clowns, and the like. And check out the truly mind-blowing replica of Cinderella Castle, made of handblown glass and selling for a mere $8,500. The miniature version of the aforementioned glass slipper can be had for $10.

These boots are made for stalking.... At **Reel Finds,** Pleasure Island, you can paw through celebrity castoffs such as gold ankle boots "from the personal collection of Cher" and fetching black leather pumps from the wardrobe of Elizabeth Taylor. There's also lots of memorabilia from *Gone With the Wind* at this eminently browsable shop. The stuff is priced high enough that only the truly celeb-obsessed would actually purchase anything here, giving the shop more of a museum feel than a retail-store atmosphere. Perhaps that's the intention. **Sid Cahuenga's One-of-a-Kind** reigns as the coolest shop at Disney–MGM, not that there's much competition. The cluttery front porch has bins full of movie posters, like cult fave ***The Matrix*** (Spanish version) and oldies such as ***The Love Bug*** and ***Chitty Chitty Bang Bang.*** Many of these are unframed and cheap, perfect for adding that touch of whimsy to a dorm room or home office. Inside the shop is a collection of stuff that proves even stars make fashion faux pas. Witness the earth-toned pantsuit and worn-down flats from Jaclyn Smith, and a dowdy Donna Karan supposedly worn by Cher. Drew Barrymore is so cool that even the stuff worn *near her* has cachet; how else to explain why anyone would want a (dreadful) sweater worn by an extra in one of her movies? Sid's also carries signed publicity pix from flavors-of-the-month such as Ricky Martin and Britney Spears. The stock changes frequently, depending on what treasures their "L.A. source" can find, I'm told. Meanwhile, **Starabilias** at Downtown Disney West Side seems to have cornered the market in dead-celeb mementos. Autographed items from the Grateful Dead, Kurt Cobain, and the Carpenters were on display during a recent visit, all priced above a thousand bucks. Cool finds include a guitar used and autographed by Pink Floyd for $6,995 and John and Yoko's *Double Fantasy* album cover and glossy pic (signed by the couple) for $2,795. Of course, all of these might have been snapped up by well-heeled fans by the time you visit. If you feel guilty about ogling this stuff and not buying, spring for an Oscar-statuette key chain bearing your name—if your name is a common one, that is. If the only thing that will do is your own mantlepiece-worthy Oscar (and you'd rather not hijack a delivery truck), visit **Universal Studios Store,** where you'll find a bunch of authentic-looking "Best Actor" and "Best Actress" awards.

Poof! There goes your money.... A magic shop with no whoopie cushions or plastic vomit? That's **Magic Masters,** in Downtown Disney West Side, featuring magic supplies minus the novelties and gag stuff. Decked out with a 10-foot-tall magician's top hat and magic wand, it's impossible to miss this store. Modeled after Harry Houdini's library, this place is totally Disney (even if it is a chain store). To get inside the hidden "teaching room," you utter the magic word—no, it's not "please"—and enter through a bookcase. They sell everything you need to make magic—except the curvaceous assistant.

Support your college team.... There's no better way than stopping by **Steve and Barry's University Sportswear,** Festival Bay. Find most of your favorite college teams represented on T-shirts, sweatshirts, and so on...and 99% of the stock is $10 or less. Go team!

I got the music in me.... Music fans will spend hours inside the two-story **Virgin Megastore,** Downtown Disney Westside. Over 300 titles are on listening stations throughout the store; sample before you buy. Thinking about buying Disney music or movies? This store usually has a better price than **World of Disney** on the other side of Downtown Disney.

For the 11th-hour shopper... Oops. You spent all your time riding and reriding Buzz Lightyear and now you're going home empty-handed? In your dreams. This is Orlando, remember? Even the airport has a mall, of sorts. The main terminal of **Orlando International Airport** has more shops than most Main Streets, including boutiques and theme stores run by Universal Orlando, SeaWorld, and Walt Disney World. Price-wise? Whadda you care? You're desperate.

Map 11: Orlando Shopping

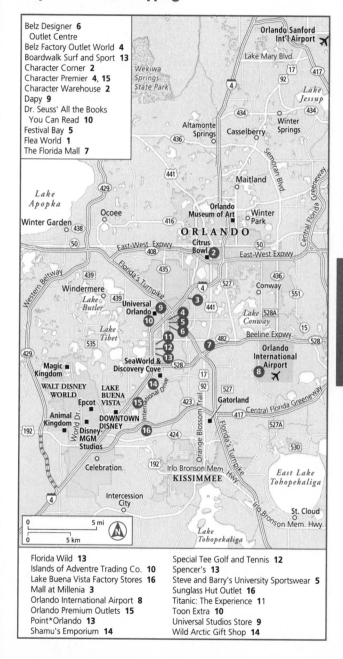

Belz Designer Outlet Centre **6**
Belz Factory Outlet World **4**
Boardwalk Surf and Sport **13**
Character Corner **2**
Character Premier **4, 15**
Character Warehouse **2**
Dapy **9**
Dr. Seuss' All the Books You Can Read **10**
Festival Bay **5**
Flea World **1**
The Florida Mall **7**

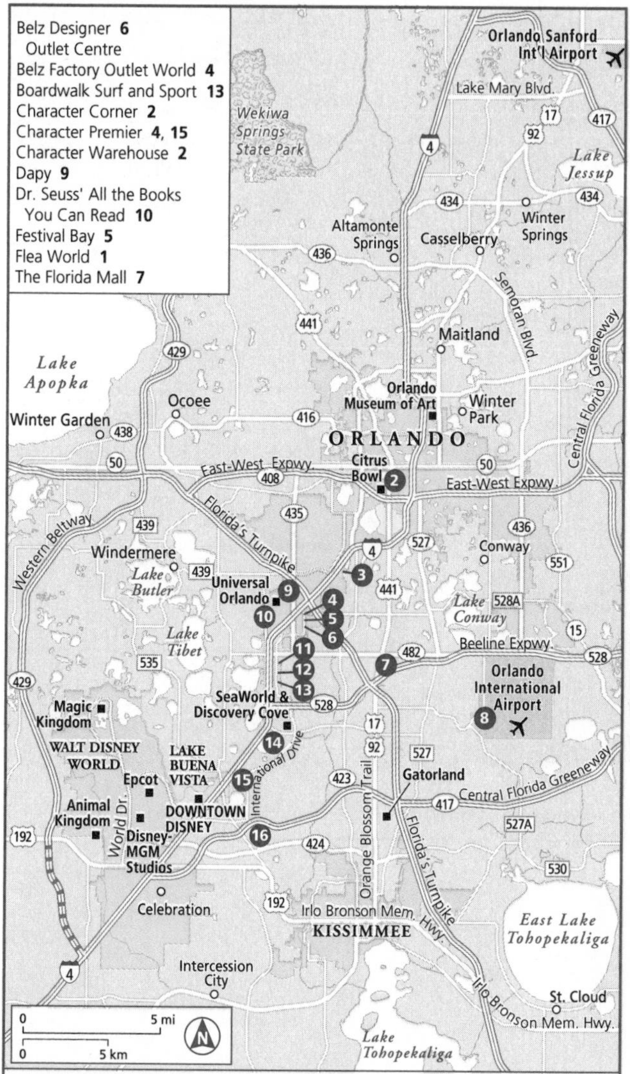

Florida Wild **13**
Islands of Adventre Trading Co. **10**
Lake Buena Vista Factory Stores **16**
Mall at Millenia **3**
Orlando International Airport **8**
Orlando Premium Outlets **15**
Point*Orlando **13**
Shamu's Emporium **14**
Special Tee Golf and Tennis **12**
Spencer's **13**
Steve and Barry's University Sportswear **5**
Sunglass Hut Outlet **16**
Titanic: The Experience **11**
Toon Extra **10**
Universal Studios Store **9**
Wild Arctic Gift Shop **14**

Map 12: Walt Disney World Shopping

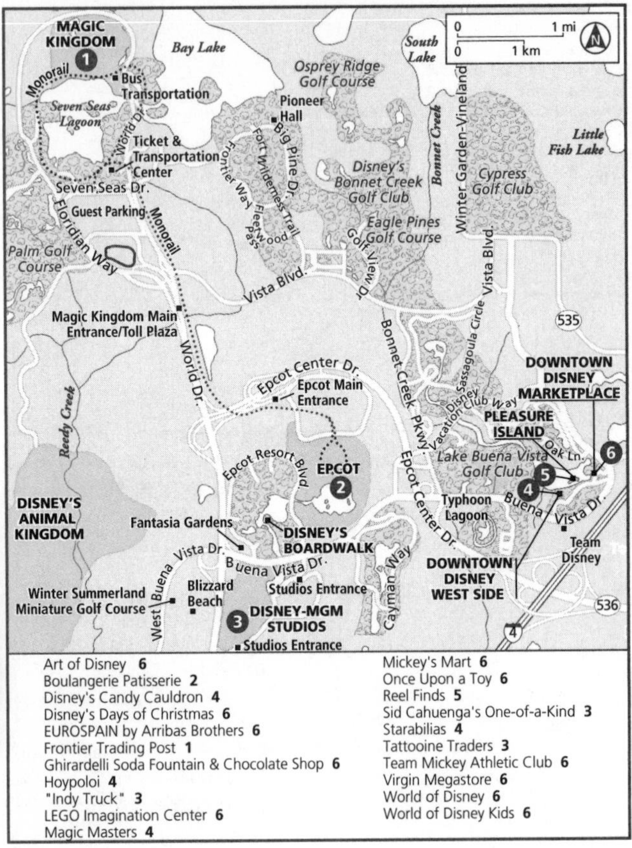

- Art of Disney 6
- Boulangerie Patisserie 2
- Disney's Candy Cauldron 4
- Disney's Days of Christmas 6
- EUROSPAIN by Arribas Brothers 6
- Frontier Trading Post 1
- Ghirardelli Soda Fountain & Chocolate Shop 6
- Hoypoloi 4
- "Indy Truck" 3
- LEGO Imagination Center 6
- Magic Masters 4
- Mickey's Mart 6
- Once Upon a Toy 6
- Reel Finds 5
- Sid Cahuenga's One-of-a-Kind 3
- Starabilias 4
- Tattooine Traders 3
- Team Mickey Athletic Club 6
- Virgin Megastore 6
- World of Disney 6
- World of Disney Kids 6

The Index

Art of Disney (p. 176) DOWNTOWN DISNEY Call it nirvana for the hard-core Disneyphile who won't bat an eye at paying, say, $1,000 and up for an original film cel from *Snow White* or *The Lion King*. Production cels can be had for $250 to $300 on average.... *Tel 407/828-3929. www.downtowndisney.com. Downtown Disney Marketplace.*

See Map 12 on p. 186.

Belz Designer Outlet Centre (p. 174) INTERNATIONAL DRIVE This outlet mall caters to label-conscious shoppers, with tenants such as DKNY, Off-5th (Saks Fifth Avenue), Kenneth Cole, Movado, and Coach.... *Tel 407/352-3632. www.belz.com. 5211 International Dr.*

See Map 11 on p. 185.

Belz Factory Outlet World (p. 174) INTERNATIONAL DRIVE For shopaholics, this may be a bigger draw than the theme parks. With 170 outlets, you're bound to find something that fits or comes in a color other than puce. Just follow the tour buses.... *Tel 407/352-9611. www.belz.com. 5401 W. Oak Ridge Rd., at north end of International Dr.*

See Map 11 on p. 185.

Boardwalk Surf and Sport (p. 178) INTERNATIONAL DRIVE The surf's always up at this shop (check out the blue wave in the window), where the look is pure Moondoggie.... *Tel 407/370-0436. www.pointeorlando.com. Pointe*Orlando, 9101 International Dr.*

See Map 11 on p. 185.

Boulangerie Patisserie (p. 179) WDW *Vive la France!* Real butter, cream, and loads of sugar... the French pastries here are worth the indulgence. A true bliss-out.... *Tel 407/824-4321. Epcot.*

See Map 12 on p. 186.

Character Corner (p. 181) ORLANDO Resist the theme-park shops and pushcarts; get your official Disney-character clothing here instead, where over-runs and last season's goods are marked down to realistic prices, sometimes up to 75% off.... *Tel 407/ 239-3690. 220 N. Orange Blossom Trail.*

See Map 11 on p. 185.

Character Premier (p. 181) INTERNATIONAL DRIVE/LAKE BUENA VISTA You'll find this Disney-affiliated discount store in two Orlando locations; shop both for different selections of merchandise.... *I-Drive: Tel 407/354-3255; Belz Factory Outlet World, Mall 1, 5401 W. Oak Ridge Rd., at north end of International Dr. Lake Buena Vista: Tel 407/477-0222; Orlando Premium Outlets; 8200 Vineland Ave.*

See Map 11 on p. 185.

Character Warehouse (p. 177) INTERNATIONAL DRIVE The second Disney discount store at the Belz Factory Outlet Mall.... *Tel 407/345-5285. Belz Factory Outlet World, Mall 2, 5401 W. Oak Ridge Rd., at north end of International Dr.*

See Map 11 on p. 185.

Dapy (p. 177) UNIVERSAL ORLANDO "Daffy" is more like it. It's a little '60s, a little nostalgia, and a lot of bad taste—everything you could possibly want in a store.... *Tel 407/363-8320. CityWalk.*

See Map 11 on p. 185.

Disney's Candy Cauldron (p. 178) DOWNTOWN DISNEY Dungeon-themed sweet shop, complete with witchy candy apples. Staff demands payment for treats in "stones" (dollars) and "pebbles" (cents).... *Tel 407/828-1470. Downtown Disney West Side.*

See Map 12 on p. 186.

Disney's Days of Christmas (p. 177) DOWNTOWN DISNEY It's Christmas in July, or whenever, at this shop chock-full of holiday ornaments (many featuring Disney characters, naturally) and decorations. Get your Quasimodo Christmas bauble here.... *Tel 407/828-3800. www.downtowndisney.com. Downtown Disney Marketplace.*

See Map 12 on p. 186.

Dr. Seuss' All the Books You Can Read (p. 180) UNIVERSAL ORLANDO Seuss-o-rama! Books, videos, software, and guest appearances by the Cat in the Hat, the Grinch, and Thing One and Thing Two.... *Tel 407/363-8000. Islands of Adventure.*

See Map 11 on p. 185.

EUROSPAIN by the Arribas Brothers (p. 182) DOWNTOWN DISNEY It's a small (glass) world after all.... *Tel 407/828-3616. Downtown Disney Marketplace.*

See Map 12 on p. 186.

Festival Bay (p. 170) INTERNATIONAL DRIVE Shop till you drop at this retail venue. Stores include the totally Florida Ron Jon Surf Shop and Steve & Barry's.... *Tel 407/351-7718. www.belz.com. 5250 International Dr.*

See Map 11 on p. 185.

Flea World (p. 175) SANFORD Open Friday through Sunday, America's largest open-air flea market is a colossal affair, with 1,700-plus dealer booths. It's a crazy scene (sometimes elephants entertain the masses), with everything from Caribbean art to zebra-print slipcovers.... *Tel 407/330-1792. www.fleaworld.com. U.S. 17–92, Sanford.*

See Map 11 on p. 185.

The Florida Mall (p. 174) ORLANDO This modern megamall features three architectural styles and more than 250 stores including Nordstrom and Saks Fifth Avenue.... *Tel 407/851-6255. www.simon.com. 8001 S. Orange Blossom Trail.*

See Map 11 on p. 185.

Florida Wild (p. 174) INTERNATIONAL DRIVE This novelty shop features (mainly) made-in-the-Sunshine-State goods, some tasteful, some tacky.... *Tel 407/903-1314. www.pointeorlando.com. Pointe*Orlando, 9101 International Dr.*

See Map 11 on p. 185.

Frontier Trading Post (p. 180) WDW One of the more interesting shops at the Magic Kingdom, offering such fun stuff as cowboy poetry books and coonskin caps.... *Tel 407/824-1247. Magic Kingdom.*

See Map 12 on p. 186.

Ghirardelli Soda Fountain & Chocolate Shop (p. 178) DOWNTOWN DISNEY Just the smell of this place will add 10 pounds to your girlish/boyish figure, so why not go for broke with the World's Largest Chocolate Bar?... *Tel 407/934-7639. Downtown Disney Marketplace.*

See Map 12 on p. 186.

Hoypoloi (p. 177) DOWNTOWN DISNEY Supremely artsy for Downtown Disney, this small shop features cool accessories for the home (for example, lamps shaped like martinis, not Mickeys).... *Tel 407/824-4321. Downtown Disney West Side.*

See Map 12 on p. 186.

"Indy Truck" (p. 180) WDW Rubber snakes (remember the Harrison Ford line in the movie, "Snakes! Anything but snakes!"?), humongous faux cockroaches, and Indy's signature hat. Now we're talking souvenirs.... *Tel 407/824-4321. Disney–MGM Studios.*

See Map 12 on p. 186.

Islands of Adventure Trading Co. (p. 180) UNIVERSAL ORLANDO This huge emporium features souvenirs from each Island, plus some gel-filled squishy cylinders that nobody knows the name or purpose of but everyone buys anyway.... *Tel 407/363-8000. Islands of Adventure.*

See Map 11 on p. 185.

Lake Buena Vista Factory Stores (p. 175) LAKE BUENA VISTA The store selection could be better, but you'll still find Liz Claiborne, Sunglass Hut, and the only Old Navy outlet in town.... *Tel 407/238-9301. www.lbvfs.com. 15591 Apopka-Vineland Rd. (S.R. 535).*

See Map 11 on p. 185.

LEGO Imagination Center (p. 173) DOWNTOWN DISNEY Wow. The things you could make out of LEGOs, if you had about a trillion of 'em (and no life). The incredible LEGO creations outside this shop—dinosaurs, aliens, and sea serpents, oh my!—should inspire you to make your own dazzling creations.... *Tel 407/934-7639. www.downtowndisney.com. Downtown Disney Marketplace.*

See Map 12 on p. 186.

Magic Masters (p. 183) DOWNTOWN DISNEY Disney unveils the secrets behind the illusions. (Didn't that masked magician on Fox already do that?) You buy the gizmos, and on-site magicians will spirit you away and show you how to use 'em.... *Tel 407/939-2648. www.downtowndisney.com. Downtown Disney West Side.*

See Map 12 on p. 186.

Mall at Millenia (p. 170) INTERNATIONAL DRIVE Why shop the Big Apple when you can shop the Big O? Names like Cartier and Chanel join anchor stores Bloomingdale's, Macy's, and Neiman Marcus at Orlando's most chichi shopping mall.... *Tel 407/363-3555. www.mallatmillenia.com. 4200 Conroy Rd., at I-4.*

See Map 11 on p. 185.

Mickey's Mart (p. 176) DOWNTOWN DISNEY Don't be fooled by the "everything for $10 or less" slogan; there are no price breaks here. Instead, it's a whole store of Disney's most inexpensive merchandise, so it's good for last-minute souvenir runs at least.... *Tel 407/828-3864. www.downtowndisney.com. Downtown Disney Marketplace.*

See Map 12 on p. 186.

Once Upon a Toy (p. 180) DOWNTOWN DISNEY This toy-lover's nirvana lets shoppers create a custom Mr. Potato Head (screw that pair of mouse ears on), and offers a huge selection of classic games and Disney toys. You won't leave empty-handed.... *Tel 407/939-2648. www.downtowndisney.com. Downtown Disney Marketplace.*

See Map 12 on p. 186.

Orlando International Airport (p. 184) ORLANDO We're not suggesting you make a trip to the airport strictly for shopping, but if you're heading there anyway, check out the boutiques and theme stores run by Universal Orlando, SeaWorld, and Walt Disney World. You could skip the theme parks altogether and just shop here, turn around, and go home.... *Tel 407/825-2001. 1 Airport Blvd., off S.R. 528 (exit 11B).*

See Map 11 on p. 185.

Orlando Premium Outlets (p. 170) LAKE BUENA VISTA If names like Hugo Boss and Versace do it for you, this upscale outdoor shopping mall is the place to head to in O-Town. Class, selection, and even a few bargains.... *Tel 407/238-7787. www.premium outlets.com. 8200 Vineland Ave.*

See Map 11 on p. 185.

Pointe*Orlando (p. 182) INTERNATIONAL DRIVE This multilevel complex houses upscale shops and pushcarts, restaurants, and bars, and a 21-screen cinema with an IMAX 3-D theater.... *Tel 407/248-2838. www.pointeorlando.com. 9101 International Dr. (near the convention center).*

See Map 11 on p. 185.

Reel Finds (p. 182) DOWNTOWN DISNEY This place is more fun than a yard sale in Malibu. They've got shoes from the closets of Liz and Cher, hats from Joan Crawford, and more. The prices encourage more gawking than buying.... *Tel 407/934-2648. Pleasure Island.*

See Map 12 on p. 186.

Shamu's Emporium (p. 180) SEAWORLD SeaWorld's largest gift shop features everything Shamu (and crew), from tub toys to telescopes.... *Tel 407/351-3600. SeaWorld (directly inside the front gate).*

See Map 11 on p. 185.

Sid Cahuenga's One-of-a-Kind (p. 183) WDW Celebrity autographs, movie props, and signed movie posters are among the goods at Disney–MGM Studios' most interesting shop.... *Tel 407/824-4321. Disney–MGM Studios.*

See Map 12 on p. 186.

Special Tee Golf and Tennis (p. 179) INTERNATIONAL DRIVE This is the largest golf store around, offering equipment and apparel from more than 100 big names, such as Nicklaus, Izod, Titleist, Ping, Norman, and Head.... *Tel 407/363-1281. www.specialtee golf.com. 8747 International Dr.*

See Map 11 on p. 185.

Spencer's (p. 174) INTERNATIONAL DRIVE More black lights, rubber feces, and lava lamps than you could shake a glow-stick at.... *Tel 407/248-1274. www.pointeorlando.com. Pointe*Orlando, 9101 International Dr.*

See Map 11 on p. 185.

Starabilias (p. 183) DOWNTOWN DISNEY This veritable museum houses one of the largest collections of celebrity memorabilia in the world. Autographs of Hollywood idols, music legends, and sports greats are among the goods for sale.... *Tel 407/827-0104. Downtown Disney West Side.*

See Map 12 on p. 186.

Steve and Barry's University Sportswear (p. 184) INTERNATIONAL DRIVE Find your favorite collegiate team's logo on almost any clothing option at this chain store.... *Tel 407/370-3810. www.steveandbarrys.com. Belz Festival Bay, 5226 International Dr.*

See Map 11 on p. 185.

Sunglass Hut Outlet (p. 179) LAKE BUENA VISTA You've seen their stores at the mall, now see what didn't sell at full retail (maybe the style was simply ahead of its time) at the outlet store.... *Tel 407/238-9801. Lake Buena Vista Factory Stores, 15591 S. Apopka-Vineland Rd. (S.R. 535).*

See Map 11 on p. 185.

Tattooine Traders (p. 181) WDW The Force will surely be with you if you shop for **Star Wars** fans here. Lots of exclusive merchandise, guaranteed to fade away the dark side.... *Tel 407/824-4321. Disney–MGM Studios.*

See Map 12 on p. 186.

Team Mickey Athletic Club (p. 176) DOWNTOWN DISNEY The Mickster and pals grace the chests, breasts, and cuffs of sweats, hats, jerseys, and other activewear.... *Tel 407/828-3364. www.downtowndisney.com. Downtown Disney Marketplace.*

See Map 12 on p. 186.

Titanic: The Experience (p. 178) INTERNATIONAL DRIVE Get your *Titanic*-logoed bathrobe here or, better yet, a little bauble like the one Kate Winslet wore in the movie. Cool earrings shaped like the doomed luxury liner, too.... *Tel 407/248-1166. www.titanicshipofdreams.com. The Mercado, 8445 International Dr.*

See Map 11 on p. 185.

Toon Extra (p. 178) UNIVERSAL ORLANDO Big shop full of gear imprinted with the likenesses of classic comic-strip denizens.... *Tel 407/363-8000. Islands of Adventure.*

See Map 11 on p. 185.

Universal Studios Store (p. 180) UNIVERSAL ORLANDO USF's biggest store is perfect for those making a last-minute dash to buy souvenirs.... *Tel 407/363-8000. Near exit gate at Universal Studios Florida.*

See Map 11 on p. 185.

Virgin Megastore (p. 184) DOWNTOWN DISNEY The largest music store in Orlando is this two-story behemoth. Spend hours listening to all 300-plus CDs on the listening stations.... *Tel 407/828-0222. www.virginmegastore.com. Downtown Disney Marketplace.*

See Map 12 on p. 186.

Wild Arctic Gift Shop (p. 180) SEAWORLD Warm cuddlies from the frozen north are stocked at this SeaWorld shop, including plush polar bears, walruses, beluga whales, harbor seals, arctic foxes, and narwhals.... *Tel 407/351-3600. SeaWorld.*

See Map 11 on p. 185.

World of Disney (p. 176) DOWNTOWN DISNEY The world's largest shop devoted to Disney-character merchandise. From shot glasses to shoes, underwear to umbrellas, it's all Mickey, all the time.... *Tel 407/934-7639. www.downtowndisney.com. Downtown Disney Marketplace.*

See Map 12 on p. 186.

World of Disney Kids (p. 178) DOWNTOWN DISNEY It's more Disney doodads, this time focused on the smallest of the small fries. Plush toys and sleepwear prominently feature Pooh and the gang.... *Tel 407/828-4983. www.downtowndisney.com. Downtown Disney Marketplace.*

See Map 12 on p. 186.

NIGHT ENTERTA

LIFE &
INMENT

6

Basic Stuff

In this less-is-definitely-not-more land of options, you'll find plenty to do after the sun sets. Granted, once the magic wears off, many folks drag themselves to bed and then collapse in a heap. Who can blame them? Other, hardier souls return to the theme parks to be chased by aliens or saved by Spider-Man. Special fireworks displays, parades, and light shows also keep folks coming back until closing hours—and sometimes beyond. But there's also plenty to do outside the confines of the major parks. Orlando is teeming with luaus, whodunit mystery theaters, Wild West shows, rodeos, comedy clubs, discos, street carnivals, magicians, jugglers, live bands, and more, more, more—all enticing you to do things that you wouldn't be caught dead doing back home, like tearing your chicken apart with your fingers while jeering a king's jousters.

Mostly, this takes the form of childlike vacation fun (never forget that Orlando's pretty much ruled by tots), rated G, cleaned up, and homogenized for the entire family. Here in the great entertainment capital of the world, the nightlife rarely gets as hot as the daytime temperatures. If you want your nightlife saucier, you'll have to venture into downtown Orlando or to nearby Winter Park. There you'll find a burgeoning nightlife scene, including a collection of live-music venues, discos, dance floors, and coffeehouses.

One-Night Standouts

When heading out for a night on the town, most visitors head to one of the one-stop entertainment complexes—a distinctly Orlando invention (though it's starting to catch on in other tourist destinations). Your choices: Disney's **Pleasure Island** and **Universal CityWalk** (universally known just as CityWalk). Each features live-music venues, dance clubs, restaurants, and shops, wrapped up in a single, contained location. You'll pay one fee at the gate, getting you into all the clubs in the complex. Forget about seeking out local color, culture, and ethnicity. At these all-in-one entertainmentplexes, you'll find a variety of clubs and restaurants that are strategically selected to offer something for everyone, but watered down to offend no one.

At **Pleasure Island,** there are 6 acres of entertainment, including nightclubs, full-service restaurants, and a variety of boutiques and shops. During the day the nightclubs are closed.

After 7pm, the gates go up, the lights go on, hands get stamped, and the music starts blasting. Tourists mill in and out of the clubs, consulting their maps and programs as they chart their pilgrimage of fun. There's 8Trax, a 1970s-themed club; Mannequins Dance Palace, a high-energy, contemporary dance club; the Adventurers Club, a quirky storytelling hangout; the Rock 'n' Roll Beach Club; Comedy Warehouse; the **BET Soundstage** club; and Motion. Loud music blasts, a few scantily clad dancers gyrate on outdoor stages, and alcohol is served on the streets. Still, the Island scene has a sterilized, fun-for-the-whole-family feel to it. You won't find much in the way of actual "live" music at most of its clubs. Only the Rock 'n' Roll Beach Club, the outdoor West End Stage, and Raglan Road regularly offer live music, and that's mostly via hardworking cover bands. Every evening at Pleasure Island ends with a New Year's Eve celebration—noisemakers, confetti, lights, countdown, the works. It's an appropriate choice; a night at Pleasure Island often leaves you feeling the underlying desperation and forced gaiety of a typical New Year's Eve. Oh yeah, you'll wait in line for the clubs and venues, too.

CityWalk, a 30-acre complex of hot-colored buildings, moving sidewalks, streetscapes, and free-form sculptures, all wrapped around a 4-acre harbor, is Universal's answer to Pleasure Island, and they do a much better job of it. Pleasure Island is largely a collection of themed venues manufactured by Disney. CityWalk sought popular entertainment leaders in different genres and gathered them under one "roof." The high-energy result is a lot of unabashed fun. CityWalk lets you choose among the world's largest Hard Rock Cafe and Hard Rock Live Orlando (a 2,200-capacity concert hall); Jimmy Buffett's Margaritaville Cafe; Bob Marley—A Tribute to Freedom; Latin Quarter, with music and food offerings from all 21 Latin American nations; CityJazz, a live-performance venue; Pat O'Brien's; the groove, Universal's hip dance club; an upcoming location of Bubba Gump Shrimp Company; Universal Cineplex; and a number of restaurants and shops.

Both Pleasure Island and CityWalk have cover charges to get into the clubs. Pleasure Island charges $22 for access to all clubs, or $11 for a pass to an individual club. CityWalk is far cheaper, charging just $10 for a pass to all clubs, or about $5 cover for individual clubs.

Other Nightlife Hot Spots

Can't commit to a one-fee, 1-night orgy of entertainment? That's okay, there are a number of other nightlife hot spots to cruise. **Downtown Disney West Side,** adjacent to Pleasure Island, is home to the top-notch House of Blues, the AMC complex of 24 movie theaters (the largest in the Southeast), a Cirque du Soleil production (a wonderful circus theatrical performance), and a host of trendy restaurants and specialty shops. It's also the location of the **Virgin Megastore,** Richard Branson's gigantic music and video shop. Now here's some cheap entertainment: You could spend most of the evening at Virgin if you wanted, listening to music and viewing videos. The store has 20 video/laser preview stations and more than 300 CD-listening stations. The West Side area is always hopping, drawing young tourists and a smattering of locals. The Disney **BoardWalk** streetmosphere is a manufactured Eastern Seaboard village, complete with beach cottages, New England–style inn, and, yes, a boardwalk—which meanders a quarter of a mile along Crescent Bay. Specialty shops, bakeries, and eateries line the plank walkway. You'll also find the ESPN World sports bar and arcade here, along with Jellyrolls Piano Bar, and the Atlantic Dance Hall, a dance hall featuring top-40 and 1980s dance hits Tuesday through Thursday, and live bands on Friday and Saturday nights.

At **Pointe*Orlando,** you'll also find a cluster of nightclubs, restaurants, a theater complex, and shopping. Most people come here to shop and eat, two of America's favorite nighttime activities. Ditto for the **Mercado,** a lively marketplace on International Drive studded with restaurants, shops, and entertainment. Street musicians, mimes, jugglers, and clowns perform in the open-air courtyard. Street entertainment, free parking, and shopping draw crowds of tourists. **Downtown Orlando,** particularly the nightclubs and bars along Orange Avenue, offers a variety of good choices; this is where locals head to escape the hordes of tourists and hear good live music. Clubs are clustered together, making it easy to sample a number of hangouts in a short span of time.

Covers

A note about cover charges: Orlando's club owners love a promotion. Ladies' nights, happy hours, wear black, wear white, bring a friend.... You name it, and they're doing it to get you in the door. If things are slow, watch for no covers, free drafts, and

More Nightlife Resources

You'll find lots of free entertainment guides and brochures cluttering up hotel counters, visitor centers, convenience stores, even gas stations. Pick them up, browse through them, and clip out any discount coupons you think you might use. But for the real scoop on local action, you'll want to pick up the free ***Orlando Weekly*** *(Tel 407/645-5888; www.orlandoweekly.com) guide to arts and entertainment. It's available at select bars, nightclubs, and restaurants. Or get hold of the monthly* ***Axis Orlando*** *(Tel 407/823-8054), more suited to the college crowd. Check the "Calendar" section of Friday's* ***Orlando Sentinel*** *(www.orlandosentinel.com) for details on local clubs, visiting performers, concerts, and events. For some of the most bleeding-edge listings, club nights, special events, highlights, and a series of photo galleries that let you check out the action in advance, check out* ***Orlando CityBeat*** *online at www.orlandocitybeat.com.*

$1.50 house drinks. If you want to start early, say before 9pm, you may get in for free at a number of clubs. Generally, expect to pay a small cover ($3–$6) at most clubs once the entertainment begins. If there are big names on stage, tickets soar to $15 to $30. Generally, it's best to call ahead.

The Lowdown

Nightlife

Where the stars shine... If you pick just one spot to do your nightcrawling, let it be **The Social** in downtown Orlando. Housed in an antique building, The Social combines style and substance. It's the strongest venue in town for diverse live music. The club's been around for a long time, though not always under the same ownership (or name). Now, under The Social marquee, the club features a wide range of live performers, from eclectic to alternative, funk to blues to jazz, including some top names. The age range and look of the crowd changes with the featured band. Drop in any night of the week and the house, which seats 300 to 400 people, will be packed wall-to-wall, standing room only. If the music doesn't send you someplace, the martinis will. How 'bout a Super Dag Daddy? This martini, named after The Dag, a band that plays here regularly, tastes like a watermelon-flavored Jolly Rancher. Or try the Dirty Donkey, a knock-your-sandals-off gin concoction.

There's the mint-chocolate-chip martini, the lemon drop—more than 25 selections in all. James Bond wouldn't approve of the drink menu, but he'd love the sexy setting. Just down the street is another favorite local hangout to catch great live music: the **BackBooth.** This "alternative entertainment" venue hosts everything from local bands to national college-radio faves to burlesque shows by the Suicide Girls. The type of crowd depends on the band. The celebrity-backed **House of Blues** (Dan Aykroyd, Jim Belushi, John Goodman, and Aerosmith were cofounders) has become one of the top music venues in the area. The complex includes a restaurant, bar, and concert hall. Top-name artists, such as Eric Clapton and L.L. Cool J, perform in the 2,000-seat concert hall. There's live music nightly, everything from rock 'n' roll, jazz, and R&B to country, swing, and the blues. I would rather see a national act at the immense **Hard Rock Live Orlando,** however, where the acoustics are better and there are no support beams blocking your view of the stage. Bad sightlines are my main source of ire with the otherwise great HOB.

Meat markets... Orlando's not on the water, but somehow beach bars feel right at home here. Devoted Parrotheads and tourists in newly purchased parrot shirts gather at **Jimmy Buffett's Margaritaville** at CityWalk, searching for a little fun. Can you possibly stand another rendition of "Margaritaville"? The mango margaritas are worth a visit, but the live bands tend to be of the not-so-worth-the-trip variety. (If you drink enough, that may not matter.) It's a tourists'-night-out crowd at the **Rock 'n' Roll Beach Club** on Pleasure Island. Live rock-'n'-roll bands play loud and try hard to get the out-of-towners to loosen up and work their way onto the small dance floor. The young crowd lingers around the billiards table and plays a little pinball until they drink away their inhibitions. It's best to wait until a little later in the evening, say 9:30 or 10pm (not too late, though—remember this is Disney country, and when the clock strikes midnight, the carriage turns into a pumpkin) and just have a little fun on the dance floor. Downtown Orlando has its share of meat markets—you know, you can't sit still for more than 5 minutes without someone trying to hit on you. If this is your goal, try any of the clubs at **Wall Street Plaza,** a complex of clubs and bars a block down from The Social; or head over to Church Street, where you'll find **Mako's** and **Chillers.** If you can't get a phone number at any of these places, just call it a night.

Dancing fool... You can almost hear the hormones sizzling at the high-energy **Club at Firestone** in downtown Orlando. This former tire store, known for its late-night revelries (it's open until 3am), is one of Orlando's top dance bars for the over-21 crowd—though of late, it's a major fave of the gay community, as well. Dress up, arrive late, and forget about getting up early the next day.... **Mannequins Dance Palace** on Disney's Pleasure Island calls itself the number-one dance club in the Southeast. I suspect the Disney PR folks worked hard to land that one. The place is interesting enough: two floors filled with eerie life-size mannequins hanging from the rafters and peeping out from corners. The rotating dance floor is lit with state-of-the-art laser lights, and the great sound system is strong enough to wake Sleeping Beauty. But the clientele, though young, is made up mostly of self-conscious tourists who need a lot of liquid courage before they'll venture out to the dance floor (maybe the mannequins are scaring them away). Still, it's probably the liveliest place on Pleasure Island. The hyperactive **Motion,** also at Pleasure Island, sports cobalt blue walls and a kaleidoscope of lights and colors to keep the dance floor pulsing. The decor's supposed to make you think you're dancing in outer space, but the effect's more like...well, a cool dance floor. Music features top-40 tunes and alternative rock; it tends to get a youngish crowd. **Atlantic Dance Hall** at Disney's BoardWalk may still look like a 1930s-style ballroom filled with twinkling lights and a parquet dance floor, but the music spun by the DJs at this adults-only dance club runs from the hot hits of the 1970s to the top-40 of the 1990s. Universal's answer to Mannequins, **the groove** (because to be hip, you've got to have that e.e. cummings spelling thing down pat) is not quite as popular as Mannequins, though it certainly competes in the volume department. And you can fill your tanks at three color-themed lounges (the spacey blue one is the coolest, though the red is kind of sexy in a bordello sort of way) when you aren't on the dance floor. Most nights, a DJ plays tunes featuring the latest in hip-hop, jazz-fusion, techno, and alternative rock.

Smoking 'gars and martini bars... Cigar clubs are popping up everywhere—even in Orlando. The concept is so old-fashioned, it's in again. The upscale **Ybor's Martini Bar** in Orlando is a fast hit with hipster puffers. Check out the Taste of Cigars event, held from 5 to 8pm on the first and third Wednesdays of each month, and featuring special liquors and complimentary cigars plus a buffet. With a full bar, **Cigarz,** on the upper level of CityWalk, is a less hectic corner of Universal Orlando's entertainment complex. Plenty of pricey 'gars have gone up in smoke here...and the scotch isn't bad either.

Do the Hustle!... At Pleasure Island's **8Trax** club, sunburned tourists dance the night away a la Travolta, under disco-ball lights, to boogie-oogie hits from the likes of KC and the Sunshine Band, Donna Summer, and the Bee Gees. This place is something of an acquired taste, and those not into the tunes may not find it as groovy.

Jamaicin' me crazy.... It's a hot and sultry night and you're on vacation...what better than a little reggae to keep you in the mood? Stop by **Bob Marley—A Tribute to Freedom** at CityWalk, patterned after Marley's home and garden in Kingston. Live bands play on the courtyard stage, surrounded by lush gardens. Order up a plate of roasted plantains and toss back a few Red Stripes.

All that jazz... Rock 'n' roll music too "loud" for you? **The Social** in downtown Orlando hosts a number of top jazz acts throughout the year. Sip on a shaken-but-not-stirred martini and wade into the crowd; this place is usually filled to the max. The **House of Blues** at **Downtown Disney West Side** features a wide range of top-name musicians, but jazz and blues artists—both top-name and anonymous—make up a large part of the lineup. Check out the monthly calendar; there's something going on every night of the week. Look, too, to CityWalk's state-of-the-art **CityJazz** to bring in a lineup of popular artists. You can check out the stories behind jazz greats at the Down Beat Jazz Hall of Fame (included in CityJazz's cover), as well. The atmospheric club is a great place to see any band, and some real top-notch talent—Wynton Marsalis, for one—has performed here.

Bar essentials... Looking for a cold drink without fanfare, froufrou, or frills? At **Top of the Palace Lounge** on the 27th floor of the Buena Vista Palace hotel, you'll have a great view of the Magic Kingdom and its nightly fireworks, plus entertainment and better-than-average drinks (read: strong). For souls craving silence and solitude, meanwhile, **Crew's Cup Lounge,** at Disney's Yacht Club resort, features slip-in, sink-in leather chairs and loads of peace and quiet.

For those who know a bodhran from a pennywhistle... The new **Raglan Road Irish Pub and Restaurant** at Pleasure Island is a huge room (it replaced the Pleasure Island Jazz Company) that features four bars and a lengthy menu of traditional Gaelic cuisine served up with modern touches. Irish music, dancing, and storytelling liven things up from the stage. Tucked away in a little strip mall near Downtown Disney, **Kitty O'Shea's Irish Pub & Eatery** offers a great beer selection, daily drink specials, and local bands nightly. Head downtown for more Irish ambience. Make a stop at **Scruffy Murphy's** (who can resist the name?) for its dark and warm-as-a-shot-of-Jameson-whiskey atmosphere, then head over to sister bar **Kate O'Brien's Irish Pub,** which offers a livelier ambience and is consistently crowded, especially during its popular happy hour (4–7pm). Finally, lovers of traditional Irish music will want to head to the hugely popular **Mulvaney's Irish Pub** to sample the atmosphere and hear live entertainment, including Irish folk music.

Red hot rhythms and saucy salsa... Latin culture and sounds have arrived in Orlando at last. I'd like to think this development is a nod to Florida's ethnic diversity, but I suspect it's more likely due to the increasing popularity of Latin music and food. Either way, the lively, hip **Latin Quarter** at CityWalk is the best Latin club in town. Music (and munchies) from all 21 Latin nations is presented here, including salsa, merengue, and Latin pop, as are costumed dance troupes. Forget about quiet conversation, however—the sound system is loud enough to blow you into the next county. At **Bongos Cuban Cafe,** you'll want to grab one of the bongo-shaped bar stools (on hot nights, head for the patio overlooking the Seven Seas Lagoon), order up a mint-drenched *mojito,* and take in the scene (which, for good measure, includes a Desi Arnaz impersonator). This Downtown Disney Latin-themed restaurant/nightclub, owned by Gloria Estefan and her husband Emilio, is a festive, brightly colored, pineapple-shaped adobe festooned with hand-painted murals of old Cuba, plenty of tile work, and lots of Latin sounds. It's pretty tame; most folks come in for dinner or a couple of drinks (though after 10pm the place does begin to sizzle a bit).

Ride 'em cowboys.... Though now heavily masked by tourist attractions, fast-food joints, and tacky T-shirt shops, there still exists a cowboy/cowgirl subculture here. Don't expect the Cowboy Bar from Jackson Hole, but there are a few places around town where you can do a little two-steppin' and line dancing. **Cowboys** isn't in the best of neighborhoods, but if you're looking for a refined flavor of redneck country atmosphere, this 15,000-square-foot country-music venue should do the trick. You can boot-scoot here from Thursday to Saturday. Cowboys regularly offers two-for-one drink specials, and a top national act occasionally drops in.

Bar-stool quarterbacks... It doesn't matter who's playing, any night is a good night at Orlando's many sports bars. Even during slow, value-season times, you'll have to wait in line to get into **ESPN World** at Disney's BoardWalk. Why miss a game just because you're on vacation? Sports-crazed visitors flock to this lounge and restaurant (*the* sports mecca in town), where they can watch just about any athletic event that might be going on at the moment—all at once. There are about a gazillion television sets in the restaurant and lounge, all tuned in to some sportscast. It's the final minutes of a close game, you've been sucking down brewskies all evening, and nature is screaming?... Not to worry. There are even sets strategically placed above the stalls in the restrooms. Next door, you can try your hand at the ESPN arcade, a fantasyland of virtual-reality and video-arcade sports games. The **Official All-Star Cafe** at the entrance of Disney's Wide World of Sports complex has—surprise!—32 gigantic video screens playing sports events, and baseball-mitt-shaped booths. The food is ho-hum and overpriced.

Universal responded to the sports-themed restaurant/bar craze with **NBA City** at CityWalk. Hoopster fans can gather here to watch NBA and WNBA action amid roundball memorabilia. Test your b-ball skills on pop-a-shot games while you down a couple of longnecks. For those who prefer the roar of engines to the roar of the crowd, just down the street in CityWalk you'll find the **NASCAR Cafe,** a restaurant that caters to driving fans. Out front, the car driven by the current NASCAR Winston Cup champion is on display, while additional famous racing cars are on view inside (have a drink under Richard Petty's car!), along with a variety of other racing memorabilia. Burgers, beer, and big games are the focus at the **Kirkman Ale House,** a branch of the popular Ale House chain. Weekends and Monday nights are packed with locals chugging buckets of beer for $5 while watching their favorite sports team on the many televisions around the building.

Just for laughs... When was the last time you sat through a live stand-up comedy routine without hearing the "F" word? You'll hear nothing naughty at Disney's **Comedy Warehouse** on Pleasure Island. This squeaky-clean improv show features house comedians and is usually pretty corny; order a Shirley Temple to get in the mood. Better comedy can be found at the **SAK Comedy Lab** or **Orlando Improv** in downtown Orlando. Guaranteed to make you smile, the award-winning shows at both clubs feature troupes of actors and boast some of the best in improvisational comedy, as well as big-name comics. CityJazz at CityWalk plays host on the weekends to **Bonkerz Comedy Club,** home to a revolving door of big-name touring comedians.

Back at Pleasure Island, the quirky **Adventurers Club** offers comedic adventures of the interactive kind. It looks sort of like an English gentlemen's club and is chock-full of artifacts: hunting trophies, shrunken heads, and a mounted "yakoose," a half yak, half moose that occasionally speaks, whether you've been drinking or not. Also on hand are a zany band of servants and globetrotters (also known as Disney actors) who interact with guests. The comedy can get corny, but this is actually a fun place to hang out, especially after you've got a few drinks under your belt.

Painting the town pink and lavender... Suffice it to say that Orlando is no San Francisco. And when it comes to societal norms, Disney World is about as conservative as it gets, even though many cast members are homosexual. Those looking for same-sex companionship are best off heading into downtown Orlando, where you'll find **Parliament House, Southern Nights,** and **The Club at Firestone.** You'll also find unofficial gay nights (Thurs) at **Pleasure Island,** during "cast member appreciation nights." And while Disney refuses to publicly acknowledge the existence of the annual "Gay Days" festival, if you want to see a lot of same-sex events, visit Orlando during the first weekend (or so) in June. During this time over 100,000 gays and lesbians converge on the theme parks for a 5-day party. For official dates and events, visit www.gaydays.com.

Entertainment

Dinner theater dynamos... One look at Orlando's dinner theaters and you'll realize that moderation is a word that's been left out of the local lexicon. Tourists flock to these over-the-top extravaganzas, though, making tickets difficult to come by during peak vacation times. Go figure. For most, the show comes first; adding dinner seems merely a way to pass off average food as a reason to jack up prices. Some, however, actually try to give you the best entertainment for your hard-earned cash. For unabashed, irony-free country kitsch, try **Dolly Parton's Dixie Stampede.** The show is very family friendly—Ms. Parton doesn't even allow alcohol to be served on the premises, which may or may not be a plus depending on how you look at it—and the grub is actually worth raving about. The show is a little on the hokey side, with a loose plot about the North versus the South. But it's really just an excuse to get the audience involved—they even bring some people into the ring to participate in the contests. Special shows around the holidays actually feature Jesus descending/ascending from the rafters. The **Arabian Nights** dinner attraction, voted number one by *Orlando Sentinel* readers, offers some of the best and most showy and extravagant entertainment—including chariot races (yes, with real horses and manure), thrilling rides, and spectacular horse acts. This over-the-top, Las Vegas–style showmanship will impress even the most jaded among you. It's mostly for the kids, but you still may end up rooting for your designated knights at the **Medieval Times Dinner & Tournament.** You may even become the princess to be rescued. The audience is divided into teams and encouraged to cheer lustily as their favorites do battle. The **Hoop-Dee-Doo Musical Revue** at Fort Wilderness Resort & Campground is Disney's very popular country-western show. My table had mixed reviews for the hoedown-type, cornball jokes (remember the ones you used to tell in second grade?), and the food wasn't all that good—especially not for the price paid. But if you're toting kids, it's very family-friendly, and the high-energy performers interact with the audience quite often.

Bravo!... If you're going to spend 1 night on the town, grab an early bite at Downtown Disney and go see the fantastic **Cirque du Soleil** production, *La Nouba* (French for "live it up," and boy does this ever). The over-the-top theatrical fantasy (no lions or tigers, but you won't care) features extraordinary costumes, high-flying wire and trapeze acts (with truly amazing 360-degree spins, somersaults, and headstands on a 90-ft.-long high wire...you'll hold your breath), gymnastics, and acrobatics. The story line is as surreal as the setting: "Once upon a time, a door opened and two worlds collided. Dreams clashed with reality. The mundane mixed with the marvelous...." Nothing mundane remains once the curtain opens on this production. If you only see one show in Orlando, this is it. (***One caution:*** The seats are quite narrow, so if you need extra room, get an aisle seat.)

Amen! And please pass the grits.... Sunday morning at the theme park? Shame on you. Instead, reserve a table at the **House of Blues Gospel Brunch.** Hallelujah for this show! First, you'll feast on a Southern-style, low-country buffet, including dishes like spicy shrimp, grits, catfish, and the not-to-be-missed bread pudding drenched in silky bourbon sauce. The live music (provided by talented choruses from around the South) is loud and rambunctious; you'll be asked to put your hands together for Jesus and coaxed to your feet the minute the singing begins. The show is guaranteed to leave you feeling good for the rest of the day.

Wanna get lei'd?... Even though Orlando is an entire continent away from Hawaii, luau devotees have several options to choose from. Popular with kids is the nightly **Spirit of Aloha Polynesian Luau** at—you guessed it—Disney's Polynesian Resort. The preshow tells the story of a young Hawaiian girl as she grows up and ends with an appearance by Lilo and Stitch. Dinner selections include items such as Lanai roasted chicken, Polynesian rice, pork ribs, and a vegetable mix. Following dessert, the show picks up with some more traditional luau fire dancing and native interpretive dances. Just as much fun is the nightly **Makahiki Luau** at SeaWorld. It starts with the arrival of the tribal chief via boat, with a ceremonial progression leading the audience into a theater located in the Seafire Inn at the Waterfront. Throughout the night, you experience the ancient customs, rhythmic music and dance, authentic costumes, and cuisine of the Pacific Islands while dining family-style on Polynesian-influenced cuisine. My only complaint: The ventilation in the theater wasn't adequate for all the smoke that was used during the show. The vapors, though harmless, can get so thick near the front that you'll have a hard time making out your dinner companions, much less the doings on stage.

Playing Sherlock Holmes... Adults who love a mystery will enjoy the **MurderWatch Mystery Dinner Theater,** staged Saturday nights in the Grosvenor Resort's Baskervilles restaurant (which has a museum dedicated to the world's most famous sleuth). Dine in a spacious Edwardian-style room and watch a talented cast perform. Subtle hints and clues dropped during the course of the evening, and a series of funny confessions, help guests solve the mystery. This somewhat sophisticated offering is one of the city's best. **Sleuth's Mystery Show and Dinner** is yet another whodunit dinner. It's a bit more lighthearted than the production at the Grosvenor, with plenty of audience participation. Unlimited beer and wine offerings tend to loosen up the crowd as the show moves on.

Piano licks and singalongs... If you're feeling a bit subdued, it's best to stay away from bars with dueling grand pianos, where two keyboardists play favorite singalong tunes and the audience is not allowed to just sit and listen. (***Warning:*** This could be sheer torture for some.) Disney's singalong venue is **Jellyrolls Piano Bar** at the BoardWalk entertainment district. It's designed to look like a giant warehouse full of mismatched chairs and tables, battered crates, and clutter. The featured musicians try to outdo each other, and the audience joins in. Loud, raucous, and sure to irritate if you're not in the mood. If you really like this kind of thing, you might want to check out **Pat O'Brien's** at CityWalk. This replica of the original Big Easy establishment prides itself on its dueling pianos; it's a magnet for tourists out on the town drinking fancy "flaming fountain" and "Hurricane" drinks (which either reduce or inflame the irritation factor).

Theater, opera, and dance... Sure, monster-truck rallies and wet T-shirt contests are popular down here, but if you look hard, you'll find some redeeming entertainment, too. The **Orlando Opera Company** has brought national and international performers to its stage for almost 30 years. Shows are performed at the **Bob Carr Performing Arts Centre** in downtown Orlando, drawing audiences from all over Central Florida. The **Orlando Broadway Series,** a schedule of touring Broadway productions, is also performed at the Bob Carr Performing Arts Centre. The **Civic Theatre of Central Florida** presents Broadway, off-Broadway, and family classics on three stages. The theater is located in pretty Loch Haven Park, a quiet, tree-lined oasis that is also home to the Orlando Science Museum, the Orange County Historical Museum, and the Orlando Museum of Art (see the Diversions chapter). When it comes to dance, Orlandoans and visitors have one choice: the **Orlando Ballet,** the only professional dance company in Central Florida. Its varied selection of scores tries to please traditionalists as well as those with more modern tastes. Performances are at the Bob Carr Performing Arts Centre.

Map 13: Orlando Area Nightlife & Entertainment

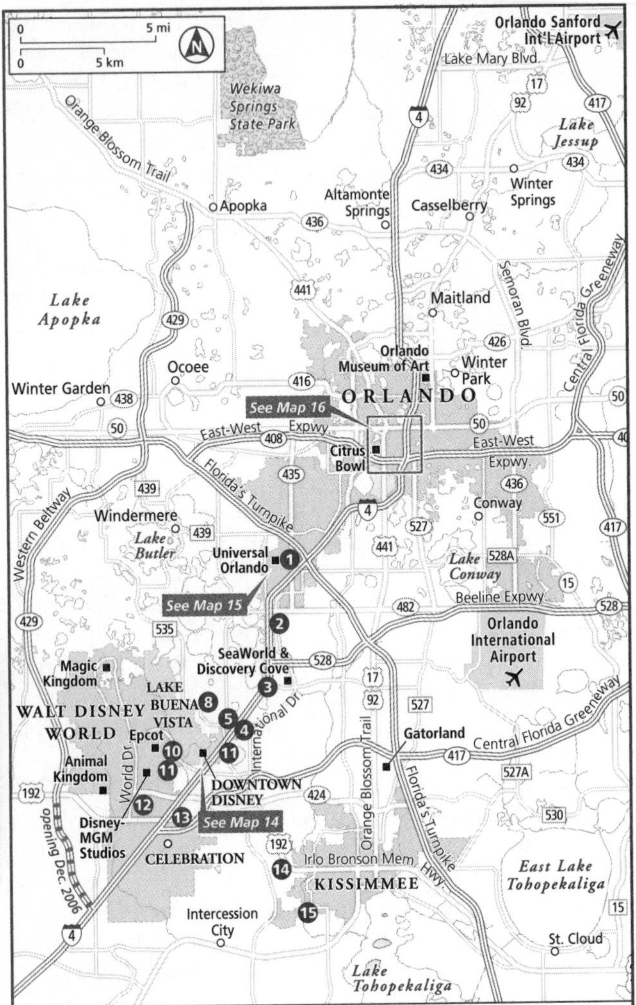

Arabian Nights **13**
Atlantic Ballroom **11**
Crew's Cup Lounge **10**
Dolly Parton's Dixie Stampede **4**
ESPN World **11**
Hoop-Dee-Doo Music Review **6**
Jellyrolls Piano Bar **11**
Kirkman Ale House **2**
Kitty O'Shea's Irish Pub & Eatery **5**
Makahiki Luau **3**
Medieval Times Dinner & Tournament **14**
MurderWatch Mystery Dinner Theater **9**
Official All-Star Cafe **12**
Sleuth's Mystery Show and Dinner **2**
Spirit of Aloha Polynesian Lounge **7**
Top of the Palace Lounge **8**

Map 14: Downtown Disney Nightlife & Entertainment

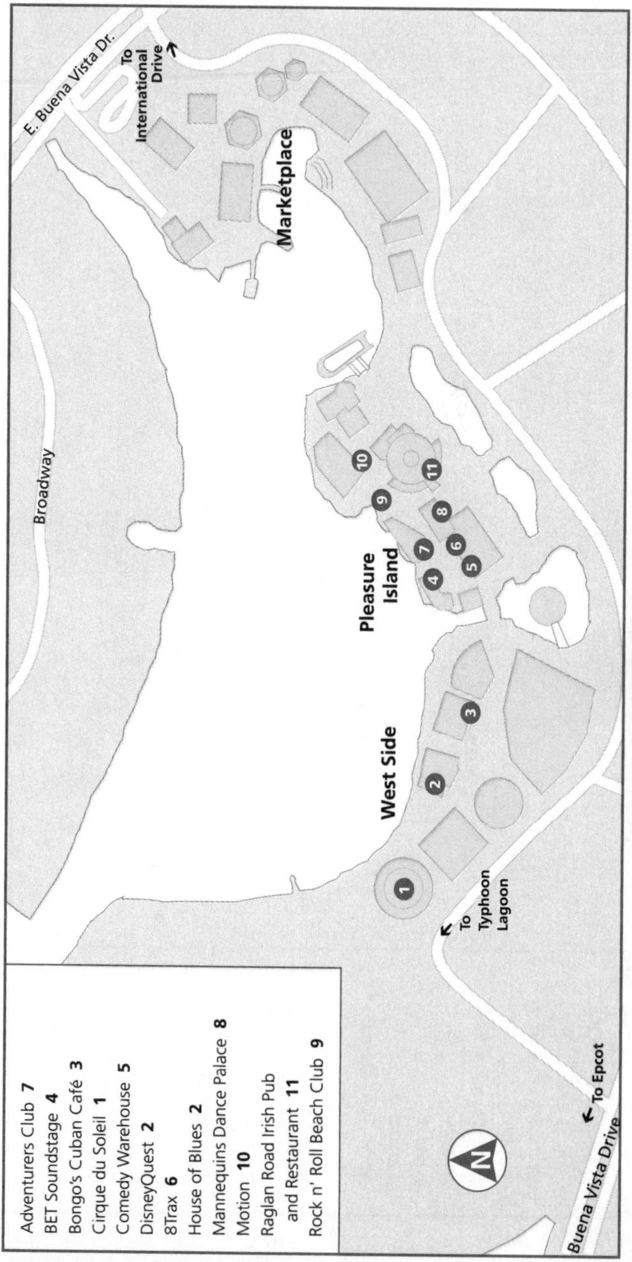

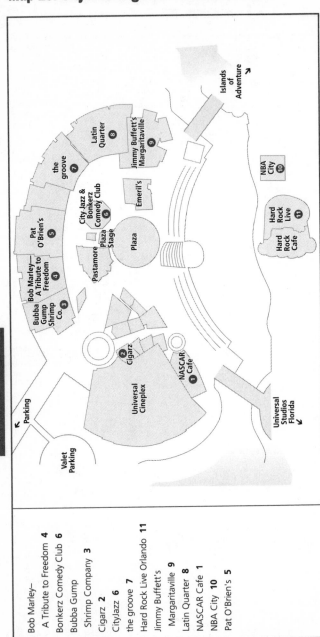

Map 15: CityWalk Nightlife & Entertainment

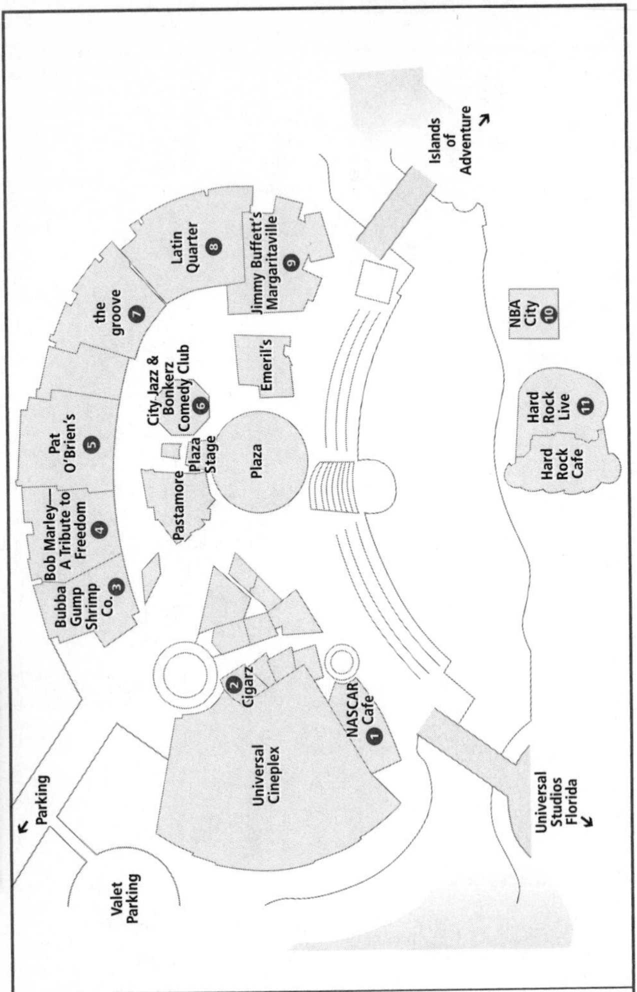

Bob Marley–
A Tribute to Freedom **4**
Bonkerz Comedy Club **6**
Bubba Gump
Shrimp Company **3**
Cigarz **2**
CityJazz **6**
the groove **7**
Hard Rock Live Orlando **11**
Jimmy Buffett's
Margaritaville **9**
Latin Quarter **8**
NASCAR Cafe **1**
NBA City **10**
Pat O'Brien's **5**

Map 16: Downtown Orlando Nightlife & Entertainment

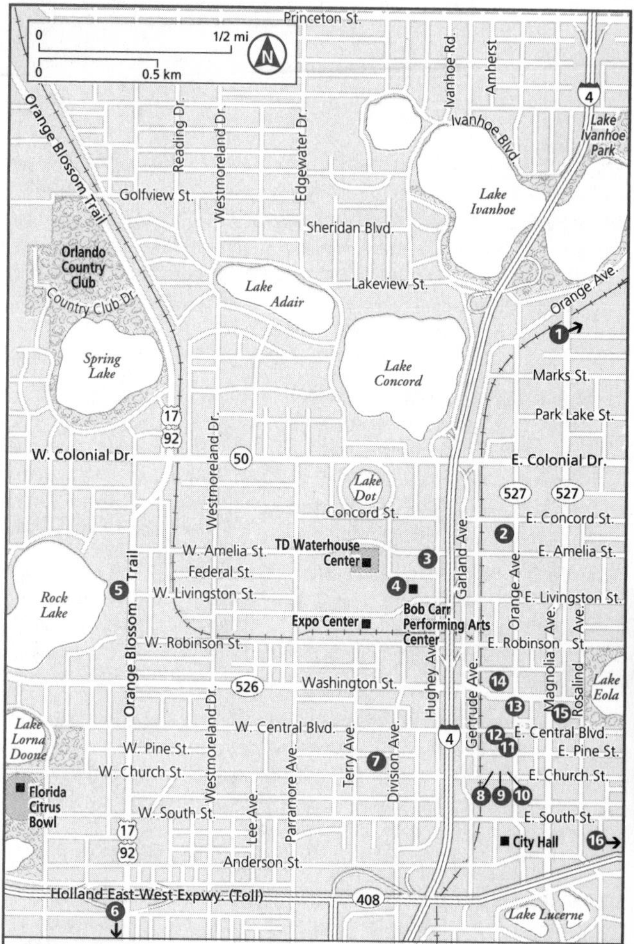

Backbooth **11**
Bob Carr Performing Arts Centre **4**
Chillers **9**
Civic Theatre of Central Florida **1**
The Club at Firestone **2**
Cowboys **6**
Kate O'Brien's Irish Pub **12**
Mako's **10**
Mulvaney's Irish Pub **10**
Orlando Ballet **4**
Orlando Broadway Series **4**
Orlando Improv **7**
Orlando Opera Company **4**
Parliament House **3**
SAK Comedy Lab **3**
Scruffy Murphy's **14**
The Social **13**
Southern Nights **16**
Wall Street Plaza **15**
Ybor's Martini Bar **8**

The Index

Adventurers Club (p. 205) DOWNTOWN DISNEY Pleasure Island's most quirky venue offers comedy, cabaret, and madcap interactive fun. Sip one of the potent tropical drinks in the library or the bar, where elephant-foot bar stools rise and sink mysteriously.... *Tel 407/934-7781. Pleasure Island, Downtown Disney.*

See Map 14 on p. 211.

Arabian Nights (p. 206) KISSIMMEE If you want to take in a dinner show, this should be the one. Fifty horses and expert riders put on a colorful, amazing extravaganza that can give Las Vegas a run for its money.... *Tel 407/239-9223. www.arabian-nights.com. 6225 W. Hwy. 192. Tickets $46–$57 adults, $21–$32 kids 3–11.*

See Map 13 on p. 210.

Atlantic Dance Hall (p. 201) WDW Dance to big-band sounds at this 1930s-style retro lounge and ballroom. Martinis and twinkling lights set the stage.... *Tel 407/824-4321. Disney's BoardWalk, 2101 N. Epcot Resorts Blvd., off Buena Vista Dr. No cover.*

See Map 13 on p. 210.

BackBooth (p. 200) DOWNTOWN ORLANDO The onetime campus legend has bigger digs now in downtown Orlando. Books bands of all genres, both local and national, as well as specialty shows like the Suicide Girls burlesque.... *Tel 407/999-2570. www.backbooth.com. 37 W. Pine St. Cover varies.*

See Map 16 on p. 213.

BET Soundstage (p. 197) DOWNTOWN DISNEY This club grooves—loudly—to the sounds of reggae, R&B, and hip-hop. Boogie on an expansive dance floor or kick back on an outdoor terrace. If you like the BET Cable Network, you'll love it.... *Tel 407/934-7666. Pleasure Island, Downtown Disney.*

See Map 14 on p. 211.

Bob Carr Performing Arts Centre (p. 209) DOWNTOWN ORLANDO Part of the taxpayer-funded Centroplex, which also boasts the T.D. Waterhouse Arena and an expo center, Bob Carr is Orlando's big-time stage for the performing arts.... *Tel 407/849-2577. 401 W. Livingston St. Ticket prices vary.*

See Map 16 on p. 213.

Bob Marley—A Tribute to Freedom (p. 202) UNIVERSAL ORLANDO Head here on a hot night for reggae and to pay homage to the man. Live music and lots of memorabilia.... *Tel 407/224-3663. CityWalk. Cover varies.*

See Map 15 on p. 212.

Bongos Cuban Cafe (p. 203) DOWNTOWN DISNEY Gloria Estefan and hubby Emilio own this Latin-themed restaurant/nightclub. Festive and lively, especially after a couple of *mojitos.... Tel 407/828-0999. Downtown Disney West Side. No cover.*

See Map 14 on p. 211.

Bonkerz Comedy Club (p. 205) UNIVERSAL ORLANDO The humor flows Thursday through Saturday nights at CityJazz.... *Tel 407/629-2665. www.bonkerscomedyclub.com. CityWalk. Cover varies.*

See Map 15 on p. 212.

Chillers (p. 201) DOWNTOWN ORLANDO Great drink specials, but the bar is always packed so it takes a while to get another round.... *Tel 407/649-4270. 33 W. Church St. No cover.*

See Map 16 on p. 213.

Cigarz (p. 202) UNIVERSAL ORLANDO Huff and puff away in this corner bar at CityWalk, which offers smooth scotch and occasional acoustic performances by local musicians.... *Tel 407/370-2999. CityWalk, 1000 Universal Studios Plaza, Orlando. No cover.*

See Map 15 on p. 212.

Cirque du Soleil (p. 207) DOWNTOWN DISNEY Their *La Nouba* production is the best show in town. Extraordinary mix of costumes, music, high wire, trapeze, and acrobatics. Worth the steep admission price, though it occasionally offers hefty discounts on multiple tickets bought at the same time.... *Tel 407/939-7600. Downtown Disney West Side. Tickets $61–$95 adults, $49–$76 kids 3–9.*

See Map 14 on p. 211.

CityJazz (p. 202) UNIVERSAL ORLANDO Universal's venue for jazz lovers is also home to the Down Beat Jazz Hall of Fame. Look for big-name artists and fine jazz players.... *Tel 407/363-8000. CityWalk. Cover varies.*

See Map 15 on p. 212.

CityWalk (p. 196) UNIVERSAL ORLANDO Universal's entertainment complex boasts 30 acres of nightclubs, restaurants, a multiscreen cineplex, and specialty shops. Check it out.... *Tel 407/363-8000. www.citywalk.com. 1000 Universal Studios Plaza, Orlando. Club and restaurant hours vary. Party Pass to all clubs costs $10.*

See Map 15 on p. 212.

Civic Theatre of Central Florida (p. 209) DOWNTOWN ORLANDO Professional-quality Broadway, off-Broadway, and family classics are performed throughout the year.... *Tel 407/896-7365. 1001 E. Princeton St. Ticket prices vary.*

See Map 16 on p. 213.

The Club at Firestone (p. 201) DOWNTOWN ORLANDO Currently home to a revolving list of dance parties every night of the week. Continuously books some of the best DJs on the dance scene to spin for the crowd and hosts a popular "gay night" dance party on Saturday (all are welcome).... *Tel 407/426-0005. www.clubatfirestone.com. 578 N. Orange Ave. Cover varies.*

See Map 16 on p. 213.

Comedy Warehouse (p. 205) DOWNTOWN DISNEY The cleanest comedy you'll ever hear, performed by Disney's house comedians.... *Tel 407/934-7781. Pleasure Island, Downtown Disney.*

See Map 14 on p. 211.

Cowboys (p. 204) DOWNTOWN ORLANDO Less of a redneck vibe than you might expect, this huge bar offers nightly drink specials sure to loosen your bolero.... *Tel 407/422-7115. www.cowboysorlando.com. 1108 S. Orange Blossom Trail. Cover varies.*

See Map 16 on p. 213.

Crew's Cup Lounge (p. 203) WDW This quiet and comfy lounge, tucked away in Disney's Yacht Club resort, is a cozy place to escape the madness.... *Tel 407/824-4321. Disney's Yacht Club Resort, 1700 Epcot Resorts Blvd., off Buena Vista Dr. No cover.*

See Map 13 on p. 210.

Dolly Parton's Dixie Stampede (p. 206) ORLANDO Disney's newest dinner theater is a great choice for families; cheer for the North or South while you eat your vittles.... *Tel 866/443-4943. 8251 Vineland Ave. Tickets $49 adults, $22 kids 3–11.*

See Map 13 on p. 210.

Downtown Disney West Side (p. 202) DOWNTOWN DISNEY Disney's entertainment complex adjacent to Pleasure Island. Home to the House of Blues, Cirque du Soleil, and a variety of restaurants and shops.... *Tel 407/828-3058. Buena Vista Dr.*

See Map 14 on p. 211.

8Trax (p. 202) DOWNTOWN DISNEY Get down and boogie to '70s classics; can be a lot of fun with the right people.... *Tel 407/934-7781. Pleasure Island, Downtown Disney.*

See Map 14 on p. 211.

ESPN World (p. 204) WDW A huge sports-themed bar at Disney's BoardWalk entertainment district.... *Tel 407/939-6200. Disney's BoardWalk, 2101 N. Epcot Resorts Blvd., off Buena Vista Dr. No cover.*

See Map 13 on p. 210.

the groove (p. 201) UNIVERSAL ORLANDO Not as hip as it aspires to be, but the high-tech sound system and the themed lounges and drinks pack 'em in.... *Tel 407/224-2227. www.citywalk.com. CityWalk. Cover varies.*

See Map 15 on p. 212.

Hard Rock Live Orlando (p. 200) UNIVERSAL ORLANDO Large concert hall drawing top-name national and international artists.... *Tel 407/351-5483. www.hardrock.com. CityWalk. Ticket prices vary.*

See Map 15 on p. 212.

Hoop-Dee-Doo Musical Revue (p. 207) WDW This hoedown, ho-hum dinner show is booked up months in advance. Not my first choice for dinner-theater options, but not the worst, either.... *Tel 407/939-3463. Disney's Fort Wilderness Resort & Campground, 3520 N. Fort Wilderness Trail. Tickets $51 adults, $26 kids 3–9.*

See Map 13 on p. 210.

House of Blues (p. 200) DOWNTOWN DISNEY A top-notch venue for all kinds of music—rock 'n' roll, jazz, R&B, country, swing, and lots of blues. Try to make their Sunday Gospel Brunch, or drop by anytime for their good Southern cuisine.... *Tel 407/934-2583. www.hob.com. Downtown Disney's West Side. Ticket prices vary.*

See Map 14 on p. 211.

Jellyrolls Piano Bar (p. 209) WDW Two pianists battle it out while the audience cheers, claps, and sings along.... *Tel 407/939-6200. Disney's BoardWalk, 2101 N. Epcot Resorts Blvd. Cover varies.*

See Map 13 on p. 210.

Jimmy Buffett's Margaritaville (p. 200) UNIVERSAL ORLANDO Parrotheads flock to this tourist-magnet, which offers three bars and the occasional live band. Mango margaritas are great, the rest of the place, merely so-so.... *Tel 407/363-8000. www.margaritavilleorlando.com. CityWalk. Cover varies.*

See Map 15 on p. 212.

Kate O'Brien's Irish Pub (p. 203) DOWNTOWN ORLANDO Popular Irish bar with lively music, crowds, and happy-hour specials. Orlandoans love it.... *Tel 407/649-7646. www.kateobriens.net. 46 W. Central Blvd. Cover for special events varies.*

See Map 16 on p. 213.

Kirkman Ale House (p. 205) ORLANDO A great place to watch your favorite game. Plenty of good munchies and friendly locals.... *Tel 407/248-0000. www.alehouseinc.com. 5573 S. Kirkman Rd. No cover.*

See Map 13 on p. 210.

Kitty O'Shea's Irish Pub & Eatery (p. 203) ORLANDO Popular Irish bar with lively music, crowds, and happy-hour specials; all within punting distance of Disney.... *Tel 407/238-9769. www.kittyosheaspub.com. 8470 Palm Pkwy. No cover.*

See Map 13 on p. 210.

Latin Quarter (p. 203) UNIVERSAL ORLANDO This venue is tops for Latin music, and the food's not bad either. Live music from 21 South American nations fills the bill.... *Tel 407/224-3663. CityWalk. Cover varies.*

See Map 15 on p. 212.

Makahiki Luau (p. 208) SEAWORLD This 2-hour Polynesian dinner show at SeaWorld is one of city's better offerings, featuring an all-you-can-eat buffet, even a fire dancer or two!... *Tel 800/327-2420. www.seaworld.com. The Seafire Inn at SeaWorld, 7007 SeaWorld Dr. Tickets $49 adults, $32 kids 3–9.*

See Map 13 on p. 210.

Mako's (p. 201) DOWNTOWN ORLANDO Its motto is "anything goes at Mako's." Nothing more than a meat market with a dance floor and girls on swings.... *Tel 407/872-3296. www.anythinggoesatmakos.com. 27 W. Church St. Cover varies.*

See Map 16 on p. 213.

Mannequins Dance Palace (p. 201) DOWNTOWN DISNEY Pleasure Island's hottest dance venue.... *Tel 407/934-7781. www.disneyworld.com. Pleasure Island, Downtown Disney.*

See Map 14 on p. 211.

Medieval Times Dinner & Tournament (p. 207) KISSIMMEE Finger-lickin' fun: Knights in shining armor compete on horseback as you tear into chicken and ribs with your bare hands.... *Tel 800/229-8300. www.medievaltimes.com. 4510 W. Hwy. 192. Tickets $50 adults, $34 kids 3–11.*

See Map 13 on p. 210.

Motion (p. 201) DOWNTOWN DISNEY Pleasure Island's Space Age dance club tries hard to be hip and trendy, but the tunes run from alternative to top 40 to please the T-shirt-and-sneakers theme-park crowds.... *Tel 407/934-7781. www.disneyworld.com. Pleasure Island, Downtown Disney.*

See Map 14 on p. 211.

Mulvaney's Irish Pub (p. 203) DOWNTOWN ORLANDO Considered by many to be the best Irish pub in Orlando. Lots of authentic music and crowds.... *Tel 407/872-3296. 27 W. Church St. No cover.*

See Map 16 on p. 213.

MurderWatch Mystery Dinner Theater (p. 208) LAKE BUENA VISTA Dinner, a murder, and you—along with the rest of the guests—try to solve the case.... *Tel 407/827-6534. www.murderwatch.com.*

Grosvenor Resort, 1850 Hotel Plaza Blvd. Tickets $40 adults, $11 kids under 10.

See Map 13 on p. 210.

NASCAR Cafe (p. 205) UNIVERSAL ORLANDO Racing fans flock to this car-lover's haven. The restaurant/bar is known more for its memorabilia than its food.... *Tel 407/224-3663. www.nascarcafeorlando.com. CityWalk. No cover.*

See Map 15 on p. 212.

NBA City (p. 205) UNIVERSAL ORLANDO Universal's nirvana for hoops-obsessed fans. This restaurant/bar pays tribute to every aspect of b-ball action..... *Tel 407/363-5919. www.nbacity.com. CityWalk. No cover.*

See Map 15 on p. 212.

Official All-Star Cafe (p. 204) WDW One of the dozen celebrity-owned chain sports bars/restaurants in the country..... *Tel 407/939-3463. www.disneyworld.com. Walt Disney's Wide World of Sports, 6910 S. Victory Way. No cover.*

See Map 13 on p. 210.

Orlando Ballet (p. 209) DOWNTOWN ORLANDO This troupe puts on traditional shows such as *The Nutcracker* using guest artists to augment local talent.... *Tel 407/426-1739 for information; 877/803-7073 or 407/839-3900 to get tickets. 111 N. Orange Ave. Ticket prices vary.*

See Map 16 on p. 213.

Orlando Broadway Series (p. 209) DOWNTOWN ORLANDO The latest hits from the Great White Way, staged at the Bob Carr Performing Arts Centre by touring companies.... *Tel 800/448-6322 (Broadway Across America) or 407/423-9999 (Ticketmaster) for tickets. www.broadwayacrossamerica.com. Bob Carr Performing Arts Centre, 401 W. Livingston St. Ticket prices vary.*

See Map 16 on p. 213.

Orlando Improv (p. 205) DOWNTOWN ORLANDO Comedy club in downtown Orlando that features national and touring comedians.... *Tel 321/281-8000. www.orlandoimprov.com. 129 W. Church St. Ticket prices vary.*

See Map 16 on p. 213.

Orlando Opera Company (p. 209) DOWNTOWN ORLANDO Though mostly composed of local stars, this company has brought national and international stars to the stage, including mezzo-soprano Cecilia Bartoli.... *Tel 407/426-1700 (toll-free 800/336-7372). www.orlandoopera.org. 401 W. Livingston St. Ticket prices vary.*

See Map 16 on p. 213.

Parliament House (p. 206) DOWNTOWN ORLANDO A club with drag shows attached to a motel—what more could you want for a night of all-out gay partying?... *Tel 407/425-7571. www.parliamenthouse.com. 410 N. Orange Blossom Trail. Cover varies.*

See Map 16 on p. 213.

Pat O'Brien's (p. 209) UNIVERSAL ORLANDO Hoist a Hurricane and listen to the dueling pianists at this replica of the Big Easy's famous bar. You have to be in the mood.... *Tel 407/363-8000. www.patobriens.com. CityWalk. Cover varies.*

See Map 15 on p. 212.

Pleasure Island (p. 196) DOWNTOWN DISNEY Disney's one-stop, one-price entertainment complex, where every night is New Year's Eve..... *Tel 407/934-7781. www.disneyworld.com. Downtown Disney, Buena Vista Dr. Admission $21.*

See Map 14 on p. 211.

Raglan Road Irish Pub and Restaurant (p. 203) DOWNTOWN DISNEY It's a giant-sized Irish pub, complete with traditional music, dancing, beer, and shepherd's pie.... *Tel 407/938-0300. www.disneyworld.com. Pleasure Island, Downtown Disney.*

See Map 14 on p. 211.

Rock 'n' Roll Beach Club (p. 200) DOWNTOWN DISNEY Disney trying to be hip. The decor is surfboards, billiards, and dart boards. Rock bands entice tourists to move onto the dance floor.... *Tel 407/934-7781. www.disneyworld.com. Pleasure Island, Downtown Disney.*

See Map 14 on p. 211.

SAK Comedy Lab (p. 205) DOWNTOWN ORLANDO One of the best places for improv comedy in Orlando.... *Tel 407/648-0001. www.sak.com. 380 W. Amelia St. Ticket prices vary.*

See Map 16 on p. 213.

Scruffy Murphy's (p. 203) DOWNTOWN ORLANDO This warm and wonderful Irish pub features dark woods and potent potables. Popular with locals.... *Tel 407/648-5460. www.scruffys.com. 25 S. Magnolia Ave. No cover.*

See Map 16 on p. 213.

Sleuth's Mystery Show and Dinner (p. 208) INTERNATIONAL DRIVE Guests are called upon to solve a mystery from clues dropped by cast members.... *Tel 407/363-1985. www.sleuths.com. 8267 International Dr. Tickets $48 adults, $24 kids 3–11.*

See Map 13 on p. 210.

The Social (p. 199) DOWNTOWN ORLANDO The best spot in town for live music changes dramatically from night to night, depending on the act.... *Tel 407/246-1419. www.thesocial.org. 54 N. Orange Ave. Ticket prices vary.*

See Map 16 on p. 213.

Southern Nights (p. 206) DOWNTOWN ORLANDO A local hangout for gays and lesbians in downtown Orlando.... *Tel 407/898-0424. www.southern-nights.com. 375 S. Bumby Ave., Orlando.*

See Map 16 on p. 213.

Spirit of Aloha Polynesian Luau (p. 208) WDW Disney's popular version of a Polynesian luau.... *Tel 407/939-3463. www.disneyworld.com. Disney's Polynesian Resort, 1600 Seven Seas Dr. Tickets $51 adults, $26 kids 3–9.*

See Map 13 on p. 210.

Top of the Palace Lounge (p. 203) LAKE BUENA VISTA Go for the view. This is the best place to stay and watch the Magic Kingdom's nightly fireworks show.... *Tel 407/827-2727. Buena Vista Palace, 1900 Buena Vista Dr. No cover.*

See Map 13 on p. 210.

Wall Street Plaza (p. 200) DOWNTOWN ORLANDO This crowded downtown complex is comprised of eight clubs, restaurants, and lounges. Enjoy a variety of atmospheres from dance to live music..... *Tel 407/420-1515. 25 Wall Street Plaza. Covers vary.*

See Map 16 on p. 213.

Ybor's Martini Bar (p. 202) DOWNTOWN ORLANDO Hip and upscale place to sip 'tinis and smoke stogies.... *Tel 407/316-8006. 41 W. Church St. No cover.*

See Map 16 on p. 213.

HOTLINES & OTHER BASICS

Airport... Orlando is served by two airports. The main airport is **Orlando International Airport (MCO)** (Tel 407/825-2001; www.state.fl.us/goaa). More than 44 scheduled airlines and 41 charters provide service to more than 100 cities worldwide. The airport is located about 15 miles from the major attractions and downtown Orlando. Some charters and budget airlines are now flying into **Orlando-Sanford International Airport** (Tel 407/585-4500; www.orlandosanfordairport.com), more than an hour away from Disney.

Airport transportation to the city... If your Orlando package doesn't include transportation and you don't plan to rent a car, contact **Mears Transportation Group** (Tel 407/423-5566 or 800/759-5219; www.mearstransportation.com), which operates shuttles from Orlando International to all area hotels and attractions. They depart from the baggage-claim level of the airport 24 hours a day. Round-trip shuttle fares from the airport to International Drive,

Lake Buena Vista, and downtown Orlando range from $26 to $30 per adult, $19 to $22 per child age 4 to 11; cabs are $2.75 for the first mile and $1.50 for each additional mile. From the Universal Orlando area to downtown Orlando, the fare is around $24.

All-night pharmacies... To pick up a bottle of cough syrup at 3am, try **Walgreen's** 24-hour pharmacy at 7650 W. Sand Lake Rd. (Tel 407/345-9497). Other locations can be found near Universal Orlando and Kissimmee by logging on to www.walgreens.com.

Babysitters... Have kids along for the ride? Many Orlando hotels, including all of Disney's resorts, offer babysitting services, usually from an outside service such as **Kids Nite Out** (Tel 407/828-0920 or 800/696-8105; www.kidsniteout.com) or **All About Kids** (Tel 407/812-9300 or 800/728-6506; www.all-about-kids.com). Child-care rates usually run $12 per hour for the first child and $1 per additional child, per hour. Several of Walt Disney World's expensive resorts also have child-care centers that cater to kids ages 4 to 12. If you'd like to park your children here for a few hours, advance reservations are a must; call Tel 407/939-3463.

Buses... Don't use the public Lynx buses or you'll spend your entire vacation en route to somewhere. The **I-Ride** trolleys (Tel 407/248-9590; www.iridetrolley.com) serve International Drive, departing every 15 minutes from 8am to 10:30pm. The 54 stops include SeaWorld on the south end and Belz Factory Outlet World on the north. Look for I-RIDE on markers. The fare is $1 per ride (kids under 12 ride free); multiday passes are available. **Lymmo** (Tel 407/841-8240; www.golynx.com) is a downtown-only bus service operated by Lynx that circulates through the main drags (including Orange Ave.) about every 10 minutes. Lymmo operates from 6am to 10pm Monday to Thursday, 6am to midnight on Friday, 10am to midnight on Saturday, and 10am to 10pm on Sunday and holidays. The fare is $1.50 one-way.

Car rentals... Even if you're staying at Walt Disney World, you might end up wishing upon a star for a car. If you're planning to park-hop, you'll be feeling Grouchy and Sleepy during the long waits for Disney buses. Plus, if you have wheels, you're free to make grocery runs and find cheaper and/or better restaurants. Rates vary depending on the season, but be prepared to pay a sales tax, an airport tax, and a state surcharge on top of your rental fee; that $20 per day (or whatever) is just the beginning. Try to book way in advance to get the best selection and rates. And remember, this is the number-one tourist destination in the world; ask for something fuchsia and metallic to stand out in the sea of vehicles at the Goofy lot at Disney. All of the major car-rental companies operate out of Orlando (mostly at or near the airport), including **Alamo** (Tel 800/522-9696; www.goalamo.com), **Avis** (Tel 800/230-4898; www.avis.com), **Budget** (Tel 800/527-0700; www.budget.com), **Dollar** (Tel 800/800-4000; www.dollar.com), **Hertz** (Tel 800/654-3131; www.hertz.com), and **National** (Tel 800/227-7368; www.nationalcar.com).

Climate... No, it's not always 75 and balmy. It can get downright chilly in late December and early January, though day temps in the mid-60s to 70s (upper teens to low 20s Celsius) are more common. Spring and fall are generally pleasant, with day temps hovering in the 80s (upper 20s Celsius). But once June rolls around, you can count on serious heat and humidity. You'll sweat the minute you get off the plane, and you won't stop until you get back on it. Think 90°F (32°C) or more and 90% humidity, with brief but powerful afternoon electrical storms thrown in almost daily for good measure. (Central Florida is the lightning capital of the U.S., and Mother Nature makes sure that Mickey doesn't steal all the thunder in town.) Nights are a bit cooler, and if you retreat indoors, you can count on goose-bump-inducing air-conditioning, especially in grocery stores and movie theaters, although Floridians often crank up the heat when the temperature dips to 50°F (10°C).

Convention center... Orlando's **Orange County Convention Center** (Tel 407/345-9800; www.occc.net) is located in southwest Orlando in Plaza International. It currently provides more than 1.1 million square feet of exhibit space. The center has its own food court and in-house telephone service, and it's located within eight blocks of several thousand hotel rooms. Many more rooms are located within a 15-minute drive of the center.

Dentists... Nothing like a broken crown or throbbing molar to ruin your day. To find an emergency dentist in Orlando, contact **Dental Referral Service** (Tel 800/235-4111; www.dentalreferral.com).

Discounted tickets... For discounted attractions tickets and same-day cultural-performance tickets that don't require a daylong tour of a timeshare property, visit the Orlando/Orange County Convention and Visitors Bureau's **Official Visitor Information Center,** 8723 International Dr., Suite 201 (Tel 407/363-5872), at the corner of International Drive and Austrian Row. The center also offers bilingual brochures and accommodations information, and its (unbiased) staff can answer virtually any question you might ask about Orlando. It's open daily 8am to 7pm year-round, except on Christmas Day. While you're there, ask for your free **Orlando Magicard,** a piece of plastic that provides savings of 10% to 50% at 102 area businesses, including attractions, accommodations, and restaurants. To order a Magicard by phone (it comes with a complete visitor information kit), call Tel 800/551-1081 or visit www.orlandoinfo.com.

Doctors... For minor problems that occur during a theme-park visit (blisters, allergic reactions), visit the park's **First Aid Center;** these are noted on the park maps you pick up when you enter. If you have a serious emergency, go directly to a nearby hospital emergency room. **Sand Lake Hospital,** 9400 Turkey Lake Rd. (Tel 407/351-8500), is a full-service hospital with a 24-hour emergency department. **Doctors on Call Service** (Tel 407/399-3627) makes house and room calls in most of the Orlando area. **Florida Hospital Centra-Care** has several walk-in clinics, including ones on Vineland Road (Tel 407/351-6682) and at Lake Buena Vista near Disney (Tel 407/934-2273).

Driving around... If you are going out drinking, take along a designated driver. Under Florida law, those caught driving with a blood-alcohol level of .08 or higher, or who refuse to take a requested breathalyzer test, will have their driver's license suspended immediately by the arresting officer. It can be a long walk home. Florida law also requires drivers and front-seat passengers, regardless of

ORLANDO ONLINE TOOLBOX

CitySearch, http://orlando.citysearch.com *The local branch of Microsoft's city-guide network.*

Florida Traveler Discount Guide, www.travelerdiscountguide.com *Send in $3 (for shipping) to get this otherwise free booklet of discounts on hotels, restaurants, and attractions.*

Metroblogging Orlando, http://orlando.metblogs.com *Group blog of all things Orlandoan, from food to events to local news.*

Mousesavers, www.mousesavers.com *Encyclopedic and constantly updated list of discount offers and reservation codes available at Disney hotels and resorts.*

Orlando Magazine, www.orlandomagazine.com *A glossy city mag on local culture, news, and politics, with a few restaurant reviews thrown in.*

Orlando Magicard, www.orlandoinfo.com/magicard *Massive discounts on non-Disney hotels, transit, shopping, and theme parks.*

TouringPlans.com, www.touringplans.com *Create customized theme-park touring plans that save you time and money.*

Universal Excitement, www.universal-excitement.com *Slick fan site devoted to all things Universal.*

Walt Disney World Information Guide, www.allearsnet.com *Almost obsessive level of detail on every square inch of the World, all collected by independent enthusiasts.*

age, to wear a seat belt. Children 5 and under must ride in a safety seat (most rental-car companies can provide you with a car seat).

Emergencies... Call Tel **911** in an emergency for an ambulance, the fire department, or the police.

Festivals & Special Events

Orlando boasts a variety of annual events, about 140 in all. Here's a sampling:

JANUARY: The **Capital One Florida Citrus Bowl** (Tel 407/423-2476 or 800/297-2695) pits the second-ranked teams from the Southeastern and Big Ten conferences against each other.

FEBRUARY: The 3-day **Silver Spurs Rodeo** (Tel 407/847-4052) kicks off twice a year, in February and October, at Silver Spurs Arena, 1875 E. Irlo Bronson Memorial Hwy. (U.S. 192), Kissimmee. The biggest rodeo in the East, it features real yippee-I-O cowboys calf roping, bull riding, barrel racing, and more. Tickets range from $12 to $30.

MARCH: Winter Park celebrates the arts midmonth with a free **Sidewalk Festival** (Tel 407/672-6390; www.wpsaf.org) in Central Park. This prestigious 3-day event features the work of more than 250 artists who compete in nine categories. Music is provided by such jazz notables as Herbie Hancock, Nestor Torres, and Spyro Gyra. The **Florida Film Festival** (Tel 407/629-1088; www.floridafilmfestival.com) showcases the work of Sunshine State filmmakers and screens more than 100 films from across the globe, for both juries and the public. Most events are held at the Enzian Theater, 1300 S. Orlando Ave.

APRIL: Lake Eola, in downtown Orlando, is the setting for **Spring Fiesta in the Park** (Tel 407/246-2827), a regional arts-and-crafts festival along Robinson Street and Eola Drive. You can also enjoy the incredible topiaries at the **Epcot International Flower and Garden Festival** (Tel 407/WDW-FEST) that runs from mid-April until June. It's free with admission to the park.

MAY: It gets spicy in May over at SeaWorld for the **Viva La Música Festival** (Tel 407/363-2259). But to get really crazy, you need to attend the **Orlando Fringe Festival** (Tel 407/363-2259; www.orlandofringe.org), a 10-day escapade of "theater, art, music, and madness." Admission to all outdoor events is $30.

JUNE: More than 100,000 gays and lesbians can't be wrong—the annual **GayDays** (Tel 407/896-8431) festival is one big weeklong party. Visit www.gaydays.com for all the details.

JULY: Celebrate Independence Day with lots of flag-waving Orlandoans at the **Lake Eola Picnic in the Park.** Games, family activities, entertainment, and fireworks make it a festive event. Or just go to Disney and watch the fireworks fly at its Fourth of July celebrations.

AUGUST: Get your feet dirty during the **August Stomp** (Tel 800/768-9463) at the Lakeridge Winery in Clermont. Enjoy live music while participating in a group grape stomp in the vineyards. Admission is $2.

SEPTEMBER: The second weekend of the month, both Disney and Universal praise the Lord in all-weekend festivals. **Night of Joy Festival** (Tel 877/534-2309) is a 3-day fest at the Magic Kingdom. Across town, Universal hosts **Rock the Universe Festival** (Tel 407/363-8000) the same weekend.

Lord, have mercy! Rather dance a little salsa? Head over to SeaWorld for the second round of the **Viva La Música Festival** (Tel 407/363-2259).

OCTOBER: During **Halloween Horror Nights** (Tel 407/363-8000), Islands of Adventure turns into a happy haunting ground with a spooky maze, haunted houses, and assorted monsters, mutants, and misfits. Or eat, drink, and be merry at the **Epcot International Food and Wine Festival** (Tel 407/WDW-FEST), which runs through mid-November.

NOVEMBER: The **Orlando Magic season opener** is usually the can't-miss event of the month, the team's generally poor record notwithstanding. For tickets, call Ticketmaster (Tel 407/839-3900).

DECEMBER: The First Baptist Church of Orlando's **Singing Christmas Trees** (Tel 407/425-2555) event is a beloved local tradition. Two 45-foot Christmas trees are decked with 204 "singing" ornaments, enhanced with spectacular lighting and holiday music (thanks to a pipe organ and full orchestra). And, of course, the theme parks are a-dazzle in holiday finery. **Mickey's Very Merry Christmas Party** (Tel 407/824-4321) at the Magic Kingdom (early Dec) is always enchanting. The night is so magical, who knows? It may even "snow" on Main Street U.S.A.

Gay and lesbian resources... A good source of information on local clubs and events is the **Gay, Lesbian & Bisexual Community Center** (Tel 407/228-8272; www.glbcc.org), located at 946 N. Mills. Even though the **Gay-Days** event only happens once a year, the website (www.gaydays.com) is a great resource year-round.

Liquor laws... You must be 21 to buy alcohol in Orlando. Alcohol is sold in supermarkets and liquor stores daily from 9am to 2am. It's served at bars and restaurants from 11am to 2am.

Newspapers... The major daily newspaper is the ***Orlando Sentinel*** (www.orlandosentinel.com), published daily. Weekly local papers include the African-American–centered ***Orlando Times*** (www.orlando-times.com) and the alternative news/arts/entertainment ***Orlando Weekly*** (www.orlandoweekly.com).

Opening and closing times... At many parks and attractions, hours stretch to accommodate heavy tourist flow. In general, stores are open from 9am to 9pm and bars are open from 11am to 2am. Restaurant hours vary, but many serve dinner until 10pm. Theme-park hours vary with the season. To beat the crowds, arrive early; the hordes usually arrive around 10am.

Parking... Unlike many tourist meccas, Orlando has plenty of parking. Most restaurants and shopping centers have free lots. Theme parks and attractions have massive lots, but they fill up fast. The parks close when their parking lots are full (another reason to arrive early). The typical parking fee for these is $9, but Walt Disney World resort guests with cars do not have to pay for parking at its lots. Handicapped spaces are reserved near the park entrances; ask the gate attendant to direct you to them. Parking in downtown Orlando is a bargain compared to the prices in most major cities—as little as $5 per day in many lots.

Radio stations... To get the theme from It's a Small World out of your head, try one of these Orlando-area radio stations: **WOMX-FM 105.1** and **WMFG-FM 107.7** play "lite" rock favorites; **WUCF-FM 89.9** is a favorite of jazz fans; try **WHTQ-FM 96.5** for classic rock; **WMFE-FM 90.7** plays classical music; for country, dial up **WWKA-FM 92.3;** rock out at **WJRR-FM 101.1** and **WOCL-FM 105.9**; listen to Top-40 hits at **WXXL-FM 106.7, WJHM-FM 102.9,** and **WPYO-FM 96.5;** catch up on news and talk on **WTKS-FM 104.1;** and find out what the Magic are doing on all-sports station **WQTM-AM 540.**

Smoking... You can forget about lighting up inside most bars, restaurants, clubs, and public buildings around Orlando. At Walt Disney World and Universal Studios Orlando, smoking policies are basically the same: Smoking is prohibited on all attractions, in all attraction waiting areas, and in all restaurants and shops. At the Disney theme parks, you'll even be sequestered into separate areas within the park (designated on the park maps you get upon entry).

Taxes... You'll need to add 6.5% or 7% (depends on which county you're in) sales tax on all merchandise except "necessary" grocery items and medicine. (That means "extras" such as soda and ice cream are taxable.) The tax is added to the price marked on the merchandise. In addition to the sales tax, a 2% to 5% resort tax is added to hotel room rates.

Taxis... If you take a taxi, either use a metered cab or confirm the cost of the trip with the driver before beginning your trip. **Yellow Cab Company** (Tel 407/422-2222) is Orlando's oldest, largest cab company and offers metered rates at $5.05 for the first mile, $2 per mile thereafter.

Telephone... The main area code for Orlando is **407,** although calls to the **321** area code are often considered local as well. ***Note:*** When calling within Orlando, you must always dial the full 10-digit phone number (including the area code). Pay-phone calls cost 35¢.

Time... Orlando runs on Eastern Standard Time (EST). Call Tel 407/646-3131 for the correct time and temperature.

Tipping... Gratuities are generally not included in restaurant or bar checks (unless you have a party of eight or more, when 15% is customarily added to the bill), but it pays to read the fine print, just in case. About 20% is typical at restaurants; taxi drivers get 15%; skycaps and bellhops get $1 per bag (or more, if the bags are huge); and $1 to $2 per day for housekeeping is advised—you *do* want clean sheets tomorrow, right?

Trains... Amtrak trains (Tel 800/872-7245; www.amtrak.com) pull into stations at 1400 Sligh Blvd. in downtown Orlando (23 miles from Walt Disney World), and 111 Dakin Ave. in Kissimmee (15 miles from WDW). Don't want to give up your set of wheels? Amtrak's **Auto Train** overnight express begins in Lorton, Virginia—outside of Washington, D.C.—and ends at Sanford, 23 miles northeast of Orlando. (There are no stops in between.) Reserve early for the lowest prices. Fares average $530 ($1,100 with a berth) for two passengers and a car.

Travel agents... Though it's gotten much easier to plan a Disney World vacation, sometimes you just want a little help. In terms of logistics, group trips and special occasions can be particularly hairy in the World, and Disney's agents, while courteous to a fault, will rarely volunteer information about hidden deals, extras, or ways to make your agenda less pricey. Certain travel agents are Disney World experts, spending most or all of their time helping visitors negotiate this potentially perilous terrain. Agents that we've found enormously helpful include **Sue Pisaturo** (sue@wdwvacations.com), **Sue Ellen Soto-Rios** (sueellen@wdwinfo.com), **Lynne Amodeo** (lynnetravel@verizon.net), **Steve Schrohe** (steve@ittravel.com), and **Stephanie DelVecchio** (orlandotasteph@aol.com).

Travelers with disabilities... Accessibility is generally good for travelers with special needs. **Disney**'s many services are detailed in each theme park's *Guidebook for Guests with Disabilities.* Call Tel 407/824-4321 or 407/824-2222, or check its website at www.disneyworld.com for answers to any questions regarding special needs. At **Universal Orlando** (Tel 800/837-2273; www.universalorlando.com), go to Guest Services, located just inside the main entrances, for a *Disabled Guest Guidebook.* Both Disney and Universal provide complimentary **audiotapes** and **portable tape players** for vision-impaired guests, featuring guided tours of each park, as well as **TDD** (telecommunications device for the deaf) and **studio scripts** for the hearing impaired (check before you arrive, as these may need to be reserved in advance). At the rides, special entrances are available for nonambulatory guests; guests can ride through many attractions without leaving their wheelchairs. **SeaWorld** (Tel 407/351-3600; www.seaworld.com) has a guide for guests with disabilities, although most of its attractions are easily accessible to those in wheelchairs. All of Orlando's theme parks provide close-up parking for visitor with disabilities.

TV stations... Virtually every hotel and resort has cable, so CNN won't be hard to track down (not to mention the five Disney channels you'll find at the Disney resorts). Local TV stations include **WESH-TV 2 (NBC), WKMG-TV 6 (CBS), WFTV-9 (ABC), WKCF-TV 18 (WB), WMFE-TV 24 (PBS),** and **WOFL-TV 35 (FOX).**

Visitor information... The Orlando/Orange County Convention and Visitors Bureau staffs an **Official Visitor Center** at 8723 International Dr., Suite 101 (Tel 407/363-5872 or 800/551-0181; www.orlandoinfo.com), that is open daily from 8am to 8pm. The CVB's website has lots of up-to-the-minute info you can access before leaving home. For information on Kissimmee/St. Cloud, contact the **Kissimmee/St. Cloud Convention and Visitors Bureau** at 1925 E. Irlo Bronson Memorial Hwy. (Tel 407/944-2400; www.floridakiss.com).

GENERAL INDEX

GENERAL INDEX
WALT DISNEY WORLD

Accommodations

Restaurants

Frommer's® Complete Travel Guides

Alaska
Amalfi Coast
American Southwest
Amsterdam
Argentina & Chile
Arizona
Atlanta
Australia
Austria
Bahamas
Barcelona
Beijing
Belgium, Holland & Luxembourg
Belize
Bermuda
Boston
Brazil
British Columbia & the Canadian Rockies
Brussels & Bruges
Budapest & the Best of Hungary
Buenos Aires
Calgary
California
Canada
Cancún, Cozumel & the Yucatán
Cape Cod, Nantucket & Martha's Vineyard
Caribbean
Caribbean Ports of Call
Carolinas & Georgia
Chicago
China
Colorado
Costa Rica
Croatia
Cuba
Denmark
Denver, Boulder & Colorado Springs
Edinburgh & Glasgow
England
Europe
Europe by Rail
Florence, Tuscany & Umbria
Florida
France
Germany
Greece
Greek Islands
Hawaii
Hong Kong
Honolulu, Waikiki & Oahu
India
Ireland
Israel
Italy
Jamaica
Japan
Kauai
Las Vegas
London
Los Angeles
Los Cabos & Baja
Madrid
Maine Coast
Maryland & Delaware
Maui
Mexico
Montana & Wyoming
Montréal & Québec City
Moscow & St. Petersburg
Munich & the Bavarian Alps
Nashville & Memphis
New England
Newfoundland & Labrador
New Mexico
New Orleans
New York City
New York State
New Zealand
Northern Italy
Norway
Nova Scotia, New Brunswick & Prince Edward Island
Oregon
Paris
Peru
Philadelphia & the Amish Country
Portugal
Prague & the Best of the Czech Republic
Provence & the Riviera
Puerto Rico
Rome
San Antonio & Austin
San Diego
San Francisco
Santa Fe, Taos & Albuquerque
Scandinavia
Scotland
Seattle
Seville, Granada & the Best of Andalusia
Shanghai
Sicily
Singapore & Malaysia
South Africa
South America
South Florida
South Pacific
Southeast Asia
Spain
Sweden
Switzerland
Tahiti & French Polynesia
Texas
Thailand
Tokyo
Toronto
Turkey
USA
Utah
Vancouver & Victoria
Vermont, New Hampshire & Maine
Vienna & the Danube Valley
Vietnam
Virgin Islands
Virginia
Walt Disney World® & Orlando
Washington, D.C.
Washington State

Frommer's® Day by Day Guides

Amsterdam
Chicago
Florence & Tuscany
London
New York City
Paris
Rome
San Francisco
Venice

Pauline Frommer's Guides! See More. Spend Less.

Hawaii
Italy
New York City

Frommer's® Portable Guides

Acapulco, Ixtapa & Zihuatanejo
Amsterdam
Aruba
Australia's Great Barrier Reef
Bahamas
Big Island of Hawaii
Boston
California Wine Country
Cancún
Cayman Islands
Charleston
Chicago
Dominican Republic
Dublin
Florence
Las Vegas
Las Vegas for Non-Gamblers
London
Maui
Nantucket & Martha's Vineyard
New Orleans
New York City
Paris
Portland
Puerto Rico
Puerto Vallarta, Manzanillo & Guadalajara
Rio de Janeiro
San Diego
San Francisco
Savannah
St. Martin, Sint Maarten, Anguila & St. Bart's
Turks & Caicos
Vancouver
Venice
Virgin Islands
Washington, D.C.
Whistler

FROMMER'S® CRUISE GUIDES

Alaska Cruises & Ports of Call
Cruises & Ports of Call
European Cruises & Ports of Call

FROMMER'S® NATIONAL PARK GUIDES

Algonquin Provincial Park
Banff & Jasper
Grand Canyon
National Parks of the American West
Rocky Mountain
Yellowstone & Grand Teton
Yosemite and Sequoia & Kings Canyon
Zion & Bryce Canyon

FROMMER'S® MEMORABLE WALKS

London
New York
Paris
Rome
San Francisco

FROMMER'S® WITH KIDS GUIDES

Chicago
Hawaii
Las Vegas
London
National Parks
New York City
San Francisco
Toronto
Walt Disney World® & Orlando
Washington, D.C.

SUZY GERSHMAN'S BORN TO SHOP GUIDES

France
Hong Kong, Shanghai & Beijing
Italy
London
New York
Paris
San Francisco

FROMMER'S® IRREVERENT GUIDES

Amsterdam
Boston
Chicago
Las Vegas
London
Los Angeles
Manhattan
Paris
Rome
San Francisco
Walt Disney World®
Washington, D.C.

FROMMER'S® BEST-LOVED DRIVING TOURS

Austria
Britain
California
France
Germany
Ireland
Italy
New England
Northern Italy
Scotland
Spain
Tuscany & Umbria

THE UNOFFICIAL GUIDES®

Adventure Travel in Alaska
Beyond Disney
California with Kids
Central Italy
Chicago
Cruises
Disneyland®
England
Florida
Florida with Kids
Hawaii
Ireland
Las Vegas
London
Maui
Mexico's Best Beach Resorts
Mini Mickey
New Orleans
New York City
Paris
San Francisco
South Florida including Miami & the Keys
Walt Disney World®
Walt Disney World® for Grown-ups
Walt Disney World® with Kids
Washington, D.C.

SPECIAL-INTEREST TITLES

Athens Past & Present
Best Places to Raise Your Family
Cities Ranked & Rated
500 Places to Take Your Kids Before They Grow Up
Frommer's Best Day Trips from London
Frommer's Best RV & Tent Campgrounds in the U.S.A.
Frommer's Exploring America by RV
Frommer's NYC Free & Dirt Cheap
Frommer's Road Atlas Europe
Frommer's Road Atlas Ireland
Great Escapes From NYC Without Wheels
Retirement Places Rated

FROMMER'S® PHRASEFINDER DICTIONARY GUIDES

French
Italian
Spanish